Governing Hate and Race
in the United States and South Africa

Governing Hate and Race
in the United States and South Africa

PATRICK LYNN RIVERS

Published by
State University of New York Press, Albany

For information, contact State University of New York Press
www.sunypress.com

Production by Eileen Meehan
Marketing by Michael Campochiaro

Library of Congress of Cataloging-in-Publication Data

Rivers, Patrick Lynn.
  Governing hate and race in the United States and South Africa /
Patrick Lynn Rivers.
      p. cm.
  Includes bibliographical references and index.
  ISBN 978-0-7914-7561-4 (hardcover : alk. paper)
  ISBN 978-0-7914-7562-1 (paperback : alk. paper)
   1. Racism—United States. 2. Racism—South Africa. 3. Hate crimes—United
States. 4. Hate crimes—South Africa. 5. Social problems—United States. 6.
Social problems—South Africa. 7. United States—Race relations. 8. United
States—Politics and government. 9. South Africa—Race relations. 10. South
Africa—Politics and government. I. Title.

E184.A1R55 2008
305.800973—dc22

                          2007049734

                  10 9 8 7 6 5 4 3 2 1

For my father, Eddie Lee Rivers (1933–2005)

Contents

Preface

I started thinking about writing this book in 2001, before 9/11, while directing a study abroad program in South Africa. Before this trip, I had dabbled, a bit, with hate and hate scholarship, most of which grew from my engagement with the hate speech debates so much a part of the 1990s "culture wars" in the United States. But nothing substantial really came from my early investigations.

This changed after 9/11. It was then—after what was such an unimaginable, devastating event to the American psyche—that I started to think about "how" hatred could lead to an event such as 9/11. Many in the United States knew the answer, even as some were persecuted for daring to frankly speculate about the "why" in a political climate where anyone critical of U.S. policies became aligned with "them," "the terrorists." I sought a more substantive, and productive, answer to the "why," and the "how," given the political climate, and this book is the result.

To answer that "why" and "how" about hate directed at the United States, I turned to South Africa, a place marred by hate, but definitely not defined by it. This was a South Africa, in my post-9/11 mind, that dealt with domestic hatred, racial hatred in particular, so as to make an impact on the nation as well as to make an impact on the international community. In national terms, the postapartheid state devised regulatory measures to address racial hatred at home. In international terms, the postapartheid state projected an image of national transformation of colonial and apartheid racial hatred that helped change the place of South Africa in the international imaginary, from pariah to model state.

That was where I was, intellectually, in the aftermath of 9/11; this book reflects where I am now. Although 9/11 only comes to the surface in a significant way in chapter 4, it, and all which preceded and immediately followed 9/11, was never far from my mind.

Acknowledgments

Many hands touched this book. By this I mean that the insights and encouragement of colleagues, friends, and family helped make me and this book.

At critical moments, travel and other resources were made available to me by deans and department chairs. Thanks, in this regard, go to Martha Crunkleton, Michael McCann, Carol Becker, and Terri Kapsalis.

Several colleagues read parts, or all, of the manuscript that became this book. Thanks to Mark Kessler, Michael McCann, Katherine Beckett, Steven Herbert, Karen Morris, W. Martin, Jeannine Bell, Jean Comaroff, Andrea Simpson, Mark Ellis, Austin Sarat, Linda Steiner, Stephen Tropiano, anonymous reviewers from *Studies in Law, Politics, and Society*, *Critical Studies in Media Communication*, the *Journal of Film and Video*, and the African Studies, Cinema Studies, and Race and Reproduction of Ideologies Workshops at the University of Chicago. The workshop feedback at the University of Chicago was made possible by a generous post-doctoral fellowship from Chicago's Center for the Study of Race, Politics, and Culture.

Special thanks to my dissertation advisor at Chapel Hill, Michael Lienesch. I took to heart the words that he uttered to my cohort on our very first day of graduate school—that he would retire from a political science department, but that we would not. That one comment, from my teacher, undoubtedly resulted in the multiple scholarly communities of discourse with whom I converse in this book and in my other writings. Not to mention that, at one time or another, I have taught in departments of political science, politics, American studies, African American studies, women and gender studies, ethnic studies, sociolegal studies, communication studies, visual studies, and sculpture.

Friends offered intellectual support and encouragement throughout this process. Thanks to Yvonne Welbon, Tanya Fernando, Janice and Les Rabkin, Michelle Habell-Pallan, Seyed Maulana, Anne Roxbenu, Natalie and Belinda McCaskill, Carlo Carstens, Rick Bonus, Nilüfer Patterson, Rachael Murphey-Brown, and Kai Wood Mah, my best friend.

Thanks also to my family, for believing in me, first. Thanks to my brother, Dan, my grandparents, George and Josephine McLendon, my mother, Jean Tyson, and my father, Eddie Lee Rivers, to whom this book is dedicated.

As always, thanks to the Almighty.

Parts of this book first appeared elsewhere. Chapter 3 originally appeared as "Tortious Race, Race Torts: Legal Consciousness, Intentional Infliction Cases, and Unequal Outcomes," *Studies in Law, Politics, and Society* 27 (2003): 93–115. Chapter 6 originally appeared as "Governing Sounds: Hate, Race, and Responsibility in Post-Apartheid Broadcasting," *Critical Studies in Media Communication* 23 (2006): 219–31, and as "Governing Images: The Politics of Film and Video Distribution in Late-Apartheid and Post-Apartheid South Africa," *Journal of Film and Video* 59 (2007): 19–31.

1

States of Racial Mind

States have racial minds. This book is about the racial minds of two neoliberal states: the United States and South Africa. Of particular concern is how the racial minds of these two states function as they regulate racist hate. Instead of merely considering the constitutionality of hate controls, this book is a history of recent regulatory state practices in the United States and South Africa largely beyond constitutional question.

While making use of rather everyday regulatory practices in order to regulate racist hate, state agencies in the United States and South Africa utilize particular racial constructs. These state agencies, through their banal regulatory practices, actually contribute to the legal construction of race.[1] Given that states are not monolithic, regulatory practices and racial constructs vary from state to state, from agency to agency, from context to context, and even within states, agencies, and contexts. Though varied, racial constructs wielded by the U.S. and South African states are not indeterminate.

The most intriguing thing about some state agencies that regulate racist hate in the United States and South Africa is that their regulatory practices and racial constructs might be considered racist. These state practices and constructs have prompted me to ask a series of questions: What happens when a state uses racial constructs and engages in the construction of race in an official form such as a police report? Does it matter that a police report boxes racial identity in static ways? Is it necessarily confounding when static racial constructs in one context give way to more fluid racial constructs in another context? What happens when the fixity of an administrative form and mindset leads a judge or magistrate to racially construct someone in static ways that are uncomfortably close, in form, to the racial constructs of the racist who hates, acts on that hate, and is prosecuted? Does it even matter that the racial assumptions of a state agency mirror the racial assumptions of racist haters as long as the targets of hate are ultimately shielded from immediate harm? (This, of course, assumes that the state's constructs mirror the constructs of the racist, and not the other way around.) Do social and economic changes really lead persons and groups—hated and haters—to racially construct themselves in new ways, and, if yes, how do state agencies respond to these new constructions? Does the state's response (or nonresponse) to new racial constructions and formations pivotally shape the way that the state conceptualizes racism and combats racist hate?

This book provides some answers to these questions and makes the following three points about state regulation of racist hate in the United States and South Africa. First, state bodies in the United States and South Africa, such as independent state commissions monitoring rights, understand race and racial hate in ways that are rather strictly prescribed. It is important to assert here that certain state agencies position race as construct in normative ways that can be limber but not necessarily limber enough to understand race and racist hate shaped by the social and economic conditions that Stuart Hall has linked to changing patterns of industrial capital.[2] Race and racist hate taking shape in the new global capitalist context tend to be markedly unfixed as individuals and groups come to see themselves and demand that they be seen in complex ways, as opposed to the fixity characterizing the racial notions of some state agencies in the United States and South Africa.

Beyond this, and intricately connected to the state's rather static conceptualizations of race and racism, there is a second aspect of state regulation of racist hate highlighted in this book. Specifically, the racial constructions of states illustrate a way that state offices, such as the many bias investigative units around the United States and the Bureau of Justice Assistance in South Africa, help bound race and agency in and through their regulatory practices. Bounding race and agency at certain junctures, the racial constructs of some state agencies, such as offices of public prosecutors, do not readily and officially recognize race as social construct. In addition, state agents, such as prosecutors, fail to account for the race rebel who denies white supremacy its lifeblood when the rebel constructs race outside of white supremacist binaries where supremacists construct themselves as "civilized" and "nonwhites" as "savage."

A third point is highlighted in this book, namely, that agents of the state charged with training other institutional agents to regulate hate have set out to reform their own regulatory rationales and practices. In response to social and economic change, these master trainers have frequently tried to make state agents aware of, for example, "multi-cultural" concerns leading to acts of hate as well as the "multicultural" concerns conditioning state regulation of hate. In the United States, this "multicultural" sensitivity has fallen within the range of the liberal multiculturalism recurrently problematized by African American studies scholars such as Manning Marable, who astutely characterized such strategies as enthusiastic when it comes time to deplore prejudice and "'celebrate diversity'" but unable to forthrightly deal with "troubling concepts like 'exploitation,' 'racism,' 'sexism,' and 'homophobia.'"[3] In South Africa, the call for multicultural sensitivity has a slightly different ring. The racial dynamics are different in South Africa than in the United States due to South Africa's white supremacist history coupled with the election of a black majority government in 1994. Even in South Africa, though, the liberal multiculturalism so present and prevalent in the United States has a sinister ring as the black majority government calls for a "nonracial democracy" that has, in effect, given whites the opportunity to forego a thorough reckoning with the apartheid past as present. (Here the postapartheid state has become trapped in the liberation struggle's own language, where a "nonracial democracy" was the desired end, the goal. But in postapartheid South Africa, "nonracial democracy" has been declared by whites without South African democracy being nonracial.) This is something that a scholar such as Cynthia Kros wants to avoid, so as not to follow the U.S. example, or the French example in the "headscarf affair."[4]

From Constitution to Practices

Hate Speech Scholarship

Hate speech has dominated sociolegal discussions about hate in both the United States and South Africa for too long. Scholarship on hate speech as a form of hate has revolved around constitutional debates about freedom and speech. For example, those in the United States and South Africa favoring more state regulation of hate and speech have taken this position in the name of equal protection under the law. Basically these scholars have argued that hate speech fosters social inequalities.[5] Those who have opposed increased state action designed to curb racist hate speech in the United States have rooted their opposition in free speech terms, arguing that hate speech regulations encroach upon free speech rights.[6] But U.S. and South African debates are not always this simple. For example, in the United States, a left-leaning scholar such as Judith Butler has argued that enhanced state control of hate speech actually silences subversive and transformative forms of speech. In such a subversive and transformative mode, an individual or a group might be understood to

4   *Governing Hate and Race in the United States and South Africa*

make race as social construct depart from the normative racial scripts of white supremacy, not unlike the "drag" queen who queers patriarchal gender norms.[7] The South African case is made more complex because, unlike the U.S. Constitution, the constitution protects free speech but also contains an internal limitation used to temper just how free speech can be. This has led to scholarly debates on just where this internal limitation line should be drawn.[8]

Quickly veering from the mainstream hate speech debate in the United States and South Africa, which has not really changed since the "culture wars" of the 1990s, I use this book to downplay the centrality of hate speech scholarship and debates. I do this in several ways, while still maintaining that there is a significant relationship between hate and language. For example, this book moves away from the fixation on hate speech, as this book is used to acknowledge—as do scholars writing from many different perspectives about, for example, *Wisconsin v. Mitchell*, 508 U.S. 476 (1993)[9]—that, inevitably, language is central to hate in general, not just to hate speech. Discourse thus logically factors in, at some level, the regulation of hate outside of "hate speech." Beyond this, in a sociolegal vein, routine regulatory state practices, not constitutional questions, are centered in this comparative study especially as language figures in the development and implementation of regulatory state practices. In large part this is done in order to skirt the dizzying circularity of the hate speech debate in the United States in particular but also the lawyerly dominance of the discussion in both the United States and South Africa. This places this study in line with more recent sociolegal studies by Valerie Jenness and Ryken Grattet, who consider the importance of language in the construction of what became conceptualizations of a criminalized hate warranting policing and prosecution, Jeannine Bell, who thinks about policing practices and hate, and Jon B. Gould who studies how institutional practices shape the enforcement of hate speech codes.[10]

Changing the terms of the debate in this qualitative study in which discourse is critical, and taking a different route than Gould, Bell, and Jenness and Grattet, means looking at the ways in which regulatory state practices interact, in particular, with identities. The emphasis on reiterative regulatory state practices as these practices shape identities grows out of my curiosity about and concern with law's form—notably its structures, assumptions, and functions. This concern with form is similar to the concern highlighted by Richard Schur. Specifically, had Schur considered the dimensions of hate, he would have likely concluded that a focus on regulatory state practices turns what has largely been a doctrinal debate on constitutionality into a debate about "the ideology of form." Schur's "ideology of form" is not just an exercise in constitutional exegesis where cases and precedent rule; his emphasis on form underlines the way that ideology is embedded and imbricated within law and racial constructs made, for example, in appellate courtrooms and as the beat cop prepares incident reports.[11]

"Fixing" Race

Regulatory state practices, understood through everyday artifacts such as police reports or memoranda of law submitted to courts by public prosecutors, reflect more than what they, in their banality, appear to reflect. The completion of routine paperwork by either an agent of the state regulating hate or one who is to be regulated by the state is not necessarily a major happening, but it is significant. It is customary for a police officer in St. Louis or Mafeking to arrive on the scene of a particularly egregious hate act and take a report, assign a case number, and file the investigative report with other cases. More than what they appear to be on the surface, these case reports as ideological artifacts offer "insights into the shared meanings and social practices—the distinctive ways of making sense and doing things—which are the basis of our culture,"[12] not just of our legal culture. For example, New York City created the Bias Incident Investigation Unit (BIIU) in the early 1980s, which was administratively located within the Office of the Commissioner of the New York Police Department (NYPD). Now called the Hate Crimes Task Force, and located in the NYPD's Detective Bureau, duties of what once was the BIIU include the investigation of acts of hate, collecting and analyzing police reports as intelligence reports on the dimensions of hate, communicating with other state agencies so that different agencies with different objectives and practices could work together, and training other officers to manage incidents stemming from hate.[13] Administrative "effectiveness" depends on a series of practices that can be reiterated. Specifically, police officers reiteratively record data related to hate acts on generic forms with multiple lines and boxes. The forms are but copies of copies for which there is no longer an original. But these forms are more than simulacra—copies of copies with the original both lost and insignificant. These forms encode meanings upon given acts of hate, particular rationales, in writing.

While carrying out their everyday work, bureaucrats at the South African Human Rights Commission office in Cape Town and Seattle's Office of Civil Rights make a range of routine yet culturally conditioned judgments about the racial identity of those targeted by haters, haters themselves, and those who witness hate acts. Neoliberal states, not unlike other states, base their judgments on what might be called "common sense"[14] about race and the knowledge derived from the ethno-racial pentagon (white, black, Hispanic, Asian, native) used in the United States as well as a similar pentagon (white, colored, African, Indian, Asian) officially used in apartheid South Africa and unofficially in effect in postapartheid South Africa. Prompted to make these judgments, state agents tend to arrange race within one of the aforementioned categories so that the variability of something like race can be statistically analyzed, and governed and populations regimented. While the choices made by state agents may be affected by the cultural lens of a given agent, the professionalization of agents into a given agency's practices tends to mute state agents who, because of their experiences, see race through a different lens.

It is here within the marrow of legality that regulatory practices and racial constructs of the state are produced and reproduced. For example, Lisa Frohmann addressed the reiteration of identity constructs in the decision-making processes of public prosecutors in the United States. Specifically, Frohmann argued that public prosecutors locate the identity of victims, defendants, jurors, and their communities in ways that are dependent upon dominant social constructions of race, class, and gender. Issues of form figured as socially constructed stereotypes helped determine who got prosecuted and how prosecution proceeded.[15] Have state agencies operated in this way to naturalize racial constructs? Taking Frohmann on her own terms, stereotypes influenced the practices and decisions of public prosecutors. As cultural studies scholars theorize, these state stereotypes tended to reiteratively "reduce, essentialize, naturalize, and fix difference." Further, state stereotypes worked via a splitting mechanism that, as "part of the maintenance of social and symbolic order," differentiates the " 'normal' and the 'deviant,' the 'normal' and the 'pathological,' the 'acceptable' and the 'unacceptable,' what 'belongs' and what does not."[16]

Sociolegal scholars Paul Gready and Lazarus Kgalema similarly centered bureaucratic practices and decisions in their study of the apartheid judiciary. In particular, not unlike Frohmann, Gready and Kgalema sought to "identify structures and processes" that shaped the legal and racial consciousness of apartheid magistrates, many of whom are still on the bench. "Structures and processes," according to Gready and Kgalema, preceded the magistracy's "widespread complicity in human rights abuses" during apartheid.[17] These structures and processes conditioned a magistrate culture where apartheid's racial constructs were reiterated by apartheid's judiciary. This racial consciousness, in part a result of the formal training that magistrates received at apartheid's Justice College, became naturalized in such a way that it became racial reality. This naturalized racial consciousness reinforced the racial norms of the apartheid state. Racial consciousness here elided with a supposedly neutral and objective apartheid state so as to shape not just the magistrates' sense of racial justice but their sense of justice itself.[18]

Bounding Race and Agency

That states participate in white supremacy is not surprising. As critical legal scholar Peter Fitzpatrick suggested, "Racism is compatible with and even integral to law" in liberal democracies, and this racism might even be traced to the emergence of liberalism and (white) European identity itself.[19] Critical race theorist Patricia Williams, however, thinks that the disutility arguments of Peter Fitzgerald and other critical legal scholars do nothing to materially transform the basic existence of people of color in racist societies. According to Williams, "For the historically disempowered, the conferring of rights is symbolic of all the denied aspects of their humanity."[20] In short, liberal rights discourse, and the activism inspired by this discourse, becomes the only tool available to those on the bottom.

Using the rights understood by Williams, people of color turn to state agencies and institutions when and where possible, pressuring city councillors, administrators at the state-provincial and local levels, members of Congress or Parliament, officials within a given presidential administration, and courts at all levels. For example, a U.S. interest group such as the National Association for the Advancement of Colored People (NAACP) used its bully pulpit to lobby Congress for passage of the Hate Crime Statistics Act of 1990. Beyond lobbying for passage, though, the NAACP lobbied to have its data forms incorporated into the practices operationalizing the act. As a result of the NAACP's lobbying effort, its own data collection strategies became a part of the data collection practices of the Federal Bureau of Investigation (FBI) section (the Uniform Crime Reports section) assigned the task of data collection mandated with the passage of the Hate Crime Statistics Act. This included issues of form, such as who should get placed in which racial identity category for the purpose of data collection, interpretation, and allocation of resources used to make state regulation of hate efficient as the neoliberal state defines "efficient." Similarly, in South Africa, people of color and sexual minorities helped give contour to race and sexuality as constructs in the Promotion of Equality and Prevention of Unfair Discrimination Act of 2000, which contains a significant hate speech provision. This is not to say that the inputs of interest groups representing minority groups in the United States and South Africa always reflected changing racial or gender constructions and formations taking shape in new times. Instead, it should just be noted that there was a dialogue about how race should be constructed as the state attempted to intervene in acts of racist hate.

Multiculturalism

The underlying point of this book is that in a legal culture where racist hate is regulated via racial constructs, representation matters. This is not the "representation" presented in the mainstream political science scholarship that I devoured as a graduate student in Chapel Hill.[21] Instead, this is the "representation" theorized within the cultural studies emanating from Birmingham.[22] As I contend in this book, a "racialized regime of representation" shapes hate regulation in the United States and South Africa, and this "regime" tends to utilize rather fixed racial representations.[23] This is the case even in postapartheid South Africa, where the relatively static racial representations (or constructions) of apartheid and colonial states have been vigorously interrogated.

The racial representations (or constructs) used by the states in the United States and South Africa in order to regulate hate are frequently akin to the modernist and positivist racial constructs critiqued in the work of postcolonial theorists such as Vine Deloria and Gayatri Chakravorty Spivak, ethnic studies scholars such as Michelle Habell-Pallan and Dwight A. McBride, and in the work of philosophers such as Charles W. Mills and Paul C. Taylor.[24] Dominant constructions of marginalized groups have historically depended upon certain stereotypes presented in what might be understood as the binary form. With these stereotypes reified via legal "science" and racial "science," the dominant culture has constructed identities in male-female terms, masculine-feminine terms, in terms of heterosexual-homosexual, black-white, white-nonwhite, whites as civilized-nonwhites as savage, or the catchall postmodernist shorthand of self-other. Using such polarities, or binaries, powerful interests have been able to use discourse in order to construct themselves as normal and the "other" in the polarity as deviant. And this binary has become the basis of supremacist ideologies, such as white supremacy and patriarchy, intended to systematically order the world and structure inequalities.

While these binary constructs do not necessarily play out in absolutist ways, understanding these social constructs as functioning through reified binaries is a useful theoretical starting point to understand the genealogy of race, racism, and the flow of power. The limits of such binary understandings are presently evident in both the U.S. and South African contexts where the state has successfully turned multiculturalism into a commodity. The U.S. limits are increasingly evident as immigration from the Americas and the Islamic diaspora leads state and society to view race in new, multicultural ways. In South Africa, apartheid's formal end brings to the fore multicultural divisions and differences within and between communities of black Africans, black "coloreds," English-speaking whites, Afrikaans-speaking whites, Indians, and Chinese (who are actually now seeking black status in order to claim the redistributive benefits of affirmative action). The neoliberal state's burgeoning multiculturalism, though, is not a reconstructive or transformative practice that deconstructs stereotypes by dismantling the "science" legitimating racial and other negative stereotypes. As Michael Hardt and Antonio Negri recently charged in their book *Empire*, neoliberal states can and do appropriate the slogans of their academic and activist antagonists when the neoliberal state leads chants such as "Long live difference!," and "Down with essentialist binaries!"[25]

If the neoliberal state's racial constructs largely adhere to white supremacy's racial binaries, with neoliberal states appropriating multiculturalism only when challenged by those on the bottom or their representatives, then how can neoliberal states be depended upon to remedy and transform racist hate? But, really, this is only part of the story, as my supposition and question assume that racial supremacy itself is static. After all, who is to say that the racial supremacy of haters has not changed and will not change?

Significantly, race and racist hate in the United States and South Africa have changed and will continue to change. The neoliberal state in particular has, however, approached this change in less than desirable ways. Namely, state structures in the United States and South Africa have been used to ardently regulate, for example, hate. And this regulation has occurred in the name of a multiculturalism forced on the state's agenda by social movement activists demanding rights for people of color in general, immigrants, sexual minorities, women, and other "others" targeted by haters. The state's multicultural "turn" has taken place as the state's regulatory practices continue to operate within modernist and positivist state frameworks. These have been frameworks where legal "science" and racial "science" prevail, or at least prominently figure. And, as I argue throughout this book, "scientific" discourse has served as a kind of enabler of the type of racial governance in neoliberal states that I find so problematic. State appropriation of multicultural rhetoric has conveniently allowed the neoliberal state to absolve itself of racist hate, even as the state ironically propagates a legal "science" and racial "science" promoting a social fixity and stasis antithetical to the dynamism and openness promoted by progressive multiculturalists.

Comparing U.S. and South African Contexts

Why compare hate in the United States and South Africa? The cases are similar enough to make a comparison feasible but different enough to make a comparison interesting, as evidenced by classic comparative studies of the United States and South Africa written by George M. Fredrickson and Anthony W. Marx.[26] Both the United States and South Africa share a colonial past, in which Europeans established hegemonic control over an indigenous population and over a population that was not European, all ultimately in the name of efficiently directing resources to the colonizer. New systems of social control followed the decline and formal end of colonialism in both cases. For example, in the United States, Jim Crow and segregation dictated the course of social relations between people of color and whites after the Civil War. In South Africa, Jim Crow and segregation parallels were put into place as the prospect of black power in the late nineteenth century and the reality of Afrikaner poverty in the mid-twentieth century led to the institutionalization of apartheid to secure white domination. Resistance to white supremacy in both contexts led to the emergence of prominent leaders whose cause gained international notoriety: Mandela in South Africa, and King in the United States, during the 1950s and 1960s, just as liberation movements replaced colonial regimes in the Americas, Africa, and Asia. Dissent about the shape of the mainline responses of Mandela and King came from younger activists of color in the United States (e.g., Huey P. Newton) and South Africa (e.g., Steve Biko) during the 1970s, with younger activists being inspired by Fanon, and not so much by Gandhi. Together, the leadership of struggle veterans, and more junior struggle activists, prompted change in the white supremacist order in both the United States and South Africa. In both contexts, though, the cause for which many gave their lives has been won, and not won.

It is within this larger historical context that I come to my understanding of hate regulation in the United States and South Africa. I start first with the scholarship and debates about hate speech. The U.S. and South African hate speech scholarship from the 1990s is rich, and converging, as both countries wrestled with the "culture wars" specific to their own national contexts. For example, as stated earlier, the gist of the scholarly debate in both the United States and South Africa revolves around how the regulation of hate speech impinges upon free speech and expression. The South African case, though, differs, as it regards this free speech framework. As mentioned earlier, South Africa's constitution, unlike the U.S. Constitution, contains an internal limitation forthrightly allowing the South African state to regulate speech deemed hateful. There is another critical dimension differentiating the two cases. In the United States, hate speech regulation exists in its own regulatory domain, largely separated in legal terms from the regulation of hate crime and discrimination. In contrast, in the South African case, hate speech is a crime that is understood to be a critical factor in persisting patterns of discrimination, so it is impossible to neatly parse hate in this compara-tive study, making this study *just* about hate speech. As a result, chapter 5 of this book, understood from a U.S. perspective, might be primarily understood to be about discrimination. But from a South African regu-latory perspective, it is about discriminatory forms that frequently implicate each other, and hate in general and hate speech in particular are among these discriminatory forms.

The expansiveness of the South African regulatory form, and the way that it links hate speech-hate crime-discrimination, draws me to it. It is interesting to see how a nation such as South Africa comes to terms with its past, so soon after that past, whereas there is a kind of indifference to hate and its regulation in the United States. Hate regulation in the United States is about reform, and these reform efforts are frequently dispas-sionate in tone, not to mention decentralized as, for example, federal, state, and local governments frequently have different and very proce-durally driven provisions for the regulation of hate. As a set of reform measures, hate regulation in the United States is about ending something viewed as a mere inconvenience. There is no real systemic and central-ized attempt to address that which has been identified as the source of hate in the U.S. case. Regulators in the United States, too, often see hate and hateful actions as an anomaly and not as something so embedded in the social and political fiber of the nation's essence, making it necessary to go beyond mere reform measures. The U.S. regulators seemingly approach hate as an administrative matter, where nothing beyond an administrative solution is needed.

In contrast, hate regulation in South Africa is more transformative. That is, some agents of the South African state proclaim that they regu-late hate in the name of undoing the structures of oppression giving life to hate. And this attempt to deconstruct oppressive structures in South Africa comes as state regulators repeatedly return—at least in rhetoric—to the social context giving life to the state's regulatory zeal. This is a social context where an active recognition of the historical (colonial and apartheid) basis of ongoing hate acts and inequalities is understood to be much more central than in the U.S. case. In South Africa, this is a histor-ical basis where the state does not consider hate anomalous, even as, in practice, some regulatory (state and quasistate) entities treat hate as anomalous. In any event, agents of the South African state see hate as an unacceptable norm that must be excised from the social. Further, South African regulatory practice uniquely recognizes the relationship between social constructs and material inequalities, even as, in regulatory practice, some regulatory bodies struggle with what encompasses a social construct, never mind the material inequalities stemming from social constructs.

As might be surmised by the aforementioned overview of the South African case, the South African hate regulation context, in short, is contradictory at points. These contradictions really become evident when the South African case is placed within the larger neoliberal framework increasingly characterizing the postapartheid state. Neoliberal regulatory forms seep into the regulatory practices adopted by the post-apartheid state as well as by "private" nonstate entities given "public" regulatory power by the postapartheid state. That such a neoliberal regulatory form characterizes the U.S. context, especially after the "Reagan revolution," is not terribly surprising; for more than a generation now, Americans have viewed the state as "the problem" and not necessarily "the solution." The growing privatization of regulatory practices in South Africa's hate domain, though, leads to a lessening of the very transformative ethic that makes the spirit and operational components of hate regulation in South Africa so different from the U.S. case. With privatization, hate regulation in South Africa starts to sound like a mere administrative act, or worse, when hate regulation starts to become just another management tool helping to temper mass unrest really emanating from continued material disparities that the postapartheid state has tackled only at the edges, fourteen years after the start of multiracial democracy. Burgeoning neoliberal regulatory practices in South Africa tend to lessen the salience of race and racism within the hate regulation matrix, sometimes erasing a progressive understanding of the way that race as construct and racism function. The result is a neoliberal state that increasingly governs racist hate by governing race as construct. This is a state that gradually manages racial hate and racial constructs in the name of a kind of efficiency that, in effect, decreases the possibility of progressive social change. Significantly, part of the neoliberal postapartheid state steadily absolves itself of the responsibility for undoing that which is the systemic cause of hate, because the neoliberal postapartheid state seamlessly projects itself and the society for which it acts as innocent. Innocence here comes as a neoliberal, postapartheid state points to its "objective" and "neutral" regulatory mechanisms remedying hate, when "deviant" individuals or groups hate in impermissible ways. In the end, the hated subsequently find themselves in a kind of statelessness, where the neoliberal, postapartheid state acts, but does not act at all.

Chapter Outlines

Considering hate, race, and neoliberal regulatory state practices from multiple perspectives, the chapter outlines of this book follow.

Chapters 2 and 3 highlight certain regulatory state practices in the United States—policing in particular in chapter 2 and tort in chapter 3. Of these two chapters, chapter 2 elaborates on the primary argument of this book—an explication of how and why the neoliberal state governs hate by governing racial constructs. Foucault's "governmentality" will be used and tweaked in order to make this argument. The role of "science"—legal and racial—also is significantly developed in this chapter to illustrate how governance here is about controlling discourses on race as construct and divesting the state in particular but also society of responsibility for racist hate. These parts are brought together to talk about the policing of one particular hate occurrence in Maine, a national strategy adopted by the Clinton administration in an effort to police hate, such as the hate act in Maine, and the practices enacted by the Chicago Police Department in the period following the implementation of the Clinton administration's strategy.

Chapter 3 on tort does a bit of storytelling. Here storytelling is used to ask how legal "science" in tort enables a racial "science" that bounds race and agency. Hate regulation in this chapter is considered at the intersection of race, gender, and sexuality—at that place where white supremacy, patriarchy, and heterosexism converge.

Chapter 4 articulates how and why a traumatic event such as 9/11 leads to social change in the United States, but not always change in regulatory state practices. Once again, here legal "science" has seemingly led to the state understanding race and racism in ways that do not reflect racial and racist realities after 9/11. Special attention is given in this chapter to the ways in which racial constructs in the United States are formatively influenced after 9/11 by acts of hate against those who are Muslim or "Muslim looking." A look at such post-9/11 acts of hate is paired with a look at activism by newly vocal rights claimants—especially those who are Muslim, but also those who are "Muslim looking."

Chapters 5 and 6 place reconstructive and transformative possibilities in the U.S. case next to the more reconstructive and transformative regulatory practices in South Africa. The South African practices have been introduced in order to shuck the rigid pretenses of apartheid's legal and racial "science." Interestingly, at a key moment when the state rebuked apartheid's "science," understandings of race and racism reflecting new times and new egalitarian possibilities started to come into clear political view. While more progressive practices serve as the template for postapartheid regulation of hate, traces of apartheid practices have reemerged at points in South Africa to make the path of social transformation a bit murky. These traces have been neoliberal in form, as, in late apartheid, the apartheid state began to reposition itself and those it represented for a postapartheid dispensation. Of this book's final two chapters, chapter 5 is specifically relevant in understanding the politics of a piece of South African legislation and special courts designed to regulate hate. Significantly—and very much unlike the U.S. case—this legislation has been implemented within an equality framework where systematic and systemic efforts are being made to undo racial discrimination. Chapter 6 specifically traces the development of media regulations in South Africa intended to control the proliferation of hate. A multilayered comparative analysis is used to compare state regulation of hate and a burgeoning self-regulation within the media industry. Further, a comparison is made between apartheid and postapartheid regulatory norms. The limits of transformation in media regulation here also are brought to the fore.

Finally, this book contains a brief but pointed postscript, which suggests how this study might be used to rethink policies and practices in the United States and South Africa.

2

Is Racism Burning?

Michel Foucault's "governmentality" provides a historical and theoretical foundation upon which to understand how the state governs hate by governing race. Trying to understand political power, historian and philosopher Foucault thought about the ways in which states in Europe and, more important, nonstate and quasistate entities bring about and manage change. He understood change and development in power structures to have occurred in three definable and interconnected stages, forming "a triangle [of] sovereignty-discipline-government, which has as its primary target the population and as its essential mechanism the apparatuses of security."[1]

Foucault conceptualized state power by teasing out the ebbs and flows of governance rationales within the "triangle." For example, he asserted that European mercantilism emerged as an economic system during the sixteenth century, just when European states started to control polities like sovereign patriarchs controlled their households. Foucault suggested that European states increasingly started not just to regulate polities but to microregulate polities as a father regulated his wife and children.[2] Pointing to this blurring of the lines between public and private regulation, he concluded that the change was a crucial marker indicating how and for what ends state control would be established and maintained. This "era," which Foucault conceptually connected to "sovereignty," rested upon the power of a burgeoning state that, without a highly developed state apparatus, largely had to impose its will by the mere aura of its authority as well as its ability to unleash physical force when required.

According to Foucault, state power in Europe expanded in a different way through much of the twentieth century, signifying the transition "from an art of government to a political science."[3] The new forms of state power depended on the economic use of "laws themselves as tactics—to arrange things in such a way that, through a certain number of means, such and such ends may be achieved."[4] Tactics made it possible for European states to more formally identify and routinely punish "deviant" individuals who did not pay sufficient homage to the sovereign. For those who fell outside of the lines, discipline followed, as pinpointed in Foucault's *Discipline and Punish*.[5] This was a discipline and sovereignty that could control—or at least attempt to control—bodies in "schools, manufactories, armies"[6] as well as in places such as prisons through the regimented habilation and rehabilitation of the individual. For example, the prison strictly managed the body of the prisoner by controlling the prisoner's schedule, diet, and attire, as well as controlling the physical movements of the imprisoned by regulating what the new cultural geographers would call space and place. What was going on, in effect, was the state constructing bodies via the control of bodies.

Perfect governance, according to Foucault, has come into being with the political rationale of the present (postdisciplinary) "era." The newly dominant forms of political rationality arrived with the shift "from a regime dominated by structures of sovereignty to one ruled by techniques" that could be even more subtle than the technologies used in prisons. The new economy of control materialized via, as Foucault would have understood it, technologies and tactics such as community policing and student-centered classrooms as well as other means that marked the beginning of the so-called "responsibilization"—or, really, neoliberalization—of society. Technologies and tactics here too constructed bodies in managerial ways. Responsibilization supposedly denoted the moment when the state's regulatory impetus could be removed and given to individuals who, having been taught, could govern (or "governmentalize," or construct) themselves in the name of a so-called enhanced freedom. And significantly the state here began to manifest itself through the outsourcing of its "public" regulatory prerogatives to private bodies, as well as to individuals themselves. Examples of such private bodies included the private and self-governing New York Stock Exchange as well as more inconspicuous and more innocuous sites of privatized—or neoliberal—governance, such as a self-pay parking lot (public or for profit, if there is a difference) and even the shopping center or mall.[7] Shopping centers and malls have become sites where people are "free" to move about, in an "iconoplastic" social environment of their "choice," as long as they remain within certain zones of permissibility.

While recent scholarship on Foucault's governance has ranged from the governance of crime[8] and health[9] to microcredit lending[10] and sexuality,[11] this scholarship has not been used to center race, much less hate, that might be governed by a state, nonstate, or quasistate agency.

Governance scholars omit that—when the state adds to its "art of govern-ment" a tendency to think of the "political [as] science,"[12] as Foucault put it—race is among the things being governed. Further, when the state starts to use "laws themselves as tactics—to arrange things in such a way that, through a certain number of means, such and such ends may be achieved,"[13] race is among the things being arranged in order to establish and maintain certain racial norms.

Not centering race, debates about the emergence of particular gover-nance rationales have instead revolved around how and why new forms of governance come to be, or how governance rationales operate in multi-vectored ways as opposed to unilinear ways. Notably, contributors to the most important edited volumes on Foucault's governance have written with conviction about the transition from the governance of the welfare state to the governance marking "advanced liberalism," where in advanced liberalism responsibilization takes shape next to sovereignty's laws and the disciplinary state's regimented normalization.[14] Yet these governance scholars have not really considered the centrality of race to governance rationales in, for example, a postcolonial and neocolonial moment, except, as with Pat O'Malley, for example, who considered the governance of indigenous Australians.[15] For O'Malley, though, as in an article by U. Kalpagam looking at the economy of a business practice such as accounting in colonial India,[16] race as construct is not central to the overall economy of power; race as construct for O'Malley and Kalpagam is more of an aside. Even the newest line of thinking on "governmentality," as articulated by Giorgio Agamben and those with whom he is in conversation, has not been used to center race as construct. Discussion of race in the work growing from Agamben has come almost by default, as scholars think about Guantánamo, immigration, and other post-9/11 political developments where race is not just important but central. Of scholars in conversation with Agamben, perhaps Judith Butler has understandably offered the most thorough analysis of race as construct. (Much of Butler's earlier work centered on gender and sexu-ality constructs.) Even Butler's work, though, only treats race as construct in implicit terms, as she writes about Muslim "detainees" at the U.S. mili-tary base at Guantánamo Bay, Cuba.[17]

This has been the case despite the centrality of race to state forma-tion and state formation to race, as cogently argued by Ann Stoler.[18] Stopping short of a different politics of governance, scholars studying governance rationales have downplayed the ways that liberal democratic welfare states like the United States and the United Kingdom as well as mixed states (liberal democratic with the tinges of something else, like a real revolutionary past) like South Africa have raced and been raced. This has been a race taking form as the welfare state of Lyndon Johnson and Harold Wilson became the personal responsibility critical to the economizing states of Ronald Reagan and Margaret Thatcher, and the apartheid state of P. W. Botha became the late apartheid and post-apartheid states of F. W. DeKlerk, Nelson Mandela, and Thabo Mbeki. As the transition from liberal welfarism to advanced liberalism has come into being, race has been central, with, for example, the 1980s' and 1990s' racialization of welfare "reform" in the United States, complete with economic constructions of the "welfare queen" who was represented as either the "typical" woman of color, or "white trash."[19] Reform meant a responsibilization absenting the state from a social effected by the creation of capitalism's "haves" and "have-nots." A similar economy of race and responsibility has developed in South Africa as the transition from apartheid's command-oriented capitalism to postapartheid's social democratic economic framework (Redistribution and Development Program [RDP], 1994–1997) and then the later adoption of advanced liberalism's economics (Growth Employment and Redistribution [GEAR], 1997–present). As this transition has taken shape in postapartheid South Africa, the North-South hemispheric divide perpetuating the newest dependencies is reproduced within South Africa itself as many of the "previously disadvantaged" (a euphemism for South African blacks and women in particular) are increasingly left responsible for themselves in their search for jobs and in the continental struggle with HIV/AIDS, while apartheid's privileged racial class continues to reap the residual privileges of apartheid (e.g., education, higher wealth accumulation, easy immigration, European passports, etc.).

Much is to be learned when hate, race, and responsibility are centered as some scholars thinking of governance have started to center gender as construct.[20] Studying racial governance (and moreover the economic governance of racial constructs in the United States and South Africa), allows scholarship on governance rationales to move beyond the understanding of a "political" ending at that point when we are insidiously taught to govern ourselves, and thus become responsible for ourselves, or when a traumatic event such as 9/11 prompts some state actors to claim extralegal powers consistent with sovereign power. The cases highlighted in this chapter demonstrate that politics is just beginning when a neoliberal state—through its police departments or a federal agency—discursively governs hate by governing racial constructs in order to absent itself from regulatory responsibilities.

The remainder of the chapter presents snapshots of the governance practices of three law enforcement agencies in the United States, from the mid-to-late 1990s. Two of the agencies are local police departments, and the other is a department of the federal government.

In the first snapshot, I take a close look at police and legislative practices in a Maine cross-burning case. I contend that the state governs hate and race in a way that does not reflect the ebb and flow of hate and race in a postindustrial society like the United States, where social and economic change beckons us to think of race and racism in new ways.

In the second snapshot, I look at the ways in which the federal government prescribed a method of policing hate and race. I do this through a detailed description of the training component of the U.S. Department of Justice's National Hate Crime Initiative. This curriculum for law enforcement officers serves as evidence of the duality of a federal initiative intended to help authorities handle a racist act such as a cross burning. On the one hand, the training manual for law enforcement officers promotes sophisticated and even progressive law-enforcement tactics. On the other hand, the manual contains language heralding the power of therapy, which can be productive, but only to a certain point. On the one hand, the authors of the National Hate Crime Initiative envisage a changing hate and race that might summon us to think in new ways. On the other hand, the new thinking heavily depends on "curing" the "deviant" who hates, not transforming a racist society and state.

In the last snapshot I examine the policing practices of the Chicago Police Department (CPD), which has forthrightly deployed community policing strategies in order to stanch hate. Policing hate in Chicago, though, has a problematic genealogy, that can be traced to the department's development and use of new technology explicitly used to violate rights, not to protect and extend rights.

Knowing Race to Govern Race

On June 22, 1996, Stacey Silvers raced out of her apartment in Augusta, the Maine state capitol, in order to extinguish a burning cross in front of a neighbor's home. This hallmark of the Ku Klux Klan and white supremacy prompted angry Mainers to call the police. Responding, a police dispatcher sent officers to Washington Street and Washington Street Place, across the street from St. Augustine's Roman Catholic Church in Augusta's Sand Hill neighborhood. Shortly after the police arrived, the responding officer confronted Vincent Hallowell, a resident of Sand Hill, who initially admitted to having placed and lit the cross. A representative from the Maine Department of the Attorney General arrived a short time later, and the attorney general's office started its own investigation. The department eventually requested and obtained a temporary and then a permanent restraining order against Hallowell, prohibiting him from making contact with those to whom the cross burning was directed. The baton passed from one state agency to another, from the police to the Department of the Attorney General, to a state superior court, to the U.S. Department of Justice, which later prosecuted Hallowell in a federal district court for violating the civil rights of some, but not other, residents of Sand Hill. Hallowell and his accomplice, Benjamin Newton, were never prosecuted in Maine state court for the cross burning, as, under Maine state law, they could only be prosecuted for violating the restraining order issued to them, which Hallowell actually did violate. Hallowell and Newton were, however, compelled to accept a plea agreement in the federal case, as the state disciplined two men whose hate fell outside of the bounds of permissible hate.

Policing

Instrumental to hate and racial governance, an official form (APD-Form 1) contains the initial incident report for the Silvers-Hallowell case (#9622395). Multiple compartments (or boxes) on the form have prompts to be answered with multiple strains of information. The more requested information, the more space the form allows for data. Information on the form must be recorded in code or indicated with an "X" mark next to the appropriate space, in a given box.[21]

The reporting officer, whose identification number is 115, as indicated in a box at the bottom of the form, noted that there seemed to be a "hate/bias" motive in the Silvers-Hallowell case, thus Hallowell's alleged crime was officially registered as a "hate crime" in the report. The act even received a "Nature Code," which was recorded as "90 Z." Important to the investigation was the establishment of the date and time when the incident started and ended. The cross burning on "Washington Street" was "reported on: 6/22/96" at "time 1345." The cross burning "occurred on 6/22/96" at "time 1340." The cross burning "ended on 6/22/96" at "time 1345." By giving it a time and place, the offense officially occurred and was listed as an act of "terrorizing," as terrorizing was defined by state statute.[22]

The remainder of the APD-Form 1 used in the Silvers-Hallowell case compartmentalized the identities of people, not just the space and time occupied by people. The compartmentalization on the form differed from that which occurs when fully considering the complexity of race. Whereas recognition of the complexities of race humanizes, the APD-Form 1 reduced the person to particles. Date of birth, age, sex, ethnicity, height, weight, hair, and eye color were to be requested of all witnesses who were questioned. In addition to the witness's home address, there were spaces for the reporting officer to pen the home and business phone numbers of those involved in the case.[23]

Officials, in writing, constructed race, ethnicity, and nationality in the Silvers-Hallowell case to make them appear understandable and knowable. Confident in its understanding and knowledge, the state puzzlingly concocted race. The reporting officer had four options when racially classifying those deemed "victim": "W" (white), "B" (black), "A" (Asian), or "I" (Indian). For the Augusta Police Department, "W" assumably would have included all Latinos, whether from the small Maine town of China or from a mestizo culture in Central America. The state placed Asians from China (*the* China) in the same space as Asians from India even though Asians from India, are technically "Caucasian," using the state's own crude gauges. And "I" for Indian was not the India of Nehru but Native American.

"Ethnic" labels on the incident report form were to add context to racial identities to be noted on the APD-Form 1. Interestingly, the form listed two choices in a box labeled "ethnic": "H" or "N." Given that all of the people in the Silvers-Hallowell incident report had their ethnicity recorded as "N," "N" likely marked one as "Native," not to be confused with Native American, as in American Indian, or "None," as in no ethnicity. Giving new meaning to "ethnic cleansing," those from the United States were not ethnic, ethnicity here only existing beyond the physical borders of the United States. "H," for "Hispanic," was the other ethnic choice on the form, reflecting the small but marked presence of Latinos in Maine in the mid-1990s.

As the state sought to become more precise in its understanding of race in the Silvers-Hallowell case, it continuously demonstrated that it was not racially deft. For example, an additional choice for race and ethnicity appeared in the section of APD-Form 1 where the composite of the "Suspect/Subject" was to be registered. In the "Suspect/Subject" series of boxes, specifically in the boxes for race and ethnicity, the reporting officer could have marked "U" for "Unknown," but did not, as the officer understood Hallowell to be white, as well as not ethnic. The state knew Hallowell's race as it knew his height, weight, hair color, and eye color: white, 5 feet, 7 inches, 140 pounds, brown, brown. Stacey Silvers's race and ethnicity too were as real as her height, weight, hair, and eye color, according to the police report. Silvers, listed as "Victim Type: I" (Individual), was classified as "W" (White) because she looked "white." This racial descriptor was interesting especially considering the fact that Silvers was the raced person who, according to the Augusta Police Department's incident form, suffered harm because of Hallowell's racial hatred.[24]

Stacey Silvers's identity as a twenty-two-year-old woman who is "biracial" (as she describes herself) revealed a kind of race trouble in the state's law. In reaching a conclusion about Silvers's racial identity, the state's reporting officer may have listed Silvers as a "victim," because the officer recognized that acts of racial hate can be directed from one white person to another white person. Or, perhaps Silvers was both "white" and "victim" in the report because of the race ascribed to her children. (The father of Silvers's children is African American.) The officer's report noted that Silvers's biracial children fall between and beyond the dominant culture's racial categories, though the reporting officer did not necessarily think of the children's race in such complex terms[25]; as noted in the supplementary report, the reporting officer wrote, "Stacey [Silvers] has two inter-racial (*sic*) children, and Vincent [Hallowell] knows this."[26]

Hallowell, not unlike the state, did not racially understand and know those with whom he came into contact. This lack of knowledge and understanding became apparent as Silvers positioned herself against the racist hate of Hallowell. In the affidavit Silvers submitted to Maine's Department of the Attorney General, she recounted, "Last evening, Friday, June 21, 1996," one day before the actual cross burning, she witnessed a "racial incident." Wrote Silvers, "The incident involved a black child in my neighborhood who was called 'little nigger boy' by a white man." The next day Silvers took out some trash, only to run into her downstairs neighbor, Vincent Hallowell, who according to Silvers, "stopped me and said he had seen me talking to the plice (*sic*)." In an exchange with Hallowell, Silvers acknowledged that she had given a statement to the police about the "racial incident" in which her neighbor's black child was called "little niggerboy (*sic*)." Silvers added, "Mr. Hallowell then said that he was going to get all these 'fucking niggers off of Sand Hill.'"[27] (The "little niggerboy" (*sic*) was the son of George Jones, a Sand Hill neighbor, who is black. Jones and his son were two of the "fucking niggers" Hallowell wanted to leave the Sand Hill neighborhood. The cross burning was in front of Jones's home.)

"Crossing and Blending"

Silvers constructed herself in relation to the racial and racist contexts in which she found herself. Clarifying her biracial identity, Silvers said, "My father is Puerto Rican, and my mother is white."[28] Silvers also specified that her father is not only Puerto Rican, ethnically, but also black, racially. She made this additional distinction when interviewed by a local reporter shortly after the cross burning.[29] Perhaps to Silvers, as with other *boricuas* (Puerto Ricans), to be Puerto Rican is to be black, even if one has a white mother and white skin; and to be black is to be proximate to the postcolonial hybrid culture that is Puerto Rico and its diaspora.

Latinos generally present challenges to a state either rendering race invisible or articulating race in terms of the standard racial markers used in the United States. A Latina who also is black, like Silvers, confuses the state's race even more as the state attempts to assign responsibility for the hate it has helped create. In the late 1970s, in an attempt to contain and better analyze the "race" of Puerto Ricans, for example, the U.S. Census Bureau stopped referring to Puerto Ricans as a "race." The change came as a result of U.S. Office of Management and Budget standards designed to enforce federal civil rights law, to keep tabs on race and poverty, and so on. The category "Hispanic" started to be used as a kind of technology, along with a categorical race. However, "Hispanic" and other old markers under review by the government between 1994 and 2000 lacked the dynamic qualities of Latinos as a group. This, of course, changed in the 2000 census, as the standard census form was amended to allow multiple ethno-racial identities to officially surface.[30]

Puerto Rican studies scholar Juan Flores reflected upon blackness and Puerto Rican identities. Flores wrote, "Crossing and blending of transmitted colonial cultures is not to be confused with the proverbial 'melting pot' of Anglo-American fantasy." He also noted that "crossing and blending" was not a sign that Latin cultures are free of racism. Instead, Flores emphasized the cultural synchretism between African Americans and *puertoriquenos* in New York in particular as an effort to relate to "other cultures caught up in comparable processes of historical recovery and strategic resistance"[31]—processes that the state must readily understand in order to be a reconstructive and transformative force in hate regulation.

Legislating

The racial mind of the state is apparent as the state legislates against hate, not just as the state polices and prosecutes a case like Silvers-Hallowell. Hate acts of consequence in Maine are regulated with the authority given to the Department of the Attorney General by Maine's Civil Rights Act. The act has existed as a civil statute, giving the state of Maine's attorney general the authority to request a restraining order against those who hate but whose act does not constitute a criminal act. And the attorney general has aggressively exercised this legislative authority granted to it.[32]

Race and racism nebulously figured in Maine's Civil Rights Act as the state tried to take some semblance of responsibility for the hate directed at Silvers. In 1989, when first passed, the state's civil rights legislation, for example, had no race, color, gender, sexuality, and so on. In short, there was no difference of any kind that was to be protected by statute. The only mention of "color"—and this was not "real" color—came in the first sentence of the act:

> Whenever any person, whether or not acting under color of law, intentionally interferes by physical force or violence against a person, damage or destruction of property or trespass on property or by the threat of physical force or violence against a person, damage or destruction of property or trespass on property.[33]

The act, as originally constructed, contained wording used to stress protection of person and property, not difference. The emphasis on the person as individual and on property has served to divert attention away from differentials in power based on difference.[34] (The state's centering of property matters in particular has been consistent with federal court rulings in hate cases as the regulation of hate has come into conflict with the protection of offensive speech in the name of the First Amendment. Specifically, hate speech has tended to lose constitutional protection if and only if that speech threatens persons as property or the property of persons.[35])

In response to political pressure from civil rights groups, and to comply with federal law (Hate Crime Statistics Act of 1990), Maine's legislature revised the state's Civil Rights Act in 1991 in order to assess racial difference. After the 1991 revision, the Maine Department of the Attorney General actually started to keep a record of the identity of those on the receiving end of hate. Federal legislation also prompted a 1993 amendment to Maine's Civil Rights Act. Required to statistically track hate by difference, this amendment reflected the link between difference and hate in a formal way, taking into consideration acts "motivated by reason of race, color, religion, sex, ancestry, national origin, physical or mental disability, or sexual orientation."[36] But all except one of those classified as victims from the period 1992–1998 were lodged into just one identity category, as these categories were used to attempt to contain difference. There was no consideration of, say, the black gay male whose assault stemming from hate was at the intersection of race, gender, and sexuality. Nor was there the possibility of a complex racial identity falling outside of the state's racial constructs. There definitely was no consideration of the hate act committed against someone like Silvers, who is a biracial person of color, a woman, and a single parent of biracial children. As a result, the state's regressive understanding and knowledge of difference made it difficult for it not only to acknowledge its complicity in hate, but its understanding and knowledge of difference also made it difficult to develop a collective consciousness with which states and societies set out to fight hate in a structured and systemic way.

Training against Hate and Race

National Hate Crimes Training Initiative

The Silvers-Hallowell case occurred the year before the federal government made a marked attempt to standardize training practices for state
agents regulating hate in the United States. In 1997, then attorney general
of the United States, Janet Reno, assembled a working group to put
together a curriculum reflecting the "best practices" of hate regulators.
The working group was to prepare a curriculum that would be used by
responding officers who actually investigate hate acts, their supervisors,
and others working in law enforcement who are not necessarily police
officers. Reno's working group included representatives from the U.S.
Department of Justice (DOJ) as well as representatives of state agencies
from the fifty states and Washington, D.C. After meeting during the
summer and fall of 1997, Bill Clinton used the November 1997 White
House Conference on Hate Crimes to announce that Reno's working
group would start to implement the training curriculum in the fall of
1998. Three train-the-trainer conferences took place during the fall of
1998 in Chicago, Orlando, and Phoenix. Seventy-eight teams from all of
the states and the District of Columbia received invitations to attend one
of the train-the-trainer conferences, where for two days the DOJ's
working group conducted workshops. These seventy-eight teams then
returned to their home states and trained other trainers, and so on.

The National Hate Crimes Training Curricula as technology has many
facets. It is flexible enough to give latitude to those working in contexts
as different as Chicago's white and affluent suburb of Skokie as well as
a major central city with a diverse population like a Los Angeles defined
by migration and immigration. Multiple pedagogical strategies come
into play as a result. Specifically, the course designed for a general law
enforcement audience allows the instructor to make use of lectures,
instructor-centered discussions, and student-centered discussions that
might allow other local "beat" variables to infuse the training sessions.

The curriculum workbook, or "notebook" as the authors of the
manual call it, becomes an instrument used to convey two main messages
to those who would train state officials, such as the responding officer
in the Silvers-Hallowell case. First, working group members who assembled the notebook actually understand that relaying an understanding of
context is essential to the preparation of state agents charged with regulating hate. It follows that context, in the notebook, comes with a
particular understanding of the legal context underlying civil rights and
civil rights struggles in the United States. Second, those working group
members responsible for devising the training program connect these

contextual inputs to more nuts-and-bolts practices. For example, practical instructions that aid in the identification of hate crimes and provide basic information about the psychological trauma of victims are crucial elements of the train-the-trainer curriculum.

Context, as understood by the authors of the notebook, has two significant prongs. At one level, authors of the student notebook relay an understanding of law enforcement's historical role in the shaping and misshaping of civil rights. The notebook reads, "Law enforcement and policing has been involved in or associated with hate/bias crimes and civil rights in the United States in six ways."[37] Two of these six "ways" receive particular attention in the notebook—the state's role "as protector of others' civil rights" and its role as "enforcer of civil rights."[38] Examples of the former, as illustrated in the student manual, include the role of military police in the integration of the University of Mississippi and the Boston police's role in securing schools during that city's integration battles of the 1970s. The enforcement example in the notebook is the historical role played by law enforcement officers policing hate groups such as the Ku Klux Klan and racist skinheads. Notebooks, though, also function at a different level. Namely, they become tools for critical introspection on the negative role of law enforcement in U.S. rights struggles. For example, "as a trigger or catalyst for riots/civil disturbance," those who assembled the notebook point to failures in the justice system that helped to facilitate the 1992 riots in Los Angeles. In the notebook, police receive blame for the Rodney King beating, and the judicial system receives blame for acquitting the police officers who beat King. Authors of the notebook continue by informing students about the role of the law "as an instrument of others' political agenda," as when the police acted on behalf of capitalist interests when breaking strikes during the nineteenth and twentieth centuries in cities such as Chicago as well as the state's role as a "rights violator."[39]

At a second contextual level, those responsible for writing the notebook ostensibly initiate a critique of the dominant social and political order that gives rise to hate, but only up to a certain point. The authors of the notebook acknowledge that there are "no easy answers" to remedy hate.[40] They continue, "Fear and alienation play an important role" in the making of hate.[41] As conveyed in the student manual, this fear and alienation result from "economic prejudice" that the authors connect to "the stereotype that minorities are making gains which threaten the economic and social well-being of others."[42] But beyond this "economic prejudice," which textured Hallowell's hate at some level, the authors use the notebook to attribute hate violence to "demographic changes,"[43] where whites are or are becoming racial minorities. Authors of the notebook, however, fail to connect "economic prejudice" to demographic change and what the authors identify as the "shift to a service economy."[44] That is, economic policies accompanying the U.S. transition from an industrial economy to a postindustrial economy help concentrate wealth, and opportunity, within the borders of the United States and even within the borders of a select number of U.S. metropolitan areas, counties, and zip codes.

Even as social and economic concerns figured in the hate under-stood by the authors of the notebook, the authors use the notebook to pathologize those who hate. There is a departure from the systemic and structural forces shaping hate as the authors of the notebook construct those who hate. Aside from those who hate being labeled anomalous scourges who need to be more responsible individuals, those who hate come in three basic types in the notebook: "mission offenders," "thrill[-]seeking offenders," and "reactive offenders."[45] "Mission offenders" are, as described in the notebook, "often psychotic," or some similar descriptor. "Thrill-seeking offenders," "generally," according to the authors of the notebook, are "groups of teenagers," who act to "gain a psychological or social thrill," "to be accepted by peers," or "to gain 'bragging rights.'"[46] "Reactive offenders" hate in criminal ways out of "a sense of entitlement regarding their rights, privileges, [and] way of life that does not extend to the victim."[47] While reactive offenders seemingly thrive on systemic and structural forces, such as economic inequalities, the remedy for their racist hate, as offered in the guide, is the same as that for thrill-seeking offenders who, according to the notebook's authors, merely need to become tolerant individuals instead of individuals acting in prejudicial ways.[48]

Further removing hate from social and economic structures, biolog-ical notions of race, gender, and sexuality (without intersections) are predominant in the notebook. And these notions are integral to under-standing who is responsible for hate acts as well as who or what is responsible for reconstructing and transforming hate. In the notebook, responsibility for hate is attributed to "deviant" individuals whose "deviance" is connected to the biology of the hated and perhaps even the biology of the hater. For example, "racial bias" in the notebook is

> a preformed negative opinion or attitude toward a group of persons who possess common physical characteristics (e.g., color of skin; eyes and/or hair; facial features; etc.) genetically transmitted by descent and heredity which distinguish them as a distinct division of humankind (e.g., Asians, blacks, whites).[49]

Those compiling the notebook articulate similar biological notions of gender and sexuality. Notebook authors conflate "gender" as a social construct with the biology of sex.[50] While making the case to include gender as a protected category in hate policy and regulatory practices, gender becomes just a synonym for woman instead of a concept conditioned by social constructs shaped by social and economic change. Further, authors of the notebook think that "gay" and "lesbian" are merely categories determined by "sexual attraction toward, and responsive[ness] to, other males" or "other females."[51]

Layered within biological constructions of race, gender, and sexuality, the authors of the notebook depict those who are hated as helpless victims dependent upon the state that governs hate by governing identities. For example, those hated suffer from "bias crimes" that pose "unique challenges to [law-enforcement] professionals," when "bias crimes" tend to "exacerbate existing tension within the community" of the hated.[52] "Therefore," as noted in the student notebook, "bias crimes demand a special response from the Patrol Officer and victim assistance professional."[53] Hate regulation through policing, as specified in the notebook, requires a special instinct from the law-enforcement professional, because "the victim does not always understand that he or she may have been victimized in a bias-motivated attack."[54]

The designers of the notebook understandably focus on the responding officers and their interaction with the hated in particular. Much of this focus on hate regulation, however, elevates constructs of the police as a kind of noble protector of biologically constructed victims depicted as helpless. In the case of the National Hate Crime Training Initiative notebook discussed here, Foucault's modern governance meets the multicultural police officer of the state. So, for example, authors of the manual reiterate the importance of rigid evidence collection and documentation as being "critical for a more effective response" to hate in order to achieve an "improved understanding of diversity."[55] Eliminating hate and augmenting "cultural awareness"[56] means following procedure, understanding history, responding promptly, and undertaking other investigatory methods. Culturally informed hate regulation also means being sensitive to the needs of those who are hated,[57] looking for and trying to assuage the trauma of those who are hated,[58] trying to understand the feelings of the hated,[59] and not trying to be judgmental[60] so as to cause "secondary injury."[61]

"Best Practices"

Stephen Wessler, the assistant state attorney general in Maine who managed the Hallowell-Silvers case, is an important player in the making of U.S. hate policies and practices, with its progressive and problematic dimensions. Wessler contributed to the formulation of national hate policy in his capacity as director of the Center for the Study and Prevention of Hate Violence at the University of Southern Maine, as well as through his role as consultant to the U.S. Department of Justice's Office of Justice Programs (OJP), a unit within the DOJ's Bureau of Justice Assistance (BJA). Wessler authored the Bureau of Justice Programs Hate Crime Series, published by the OJP between February 2000 (the last year of the Clinton presidency) and October 2001 (just after 9/11). The OJP consultants and staff produced the series in order to provide outlines of training practices as used by law-enforcement agencies as well as nongovernmental and nonprofit organizations throughout the United States. The DOJ efforts spearheaded by Wessler at the OJP closely followed an increasingly formalized law-enforcement practice of comparing "best practices," or technologies, which, of course, included the practices taught as a part of the National Hate Crime Training Initiative.

As a platform for the widespread circulation of "best practices," stressing kinder and gentler hate regulation, the series prepared by Wessler for the OJP contains an outline of the Juvenile Offenders Learning Tolerance (JOLT) program used by the Los Angeles County District Attorney. The JOLT programmers primarily intervene through two training programs as technologies. One uses the resources of the Simon Wiesenthal Center's Museum of Tolerance in Los Angles and the Facing History Ourselves organization in order to invite educators and educational staffs to think and speak about bias, prejudice, hate, and violence. Significantly, these programs bring together educators, nonprofit organizations committed to fighting hate in its various guises, and law enforcement agencies in order to compare strategies used to develop and implement programs. Such programs seemingly gain favor because they reproduce a brand of multiculturalism consistent with the state's hate regulation strategies. Specifically, Wessler and the OJP officials promoting JOLT and other programs herald the way their model programs aim to foster a "respect for difference," or some similar variation of the phrase, as the highest possible ideal.[62]

Approaches akin to those used by programmers responsible for JOLT circulate within a larger discourse rationalizing hate and its regulation. For example, in a more measured follow-up to their *Hate Crimes: The Rising Tide of Bigotry and Bloodshed*, Jack Levin and Jack McDevitt use their *Hate Crimes Revisited* to champion words such as "prejudice," "tolerance," "awareness," and "sensitize." This language projects a particularly neutral flare, where there is not so much a lack of blame for hate's existence as there is no one or no thing responsible for hate. Much the same rhetoric problematized by Manning Marable appears in a commissioned report by the Rand Corporation for the Los Angeles Police Department (LAPD) as a part of its 2001 Rampart consent decree with the U.S. Department of Justice. The recurrent phrase preferred by Rand is "diversity awareness," where "the LAPD must train its officers to recognize cultural differences and barriers if it is to serve its people effectively."[63] But the Rand report obscures police power and even the LAPD's institutional racism in a scandal like Rampart. In the Rand report, the core recommendation for the LAPD consists of engendering a new professionalism among officers using the governance concepts of "corporateness," "responsibility," and knowledge as "expertise," as notably deployed by Samuel P. Huntington in 1957 in his *The Soldier and the State*. (This is the same Samuel Huntington who recently authored an article on Latinos in the United States, their inability to assimilate to "American" norms, and, therefore, their challenge to the "American" way of life).[64]

"Preventing" Hate, Race, and Racism

Hate and Chicago's Alternative Policing Strategy

"Prevention" was the pertinent watchword as the CPD governed hate and race in the postindustrial city. As it historicizes its own actions, contemporary efforts to actively curb hate using governance technologies go back to 1981, when the department formed the Community Assessment Center (CAC) within its Civil Rights Unit[65] in order to, basically, monitor the effects of the postindustrial social and economic changes vividly described in William Julius Wilson's *When Work Disappears*.[66] According to the CPD, "with the prevention ideal in mind," the CAC, in a Foucauldian vein, "monitors and diagnoses community tension throughout the City of Chicago and tries to resolve potential problems before they escalate."[67] The CAC staff members receive reports from the department's Patrol Division and other units as well as reports from other city agencies and the media. These reports provide "intelligence" about the levels of hate in neighborhoods. "These varied sources of information," according to the department, "provide a system of cross-checks to ensure that appropriate data is being collected." After finding "an area of community tension" using ICAM (Information Collection for Automated Mapping) technologies, CAC staff members inform the department's Civil Rights Unit and commanders in the relevant police district so that they can start to work with community groups and community leaders to "prevent" criminal and noncriminal acts motivated by hate.[68]

The CPD started to use its "prevention" rationale and technologies to fight a different kind of "hate." In the 1980s, shortly after the formation of the CAC, CPD officials started to use CAC-like technologies to collect "intelligence" on groups that the department considered promulgators "harming relations between sections of the population." (A similar phrase, and rationale, was used by the apartheid state to justify censorship and rights violations, all in the name of regulating hate—see chapter 6 in this book.) These groups, who opposed Reagan administration policies in El Salvador in particular, were considered "terrorists." The state labeled these groups "terrorists" because they supposedly wanted to help communist-backed rebels defeat El Salvador's U.S.-supported regime. Abridging rights fundamental to political communities, and the personhood of those constituting dissenting political communities, the police sought to "prevent," by suppression, one group in particular—the Chicago Committee in Solidarity with the People of El Salvador (CISPES). The state's regulatory practices came to the fore only because those under surveillance filed a suit against the city and the U.S. attorney general, leading to a 1982 consent decree calling on the CPD to recognize and respect the right to attorney-client privilege. In the late 1980s, the Alliance to End Repression, yet another progressive group, initiated court action against the CPD. This later court action led to a 1988 permanent injunction in which the CPD was ordered to curtail police investigations interfering with political activism protected by the First Amendment.[69] In 2002, a federal court modified its oversight of CPD investigations that infringed upon First Amendment rights. The court mandated modifications that required the city to implement an audit system to, in a self-regulatory vein, check its own power.[70]

Just as the city was forced to curtail its surveillance of those considered dangerous sources of "hate" and "terrorism," the 1980s and 1990s "culture wars" were under way in the United States.[71] Court mandates and "culture wars" required that the CPD redeploy CAC's "prevention" technologies. The political climate during the "culture wars," which included fervent debates about how to regulate hate and speech, prompted the CPD to adopt a human rights policy with a hate crime and hate incident component. Instead of trying to abridge the rights and personhood of political dissidents dubbed haters and terrorists, CPD officials projected an image of the department as a protector of those socially marginalized, without recognizing the state's complicity in processes of marginalization. The department, through a 1992 general order (92-1) titled "Human Rights and Human Resources," stated its commitment "to observing, upholding and enforcing all laws relating to individual rights."[72] The CPD's addendum to this general order dealt with "hate crimes/criminal and noncriminal incidents motivated by hate." It cited relevant statutes and ordinances and outlined reporting procedures for hate crimes and incidents.[73]

General Order 92-1 and the addendum on hate came at a time when the CPD started to place a premium on its relations with communities most likely to be the targets of supremacist hate. Addendum authors sought to routinize investigative and reporting procedures for hate crimes. All officers received instructions on how they were supposed to investigate hate acts that might be criminal and file or review hate crime reports, as well as who to notify after filing a hate crime report. Beyond procedures used to regulate "hate crimes" and "other criminal/quasi-criminal incidents motivated by hate," authors of the addendum instructed police officers on a second set of procedures in "noncriminal incidents motivated by hate." The recognition of the victim's pain was an important part of investigative procedures for "noncriminal incidents." As for reporting procedures, responding officers, on-duty watch commanders, the Detective Division supervisors, and the department's Civil Rights Section investigators made up the hate regulation chain-of-command. The reporting chain of command in "noncriminal incidents" was identical to the chain in "hate crimes." Major differences, though, included the substitution of an "information report" in "noncriminal incidents" as opposed to a "case report" filed in hate cases that were deemed criminal by the police. The major difference, however, came as officers investigating "incidents" were told to investigate any underlying community tensions that may have led to the "incidents." General Order 92–1 also required CPD officers to conduct their investigations without interfering with First Amendment rights.[74]

The city's attempts to govern hate and govern race by investigating underlying community tensions culminated with the introduction of operating principles and procedures connected to Chicago's Alternative Policing Strategy (CAPS), which represented the perfection of Foucauldian governance because it helped the department formally market itself as a protector of rights while downplaying any sense of ultimate responsibility for hate. Implemented in 1993 under the stewardship of two police superintendents of color (one African American and one Latino), the department billed the "strategy" as a "new weapon in the fight against crime," like hate crime. And the "new weapon is you," according to a CAPS report, "the community," which in the CPD literature has no race or class.[75]

The "community," and individuals within the community, proved essential to this community policing plan built on neighborhood beat officers, "beat community meetings," training for officers and Chicagoans, and new technologies set up to locate "hot spots."[76] This sounded very much like CAC rhetoric, with its ICAM technologies, except that all of the negatives of the CAC—namely, the bad publicity coming from the court actions filed by progressive groups dubbed haters and terrorists by the CPD—disappeared. With CAPS, the CPD gained new partners. The "CAPS partnership," according to the department, made "tackling serious crime problems" possible, "as well as those neighborhood conditions that breed crime."[77] A report on the first five years of CAPS, from 1993 to 1998, prominently featured Luther Harrison and Arnold Mireles, CAPS community volunteers who, according to the authors of the report, actively sought to, respectively, involve African American and Latino communities in the program (Harrison is black, Mireles is Latino). That two persons of color became commodities for the CPD did not mean that they were pawns, as CAPS participants are often real neighborhood activists, not afraid to take on the police when the police harm the community. (I frequently attend my neighborhood's CAPS meetings, along with other African Americans who are both aware and watchful of the history of policing on Chicago's predominantly black South Side.) Problematic was the fact that communities in distress had to turn to state agents who helped maintain the community's distress in the first place. This distress occurred as the police overpoliced communities of color, sometimes leading to the systematic torture of men of color in particular, as recently uncovered by investigators.[78]

Responsibility for hate made possible by the social and economic changes understood by Wilson started to shift from the state constructed as a benevolent team player toward individuals and communities constructed as willing participants in their own policing. The state claimed the responsibility to police the effects of social and economic change without always foregrounding and saying exactly what it was doing: governing hate by governing race and racism. That is, the state governed hate by starting to teach those most subjected to hate to secure their own rights and personhood.

3

Tortious Race, Race Torts

An unlit Camel cigarette in hand, Stefan Chandler dove into his bed. This was his way of shifting into survival mode shortly after having returned home only to find "SPIC LOVING FAGGOT" painted on his front door. This was the toll for being "out" in the chic (some might say "icono-plastic") yet oddly populist enclave that is Sunny Beach, a world away from Augusta and Chicago. Chandler instantly realized who used a can of red spray paint to scrawl the assaulting words on the door: a male who lives in his mid-size condominium building, Chuck Renoe, an African American. Without a witness, or conclusive evidence, though, the physical and wistful Renoe avoided prosecution.

Chandler carefully lit and extinguished a third cigarette and then called the police. The reporting officer finally arrived to take a police report. The officer noted the time and date as well as Chandler's name, address, age, and race on the department's standard form. Time: 22.35; Date: 09/10/00; Name: Stefan Chandler; Address: Meridian and 11th, opposite Flamingo Park; Age: 35. Race: Black. In addition to the basics, the officer also noted that the brawny and effeminate Chandler had been verbally intimidated by Renoe two weeks prior, and that, pending further action, Renoe has been under a temporary restraining order, prohibiting him from making any contact with Chandler. Following stan-dard procedures of investigation, the reporting officer extracted from Chandler the fact that Renoe had called him a "fucking faggot" and "Española" (a derogatory reference to Latinos in the local parlance) just before promising to return to "finish the job."

Given Chandler's statement to the authorities, the reporting officer did not even have to think about what motivated whoever painted the slur on his door: homophobia. Not fully in tune with the cultural swirl that is Sunny Beach, the reporting officer missed the multiple forms of hate simultaneously at work in this case. Clearly excluded from the realm of possibility in the official investigation and official record was the following: the harm done to Chandler resulted from acts of hate simultaneously inspired by race, gender, and sexuality. Perhaps coding this as an act of homophobia was easy for the official because the reporting officer sexually coded Chandler as "gay" in the case report because he "looked" gay. And besides, "faggot" was written on his door. Beyond this, the officer concluded that there was no racial component to this hate because both Chandler and Renoe are black. Perhaps this simply demonstrated that in sunny retreats by the sea, as elsewhere, the not-so-nimble state did the best that a lumbering and fordist state can do in such instances where individuals and groups ruffle tightly bounded assumptions and social constructions.

Given that there were no available ordinances or statutes regulating hate based on sexual orientation, and without a witness to testify against Renoe, Chandler had to seek a civil remedy in state court because the state abdicated its responsibility to ensure his rights in the most direct way. His counsel understood the case in much the same way as the police officer taking the initial report; she knew what she learned in law school. That is, in seeking a permanent restraining order and compensation from Renoe, Chandler's counsel prepared a case based on sexuality, not race, gender, and sexuality. This made sense, to someone trained in a "scientific" way, due in large part to the pedagogical methods dominant in U.S. law schools, where tort is tidily and classically organized by category, tort, element, and concept. Venturing beyond the established framework meant risking loss in court. This was the starting point from which a lawyer would work, despite the diverse demographics of Sunny Beach and the larger metropolitan area, which includes a large Jewish, Latino, African American, white, and gay population, which of course could include community members who are simultaneously Jewish, Latino, white (or black, for that matter), and gay.

A stubborn Chandler wanted to do more than win in court; he wanted to make the courts see him and understand the wrong done to him. He demanded that his lawyer prepare the case to match the wrong done to him. This meant that he intended to seek a legal remedy based on hate acts driven by race, gender, and sexuality, where his hybrid status as a racial minority in the United States and as a sexual minority places him lower in the social hierarchy than the black and heterosexual Renoe. But there was one problem: his lawyer refused to cooperate. After having contacted several lawyers, all of whom refused to take his case without payment, Chandler finally found a lawyer who heard him out.

The narrative of the case that Chandler eventually relayed to the court was simple enough. Renoe acted like the typical heterosexual bent on terrorizing someone he hated. There was a clear pattern of hate that developed over several months in which Renoe habitually called Chandler either a "spic lover," "faggot," or "nigger." And Renoe made subtle use of his bodily frame to reinforce his hateful words. Renoe never physically harmed Chandler, though he instilled the kind of fear about which novelist Richard Wright wrote, where the fear stirred through the mere threat of physical harm is as bad as physical harm itself. (Wright was thinking about the terror growing from the threat of lynching in the South.) This all culminated with the paint on Chandler's door—"SPIC LOVING FAGGOT"—because Chandler identified as a black gay man, who loved Latinos and considered all of these communities his communities.

Rethinking race, tort, and inequality to highlight the ways that a state technology such as tort is used to govern hate by governing identity, I present the arguments of the chapter in the following order. In the "Race and Tort Scholarship" section, I offer an assessment of the scholarly literature on race and tort in the United States. In the "Tort (as) Structure" section, I specifically suggest a possible limitation of the race and tort scholarship. I argue that race and tort scholars have largely skirted the problematic ways by which tort (as) structure governs bodies without intersections, impeding the fullest relief for someone like the fictional Stefan Chandler, who has to use tort as a weapon against hate. Significantly, this structure is not unlike the structure of the regulatory state practices written about in the previous chapter. This is a structure where the state's "science" is used to shift responsibility for supremacist wrongs from the state to individuals. In the "Race, Tort, Genealogy" section, I explore tort in a historical and genealogical vein, teasing out bits that have helped make tort amenable to structures producing and reproducing racial supremacy. I also explore how an actual tort for racist hate speech would play out, if ever adopted, in the United States. In the "Subversive Race, Race Torts" section, I offer a different narrative of how the state might handle and eventually remedy the wrong done to subjects like Stefan Chandler without governing hate and identity in "scientific" ways.

Race and Tort Scholarship

Understanding tort in limited ways, without thinking about tort as one of the state's governance technologies, race and tort scholars have not readily captured the dynamics of tort as tort shapes identity. This is the case even though race and tort scholars do not erase or downplay difference as do mainstream tort scholars thinking in economic terms and in terms of corrective justice.[1] Frequently using critical race theory as a starting point, race and tort scholars have significantly addressed how difference leads to unequal tort outcomes for those on the bottom. There is a wide range of criticalist discourse on tort that might be used to understand hate regulation, from analyzing various tort concepts to interrogating the foundational bases of material inequalities emerging from a tort located in cognition. These progressive and criticalist discourses generally revolve around one or more of the following explanatory axes: outcomes analysis; conceptual analysis; debates over the salience of cognition versus motivation.

The explanatory axes shaping the race and tort scholarship provide the bases upon which race and tort scholars have understood the economics of tort, and the resulting material inequalities—outcomes analysis. Looking at dollars and cents, Martha Chamallas wrote about the ways in which lost income is calculated for women and people of color seeking relief through tort. She calculated the lost income of women and minorities and asserted that such calculations place women and minorities at a disadvantage. For example, Chamallas noted that women and men of color are much more likely to have work histories that include periods of work interruption. (She was thinking about inter-ruptions caused by workplace discrimination, health concerns, preg-nancy, etc.) This led her to argue that using "objective" race-based and gender-based economic data for remunerative calculations is unconstitu-tional and illustrates the ways "by which the lives of women and racial minorities are devalued, while still preserving the appearance of neutrality and rationality."[2] Chamallas recently wrote about how 9/11-related cases have led to limited changes in the way that economic data are used in order to remedy racial and gender inequalities growing from differential application of the damages element.[3] Not satisfied with this indirect remedy, though, she used a 2005 law review article to promote "the use of blended gender and race neutral tables." She characterized such tables "as an appealing solution because such an approach does not produce a false neutrality," depending "on a composite measure that incorporates the experiences of both men and women and persons of diverse races."[4]

Tort's devaluation of the "other," as understood by Chamallas, has been documented by the state, and historical explanations of this deval-uation have been offered by criticalists. Reports commissioned by administrative units of state judiciaries in the United States have pointed to what might be considered inherent inequalities reiterated in and through tort.[5] Not only did people of color win lower settlements, but according to state reports, African Americans have statistically tended to lose their cases at a higher rate.[6] Jody Armour connected such devaluation to the ways that tort concepts such as "reasonableness" have led to unequal outcomes. For example, tort has relied on "the ordinary prudent man," "the man in the street," and "the reasonable man."[7] Armour argued that these measures are not only gendered in masculinist terms but raced white, leading him to conclude that the courts "implicitly apply an impermissible racial category that gives effect to private prejudices, in violation of the Equal Protection Clause"[8] of the Fourteenth Amendment to the U.S. Constitution, assuring "the equal protection of the laws."[9] Reading injury cases from 1900 to 1949, Jennifer B. Wriggins recently concluded that black plaintiffs won lower settlements in comparison to similarly situated white plaintiffs, giving whites more license to do harm to black bodies.[10] Victor M. Goode and Conrad A. Johnson added that actual awards to people of color have been insufficient not so much because those doing the awarding deny the realness of racial harm, but that standard social science data used to calculate remuneration have not been adequate enough to capture this realness.[11]

If Frank M. McClellan is right, unequal outcomes in tort cases are shaped by actions outside of the courtroom as much as inside of the courtroom, where cases like Chandler's 2000 case are heard. (In fact, considering the small percentage of civil cases that actually make it to court, actions outside of the courtroom are arguably more important than actions inside of the courtroom.) McClellan asserted that unequal outcomes are shaped in the routine communications of lawyers within and between firms handling tort cases. In such conversations, according to McClellan, racial calculus inevitably figured. According to McClellan, these

> conversations, [in one respect,] are public because they are widespread and likely to effect the public resolution of claims. In another [respect], they are private because the speakers intend to share their real thoughts about race only with individuals of the same race.[12]

Such conversations led McClellan to wonder why a specific case, to which he was a party, led to a trial instead of to a settlement. Specifically, McClellan, a tort litigator, represented two ophthalmologists—one white and one African American—who brought claims against a computer company that sold them faulty software. McClellan suggested that the defense counsel thought that they could win without settling the case of one of the plaintiffs, because of the minority racial status of that plaintiff. Evaluation of evidence in voir dire, according to McClellan, was viewed differently for the African American plaintiff than for the white plaintiff. McClellan concluded, "If there was any distinguishing feature in the two cases other than race, I have yet to discover it."[13]

Chamallas referred to the disparities located by McClellan as part of the "architecture of bias" making up the "deep structures in tort law."[14] She went even farther than the informal conversations chronicled by McClellan, and to different depths than Jody Armour, who argued that differences in outcome are derived from "unconscious biases" encoded in language, such as the language mentioned earlier.[15] Looking for the roots of "unconscious biases" not eliminated through peremptory challenges, for example, Chamallas located the "dominant value structures, or hierarchies, in tort law" that would have surely figured in cases like the hate tort pursued by Chandler in 2000. Chamallas identified "structures" that are primarily "cognitive in nature and operate within a system that is facially neutral with respect to gender and race."[16] For example, tort has generally privileged damage to property over emotional harm and "rational" discourse over "irrational" discourse. To Chamallas, these binaries reflected power differentials not only between men and women but also between whites and people of color and, had she gone farther, between heterosexual men and gay men. It followed that (white) men who make laws protect their property. On the other hand, (white and nonwhite) women and men of color in Chamallas's analysis, excluded from the public sphere, dubbed irrational and frail, stood on the outside with little or no legal recourse for wrongs considered less significant, and even insignificant. Chamallas and Linda Kerber linked the binary logic embedded in tort to the lack of a "precise masculine analog" for emotional harm that might, for example, lead a heteromasculinist law to discount feminist legal concerns.[17]

With these sex-gender binaries in mind, Leslie Bender asked, "Is tort law male?" By this, really thinking of "deep structures," Bender maintained that certain tort concepts—in Bender's case, foreseeability—have been shaped by heteromasculinist frames that are antithetical to women's interests but also the interests of people of color generally and working-class men.[18] Similar to Bender's query, scholars who center race in their analysis of tort might easily ask whether or not tort law is white. Or, for that matter, more race and tort scholars might ask whether or not tort is simultaneously white, masculine, and heterosexual, as did Jennifer B. Wriggins in a recent law review article.[19]

Linda Hamilton Krieger and Charles R. Lawrence III would answer "yes," but they would offer two different types of "yes" as to whether or not tort is raced.[20] Digging even deeper into cognition than Chamallas, Krieger argued that, in Title VII jurisprudence, scholarship that centers cognition, not scholarship that centers motivation, gets at the foundation of disparate treatment. Basically, Krieger suggested that we have been taught to categorize everything from people to styles to tastes in order to organize our social reality, and that this is often invisible. (These systems of racial categorization constitute the new and subtler forms of racism in the United States and Europe.[21]) But because of the way that tort has been applied in the United States, cognition that contains this racism continued to be discounted in the search for intent gauges. This occurred because cognition is hard to locate in a day when racism is alive and well, but when the trace of racism can be more subtle.[22] This was true even as racism and heterosexism directed at someone like Chandler is sanctioned by a state that might have, on the cusp of the twenty-first century, denied Abraham Lincoln the "equal protection" supposedly secured by the Fourteenth Amendment.

Krieger's "deep structures" sharply departed from the work of Charles R. Lawrence III. Writing on the depths of racism in the consciousness of people in the United States, without linking the racism and the heterosexism faced by Chandler in 2000, Lawrence wrote that

> [U.S.] Americans share a common historical and cultural heritage in which racism has played and still plays a dominant role.... We also inevitably share many ideas, attitudes, and beliefs that attach significance to an individual's race and induce negative feelings and opinions [from whites and non-whites].... In other words, a large part of the behavior that produces racial discrimination is influenced by unconscious racial motivation.[23]

Whereas Lawrence accepted racism as an unconscious act, Krieger located racism in what she identified as the truly "deep structures" where cognition functions. Krieger's racism emerged in a very calculated and conscious way, even if individuals cannot see with clarity the ideological origins of their racism.

Tort (as) Structure

Centering outcomes, tort concepts, and cognition-motivation, race and tort scholars underestimate tort (as) structure. Centering individual and group cognition and motivation shifts causality and responsibility in Foucauldian ways, *away from* structural apparatuses where static constructs of race and racism are produced and reproduced, *toward* individuals and groups who, in a neoliberal context, are "deviant" and anomalous. Centering tort concepts also shifts attention *away from* tort (as) structure *to* components such as tort concepts that are but part of tort's structure. Specifically, tort concepts are vulnerable to cultural shifts, where a tort concept such as "reasonable man" can be challenged as a white and heterosexist technology that needs to be interrogated so that subjects like Chandler cannot only win cases in 2000 but can contribute to the transformation of the hate that made it necessary for him to turn to the court in the first place. How a tort concept such as "reasonable man" changes, however, is conditioned by the degree to which tort (as) structure bends. Tort (as) structure tends to change, through restatements, at a much more glacial pace. Tort (as) structure, thus, is the problem, not "deviant" individuals and groups who are the outward face of hate in the popular imaginary.

I refer to four aspects of tort when I refer to tort (as) structure. First, tort (as) structure consists of the components that make up tort. Tort's components consist of systematized tort categories, torts found within tort categories, as well as elements and concepts that give further shape to particular torts. Second, I also refer to tort (as) structure in order to denote the fixed economy of tort. Tort (as) structure, for example, is fixed so as to be unable to factor something as seemingly indeterminate, and real, as difference, whether this difference is grounded in race, sexuality, ability, and so on, and their intersections. Third, when I think of tort (as) structure, I think of how tort's components might be understood to inhibit the realization of complex individual and group identities. As a result of tort (as) structure, tort, as legal form, might lead to the managed construction of someone like Chandler as gay, male, or black—but not as a gay black male—because tort (as) structure can only process one identity variable at a time. Fourth, I use tort (as) structure in order to conceptually refer to the way that tort in and of itself, for someone like Chandler, is a source of privatized relief, when the source of the hate directed at Chandler is a public concern affecting the well-being of the social. If tort is ever to be transformative for someone like Chandler—and this is a tort that Chandler turns to as a technology of last resort because the state has largely absolved itself of regulating hate directed at a queer subject like him—then tort (as) structure must be undone.

Slow to bend, tort (as) structure is so socially significant not just because it "efficiently" constructs, and governs, race without intersections but because it also helps construct race just as subjects are trying to racially construct themselves within a public sphere that the state is increasingly privatizing in advanced capitalism. This is very different than saying that tort itself is raced, or gendered, and very different than noting that there are unequal outcomes in tort. As suggested by criticalists a raced or gendered tort denotes the way dominant social constructs have been articulated to and ingrained within tort so as to shape cognition, or motivation. While there is surely interplay between dominant social constructs and tort (as) structure, I am suggesting that tort helps govern race in ways similar to the way that technology brings something like Herbert Marcuse's one-dimensional human into being at a time of noticeable social change.[24] That is, I am suggesting that tort (as) structure, and technology, has been an apparatus helping to make the production of race and racism as economical as possible. As a result, tort has remained a place where

> the power and efficiency of [a] system, the thorough assimilation of mind with fact, of thought with required behaviour, of aspirations with reality, militate against the emergence of a new Subject[25]

at a time when "post-" societies bring new types of racial consciousness into the public sphere.

Helping to enable relatively static conceptualizations of race and subjectivity, tort does not leave room for race and its intersections. As theorized by, for example, Kimberlé Crenshaw, Angela Hooton, and Sherri Sharma, "intersectionality" has served as a "provisional concept" with which criticalists can "engage the dominant assumptions that [race and gender in particular] are essentially separate."[26] One of Crenshaw's rhetorical questions might be posed to tort scholars and practitioners. Referring to the convergence of racism and sexism, Crenshaw asked

> How does the fact that women of color are simultaneously situated within at least two groups that are subjected to broad societal subordination bear upon problems traditionally viewed as monocausal?[27]

The law has viewed women of color in overdetermined ways. As African Americans *and* women, according to Crenshaw, black women in the United States have existed as hybrid subjects courts have not always recognized in complex ways. For example, courts have sought to apply strict measures for racial wrongs in order to remedy wrongs really located at the intersection of race and gender, white supremacy and patriarchy.[28] So how has Crenshaw configured black? It must be problematized, as Crenshaw urges, with gender, class, sexuality, and so on. This "mapping [of] the margins" transforms race when race is understood in more dynamic terms, in more relational and dialogical terms. By constructing someone like Chandler in bounded ways, without intersections, the state has essentially severed a body like Chandler's in the name of a kind of efficiency not unrelated to the managerial efficiency of the Augusta Police Department as it constructed Stacey Silvers, the U.S. DOJ's National Hate Crimes Training Curriculum, and Chicago's technologies enabling racial surveillance of the self. This severing has proceeded in order to fit the way that tort (as) structure works. This severing has made it difficult to fully right wrongs done to those who live at the intersections identified by Crenshaw. Which, as Emily Grabham recently suggested, is not to say that tort plaintiffs cannot take advantage of a state that fails to recognize hybrid subjects by applying an intersectional analysis.[29]

While Crenshaw uses intersectionality in order to contextualize subject positions, a race that considers the intersections can have subversive and even liberatory possibilities in law when race as social construct is seen as synchretic and hybrid in a society in demographic transition, such as the United States, where racial subjects like Chandler queer the racial landscape in subversive ways. Specifically, Chandler falls outside of the binaries of race as predominantly understood because he is black and gay, not black, and gay. Such synchretic constructions of race, and their intersections, challenge rigid understandings of race and racism as, at particular points, Chandler primarily identifies as black, while at other moments as gay. In certain spaces and places, he thinks of himself as being both black and gay, with other identities constituting, in degrees of salience, what some political behavioralists related via schema theory.[30] Specifically, moving beyond unbending understandings of race and racism starts to undo binary and compartmentalized notions of identity; compartmentalized notions of identity become ungoverned. Theoretically, we dislodge white supremacy from its comfortable, static, and hegemonic crutch where whites are "civilized" and people of color are "savage," where heterosexual men are "normal" and homosexual men are "deviant." Challenging perceptions of the mutual exclusiveness of race, gender, and sexuality opens up a space that, as Judith Butler might suggest, "will invert the inner/outer distinction and compel a radical rethinking" of law and society's supremacies as well as to "destabilize the naturalized categories" of gender and sexuality, as well as race.[31]

The idea that law contributes to the racial construction of someone like Chandler in 2000 is not terribly new; scholarship on the legal construction of race was especially potent during the 1990s, but dated back to the mid-1980s. As informed by the social construction of race scholarship,[32] scholarship on the legal construction of race serves as a space where law's function as racial stylus has been highlighted.[33] "Law constructs races," according to Ian Haney-Lopez, "in a complex manner through both coercion and ideology with legal actors as both conscious and unwitting participants."[34]

Importantly, scholars who work on the legal construction of race point toward a dynamic race. This is an unfixed race that must be fixed by white supremacy in order for white supremacy to make its myths into truths. Further, legal construction of race scholars persuasively argue that white is a race and whiteness a racial identity that is not only unfixed in practice but also in constant play with other racial construc- tions and identities, though white supremacy presents whiteness as fixed. As something constructed, Martha Mahoney understood race to be "a relational concept" with "no natural truth, no core content or meaning,"[35] though white supremacy presents race as "natural." Because race is not necessarily fixed, Mahoney contended that those with power have used law to construct race in a fixed way, to create and perpetuate power imbalances by constructing the "other" as racially inferior and the "self" as racially superior, for example. In fact, Mahoney concluded that this is how race as social construct gains meaning as it is "created in a social system of white privilege and racist domination" that attempts to fix race to benefit dominant classes and disadvantage the subaltern.[36] Here Mahoney made rather standard critical race theory arguments, though only the "QueerCrits"[37] really center subjects like Chandler, though not necessarily in tort scholarship.

The legal construction of race might be understood in terms of the ways in which legal constructions interact with social understandings. For example, understandings of "alien" and "foreignness" arose through social and legal processes. Natsu Taylor Saito,[38] drawing directly from Neil Gotanda,[39] specifically connected the U.S. internment of Japanese Americans during World War II to the dominant racial culture's fixed construction of Japanese Americans as "foreigners." The sociolegal construction of Japanese Americans as foreigners, as encoded in the dominant popular imaginary, lessened the effectiveness of legal challenges to internment. According to Saito, this "foreignness" also colored the ways Japanese Americans were treated as they sought compensation from the government for internment.[40] Similarly, Kevin R. Johnson tied legal discourse on the "alien" to notions of noncitizens of color frequently of Mexican national origin or descent.[41] Further, before and after 9/11, as argued by Susan M. Akram and Kevin R. Johnson, as well as by Saito, Arabs and Muslims especially found them- selves facing an immigration law creating a new class of "foreigners" and "aliens."[42]

It seems rather appropriate to connect this legal construction of race literature to tort, yet this connection is seldom made to delineate how tort (as) structure constructs race. Critical race theorists who write on the legal construction of race have not necessarily addressed tort in a sustained way, much less considered tort a technology of power touching the identity of someone hated like Chandler in 2000. Usually the connec- tion between critical race theory's legal construction of race and tort is made when legal construction scholars connect race as construct to tort in footnotes.[43] Much the same can be said of criticalists looking at race and tort who acknowledge that race is a social construct that can be shaped in and through law, but the most direct acknowledgment takes place in footnotes.[44] As a result, there has not been a sustained treatment of the legal construction of race in the race and tort literature to center the way in which tort (as) structure writes on the body and even helps write the body into being.

Race, Tort, Genealogy

A Race Tort Proposal

Critical race theorists in the United States boldly placed themselves at the forefront of the fight against racist hate made possible by the modernist legal frameworks problematized in the previous section of this chapter. As defenders of those at the bottom, like Chandler, critical race theorists brought racist hate acts to the fore as an intricate part of their scholarly and activist push to transform society through law. Written by four prominent critical race theorists (Mari Matsuda, Kimberlé Crenshaw, Charles Lawrence III, and Richard Delgado), *Words That Wound*[45] has been one of the most, if not the most, forceful statements on racist hate and hate speech in particular, not unlike the hate faced by Chandler. The authors particularly implored those in positions of authority to regulate racist hate speech. They wrote a jointly authored introduction, a chapter by each of the coauthors, and a concluding chapter on *R.A.V. v. St. Paul*,[46] which was a cross-burning-as-speech case brought before the U.S. Supreme Court.

Reliance upon and mastery of the state and its law proves to be the cure for many critical race theorists in order to gain legal recourse on behalf of those who are the objects of racist hate and hate speech in particular. In one of the essays in *Words That Wound*, Delgado actually envisioned "a tort for racial slurs," which he identifies as "a promising vehicle for the eradication of racism."[47] He set forth rather strict guidelines for successful tort actions seeking to end racial hate speech. Though others have proposed hate torts,[48] Delgado's proposal proved especially significant because of the prominence of critical race theory in the legal academy in the United States, and because of his position as a leading critical race theorist.

Delgado's new hate tort as prescription is developed with the tort of intentional or reckless imposition of extreme mental distress in mind. In such a tort of intentional or reckless imposition, as presented in the *Restatement (Second) of Torts*, damages may be awarded or injunctions issued when an action is

> so extreme in degree, as to go beyond all possible bounds of decency, and to be regarded as atrocious, and utterly intolerable in a civilized community. Generally, the case is one in which the recitation of facts to an average member of the community would arouse his resentment against the actor, and lead him to exclaim, "Outrageous."[49]

Relatedly, Delgado's successful "tort for racial slurs" would definitively show that

> langauge was addressed to him or her by the defendant that was intended to demean through reference to race; that the plaintiff intended to demean through reference to race; and that a reasonable person would recognize as a racial insult.[50]

Such a hate tort, in its precision, according to Delgado, "would discourage such harmful activity through the teaching function of the law."[51]

Tort, as demonstrated in Delgado's hate tort to be used by subjects like Chandler in 2000, becomes somewhat problematic when one considers the way in which tort has helped construct race. Specifically, Delgado's race, in his race tort, would be reduced to a bit that must always be real and reiterable for a tort for racist slights to succeed, making no allowance for race that falls outside of modernist and positivist racial boundaries, and, thus, might be considered performative. One must ask how and to what effect race as construct changes when centered in a modernist legal action like a tort. Undoubtedly, race would have to be something that one could classify, probably with ease. A "reference to race" and gauging how the "plaintiff understood" would likely mark one according to the official racial schemas imposed by the state, schemas that dialogically and problematically reflect the popular racial imaginary. State schemas—and one might add to this the popular imaginary—do not necessarily reflect the fast-changing evolution and dynamism of racial identity in postindustrial societies where neoliberal economic change forces the migration of peoples across borders ranging from political borders to racial borders, from economic borders to sex-gender borders. In short, the state urges people to check a race-tight box, and not to go outside of that box, even when, for example, social change in postindustrial societies helps yield individuals and groups that might be transracial, transgendered, transclass, and so on.

The Genealogy of Tort

The tort law utilized by Delgado has its roots in English common law. Specifically, tort emerged in the English common law appeal of felony. Wrongs in common law were originally treated as criminal, not civil, offenses. If a defendant was judged to be wrong, then that defendant was not only incarcerated but the defendant's property was ceded to the Crown. The appeal of felony was eventually replaced by a writ of trespass. As action, writs of trespass allowed the wronged to pursue criminal charges and seek restitution against the individual doing wrong, all in one legal proceeding. Here, civil and criminal actions, while still intricately connected, were being differentiated in order to, eventually, be broken into civil and criminal actions that would relieve the wrong and sanction the individual doing the wrong.[52]

Tort, as racial stylus, must be placed in this modernist and positivist context that is the intellectual history of tort in the United States. In *Tort Law in America*, G. Edward White traced the emergence of tort in the United States as a "scientific" law. According to White, during the 1800s, tort in the United States emerged as an alternative to the "unscientific" system of writs viewed as antiquated and overly moralistic. Writs, argued the critics, were not systematically codified and could be manipulated by the whims of any jurist.[53] As a critic like would-be Supreme Court Justice Oliver Wendell Holmes suggested, such jurists "'think dramatically, not quantitatively.'"[54] Holmes's "quantitative" was to give law a Linnaean quality. That is, early advocates of tort in the United States saw tort as a way to classify civil wrongs not emerging from contracts, replacing the random quality of writs with what Christopher Columbus Langdell, a former head of law at Harvard, called the "constant iteration"[55] of tort as "legal science." In search of science, a taxonomy of torts came into being, with tort (and arguably certain tort litigants), shall I say, partitioned into orders, families, genera, and species.

In many respects, the history of tort has been a part of what Mary Louise Pratt considered a part of the same "Linnaean watershed."[56] This "watershed" intellectually constituted, through discourse, the emergence of racial binaries and modern racism. Carolus Linnaeus, the Swedish botanist, initiated this "watershed" with his work to name and order living things. The Swedes' human taxonomy went beyond a consideration of the biological—and this is not to suggest that the "natural" is not mediated through cultural lenses—into the cultural. This led to, for example, characterizations of blacks as lazy and whites as industrious, blacks as sexually licentious and whites as sexually controlled. In this white supremacist taxonomy, black constructions were to mark the "natural" inferiority of blacks, giving bases for the racial supremacy of whites.

With a different theoretical acumen than postcolonial studies scholars like Pratt, sociolegal scholars have addressed the "'science' of legal science" in recent articles in ways that seemingly add nuance to the "natural" in "legal science." Howard Schweber linked the scientific turn in law to what he has called a "Protestant Baconianism" present in natural science discourses at lyceums and in academic writings in the United States before the U.S. Civil War.[57] According to Schweber, early advocates of this "legal science," like Langdell, drew from these discourses and perpetuated such discourses at Harvard University in his capacity of professor and dean to generations of the most elite students of law in the United States. Professional associations and institutions also helped make legal "science" pervasive in legal practice. G. Edward White wrote about legal "science" and the American Law Institute's Restatement project, which resulted in the restatement of the tort for intentional or reckless imposition. According to White, the institute's founders "viewed the law as an entity whose shape changed with time and whose content was molded by human beings."[58]

Tort in Practice

Intellectually, in the United States, Linnaeus and Bacon touch law in general, and tort in particular, even the race tort of a radical lawyer like Delgado. Specifically, when a tort such as Delgado's hate tort is used to center race, race would take on the characteristics of tort as legal form, with all of its "scientific" attributes. Not surprisingly, racial identities in Delgado's tort would rely upon an iron matrix of clear racial categories derived from modernist racial "science" with distinct lines between victim and victimizer. As in all tort, questions would persist about the exact measurement of harm beyond the impression of human judgment, whether an action was extreme or outrageous, culpability, and causation. Measurements and standards for measurement, however, would become extremely problematic when the relative stiffness of a tort is coupled with something as sociolegally constructed and ethereal, yet real, as race and racism with their interlocking intersections. Further, the vagaries of language would complicate Delgado's particular tort for racial slights. In order to adjudicate such a tort for racist hate, variables such as race and the language used to articulate race and racism would have to be held relatively constant and reiterable.

Delgado illustrates how his hate tort would work, and unintentionally how his hate tort would construct and govern race in Foucauldian ways. Specifically, Delgado differentiates between a successful and an unsuccessful tort to remedy racist hate speech. According to Delgado, "'you damn nigger' would almost always be found actionable, as it is highly insulting and highly racial." In Delgado's hate tort, such a slight would be actionable when uttered by a white to a black, but not when uttered by a black to another person of color.[59]

What, however, is "race" in Delgado's race tort? Would Delgado's racial insult here be different when the "'n' word" is uttered by one African American and directed to another African American in a demeaning manner? And would such an utterance take on a particular racial dimension when "nigger" is used to refer to a "wigger" (a so-called "white nigger") or a deviant black, such as a working-class lesbian who acts out of black and bourgeois norms and occupies a very particular racial intersection? Further, according to Delgado, "'you incompetent fool' directed at a black person by a white, even in a context which made it highly insulting, would not be actionable because it lacks a racial component."[60] This would be the case even if the "black person" is a black lesbian and the "white" is straight and male.

But what is, once again, "race" in Delgado's race tort? Delgado's "race," in the latter scenario, is depicted as politically neutral, if not "natural," beyond the reach of humans who give moral meaning to race. Race, however, is never neutral and can never be neutralized, or "naturalized." But race has to be neutral, and natural, at some points, as a race tort (or any tort) is used to shift responsibility for judging moral wrongs away from a state administered by humans to a "science" supposedly beyond humans who would otherwise interfere with justice. This holds true especially when "objectively" adjudicating a race tort dealing with racist speech as sign, or the courts would be overrun with tort litigation, as hate speech is a part of everydayness in a racist society such as the United States.

In all fairness to Delgado, I must place his tort in a different, but still not an unproblematic, light. Notably, he clearly rejects the notion that race is neutral or "natural," and he would surely not be an advocate of a tort that constructs, and governs, race in Foucauldian ways. Thinking of race as neutral and natural is against every intellectual principle that Delgado, as a critical race theorist, is about. Specifically, critical race theorists debunk the modernist myth that race can be placed to the side in a judicial system claiming to be objective and colorblind. Delgado's race comes about as he thinks about building a tort for racist hate slurs that meets the muster of tort standards, of tort structure, if not tort (as) structure. For example, he concerns himself with the measurement of damage, how damage would be apportioned, the possibility of fraudulent claims, and objections to a race tort based on claims that a tort for racist hate would violate the right to free speech protected by the First Amendment to the U.S. Constitution.[61] These issues concern Delgado, especially as he thinks of cases where courts have ruled against plaintiffs of color in racist hate speech cases.[62]

In order to avoid previous negative tort outcomes, where courts have found insufficient evidence of harm, Delgado details at length the psychological and sociological effects of racism. He does this in order to differentiate what courts might consider frivolous suits as opposed to more substantive suits. Detailing the effects of racism also gives courts something upon which to measure and apportion damage. He poignantly likens the harm stemming from racism to physical disfigurement. And when linking harm to disfigurement he emphatically injects a moral dimension into the fray that makes humans responsible for both the harm and responsible for righting the wrong. For example, minority children who are told that they are in some way defective can start to think of themselves as being defective. Harm, according to Delgado, hurts not only the psyche but also can lead to material inequalities as, for example, kids who think of themselves as defective have aspirations that match their supposed defect. Beyond the harm to young people, the harm of racism becomes physical harm as well. Delgado, using science for progressive ends, points to studies of race and high blood pressure. Studies suggest that a physical price of racism for African Americans is high blood pressure.[63]

Without a doubt, those who suffer as a result of racism pay a heavy toll, and this toll results in various types of harm that might be remedied with Delgado's tort for racial slurs. My intent is not to propose a solution to the proper measurement of harm as this problem arises in tort. I raise my concerns about tort and tort (as) structure, however, in order to raise the specter of another harm done when tort is used to remedy racism. Notably, I am asserting that in order to remedy the harm of racism and racist hate, a tort for racial slurs might be understood to necessitate racial construction and governance of "othered" subjects in narrow ways that shift responsibility for racism and undoing racism away from the state and the interests it protects onto a "science" that can be skillfully used by a white supremacist state and white supremacist interests. How much attention tort scholars pay to this other harm is up to them, but it is necessary to try to make this dilemma more a part of criticalist discourse as we tell a different story about the law in general and tort in particular.

Subversive Race, Race Tort

An unlit Camel cigarette in hand, Stefan Chandler dove into his bed. This was his way of shifting into survival mode shortly after having returned home only to find "SPIC LOVING FAGGOT" painted on his front door. This was the toll for being "out" in the chic (some might say "iconoplastic") yet oddly populist enclave that is Sunny Beach, a world away from Augusta and Chicago. Chandler instantly realized who scrawled the assaulting words and triangle on the door: a black male in his mid-size condominium building, Charles Renoe. Without a witness or evidence, though, conclusive proof evaded Chandler's grasp. The physical and wistful Renoe avoided prosecution for the slur and triangle because there were no witnesses and lack of evidence. This was the case despite Chandler's property being damaged and his person-hood being harmed.

As Chandler carefully lit and extinguished a third cigarette, the reporting officer arrived in order to understand the harm done to him and to try to help him remedy this harm making use of the law. The officer noted the time and date as well as Chandler's name, address, and age on the department's standard form. Time: 22.35; Date: 09/10/00; Name: Stefan Chandler; Address: Meridian and 11th, opposite Flamingo Park; Age: 35. Beyond this, the officer asked Chandler about the way or ways in which he self-identifies and how this self-identification may have caused and shaped the harm done to him. After being asked, in an open-ended way, Chandler identified as a gay black male. After some questioning, the reporting officer also learned that Renoe had called Chandler a "fucking faggot" and "Española" (a very particular and derogatory reference to Latinos in Sunny Beach parlance) just before promising to return to Meridian and 11th.

Given Chandler's statement to the reporting officer, and the officer's own cultural sense of the community served, the reporting officer tenta-tively concluded that the act of hate directed at Chandler was not just motivated by homophobia. This act of hate—not unlike others—rested at the intersection of many "-isms." In Chandler's case, this was under-stood to be somewhere at the intersection of heterosexism, racism, and even patriarchy—or at least this appeared to be the case, though it is difficult to always be exacting in what really motivates someone to hate and to hate in violent ways. In any event, identity was not essentialized by the state in a reiterative way so as to officially produce and reproduce racist constructions. Without essentializing identity, the police enhanced their understanding of that which is to be eliminated, not just governed: hate. As a result, the unit was able to adjust its practices and policies in progressive ways that start to transform a racist society by changing its notions of race and racism in new times.

Sunny Beach police officers received training to help them understand the circulation of culture and power in cultural studies ways. However, local ordinances and state statutes failed to reflect this progressive cultural outlook adopted in response to interest group pressure from local activists. As a result of the conservatism of ordinances and statutes, and as a result of Chandler's refusal to be forced out of his home, Chandler decided to seek a civil remedy in the form of an enhanced restraining order and remuneration.

Before and after deciding to pursue this alternative legal avenue, Chandler's counsel had lengthy discussions with him in order to understand the act of hate directed toward him. Chandler thought that Renoe knew of his sexuality and, as a result, constructed him to be a "nigger," and not black or African American. Renoe, not unlike many in the black community, saw Chandler as "funny," "sweet," and "that way," all expressions for gay. An African American like Renoe, as a result, saw a black gay male who loved Latino men, like Chandler, as less than black and even disloyal to the race. With the construct, many members of the black community simultaneously constructed and governed race and sexuality in inflexible ways. Certain members of the black community ended up doing the work of the state and society's dominant cultures without it appearing as if the state did anything at all. Supremacies persisted, because the state taught the "other" how to "other."

The narrative of the case that Chandler relayed to his lawyer, and eventually would communicate to the court, was simple enough. According to Chandler, Charles Renoe acted in a racist and heterosexist manner and was bent on terrorizing someone who falls outside of the constructs of the state and dominant social groups. There was a clear pattern of hate that developed over several months during which Renoe habitually called Chandler either a "spic lover," "faggot," or "spic-loving faggot." And Renoe made subtle use of his bodily frame to reinforce his hate. He never physically harmed Chandler, though his actions engendered the kind of fear about which the writer Richard Wright wrote, where the fear stirred through the mere threat of lynching is as bad as lynching itself.

Chandler's radical lawyer easily understood the case that Chandler envisioned. In fact, Chandler's lawyer instinctively sensed that the black Renoe, not unlike others who hate in supremacist ways, essentialized Chandler in racial and sexual terms. This led Chandler's counsel to act against his formal training by disrupting the way that the intentional infliction tort is used in such cases. Counsel did this by making identity an essential part of Chandler's case, moving slightly away from the harm to property and person as property basis upon which many intentional infliction cases and restraining orders are frequently grounded and regularly won. Counsel presented much of the old argument but introduced a new twist by re-presenting identity in the case. Specifically, in addition to the usual property arguments, Chandler's counsel introduced him as person with a complex identity resting at intersections that cannot be essentialized. This construction was then placed next to the way that Renoe constructed and attempted to be a part of state and society's governance of bodies such as Chandler's. Counsel for Chandler presented Renoe's construction of Chandler as being similar to the disempowering constructs of supremacists as pinpointed by legal construction of race scholars.

While race inevitably gets constructed in and through legal apparatuses, such constructs would be less problematic if tort structure itself was loosened. This would mean that tort (as) structure become more fluid. For example, undoing tort (as) structure would lead to a new tort, where elements of one tort category could readily be applied to other tort categories. The effect would be to jigger the categories, making them more limber and, arguably, better able to handle the indeterminacy that is identity and difference as well as the brutality that is white supremacy and heterosexism. Here, for example, the intentional infliction element of intent, in which difference may most likely figure in measuring purpose or desire to do harm, can be more easily connected to the product liability element of duty. Here the duty element in product liability might be more formally colored by the intent to do harm to a customer who is different. And in the process, a legal mechanism that works like society—with society's evils and human potential for undoing evils—comes not just into view but into plain view.

Thinking about intersections, and interlocking oppressions, Chandler and his lawyer envisioned a progressive tort without absolute structures that construct someone like Chandler in problematic ways. A progressive tort would not offer Chandler remedies that construct and govern him in static terms. Such a tort would allow spaces for a race that is performative to take shape, as subjects like Chandler socially construct themselves. In this tort, where so-called scientific notions of race are jiggered, the plays for power buried in an old tort (as) structure that sought to construct and govern Chandler in static ways would be brought to the surface and interrogated. As a result, tort outcomes—who gets what—would not tend to reinforce the oppressive bounds of a modernism that marks someone like Stefan Chandler. Perhaps most important, tort and its remedies would become a site for the flourishing of a radical justice for someone like Chandler, as post-Marxists Laclau and Mouffe might envision it, where the hegemonic power of unitary identity constructions are displaced.[64] This would be a space where those who trouble modernism's race will prevail. Perhaps this would be a space where tort ceases to be, tort becoming something else.

4

After 9/11

Well before 9/11, legal scholars wrote about the utility of U.S. civil rights regulations intended to protect Stacey Silvers and Stefan Chandler. Angelo Ancheta, Juan Perea, Eric K. Yamamoto, and others persuasively portrayed U.S. civil rights as being paradigmatically understood in black-white ways. The black-white civil rights binary, according to Ancheta, placed Asian Americans, for example, in a kind of political limbo where blacks and whites can speak about race and rights but where the struggles of othered "others" are not earnestly acknowledged.[1]

As it directly relates to hate, Robert Chang, too, problematized the black-white civil rights binary in his recent book *Disoriented: Asian Americans, Law, and the Nation-State*. Chang pointed to the link between hate directed toward African Americans and the hate directed toward a Chinese American like Vincent Chin. Chang contended that the hate directed toward Chin was not just a case in which two white autoworkers angry about the rising level of Japanese imports beat a "Japanese-looking" American with an ("all-American") baseball bat. Instead, Chang understood the Chin murder as an act of hate committed by white men who saw Chin as a kind of black man with sexual power over white women. Why? The whole conflict leading to Chin's murder started in a strip club where Chin might be understood by white supremacists to have not only desired but used money in order to possess white women. In essence, Chang associated the Chin murder as a hate crime not unlike the lynching of African American males accused of desiring and raping white women. To Chang, Chin's lynching demonstrated how the apparatus of oppression remained quite constant, even as the individual who could be situated within the racial constructs of that apparatus might vary.[2] Chang, not unlike Janine Kim, essentially asked, "Are Asians black?"[3]

September 11 and its aftermath "disoriented" the black-white civil right binary in another noteworthy way. Post-9/11 hate notably prompted the murder of a Sikh in Arizona, made Muslim American women in Minnesota afraid to publicly wear the hijab, and ironically led someone in the state of Washington to tell Native American filmmaker and writer Sherman Alexie to go back to his own country. Clearly, directing such acts of hate toward people of color was not a new U.S. phenomenon.[4] What was new became evident with the mobilization of those most directly subjugated to post-9/11 hate. Specifically, after 9/11, those in the United States constructed as "Muslim looking" and "Arab looking" organized against murderous hate and mosque vandalism as well as collectively castigated a state (as) structure that became a party to hate in more overt ways through its own regulatory state practices. In short, as they claimed rights outside of the black-white civil rights binary, those with the post-9/11 "look" directly placed responsibility for racist hate onto the dominant racial culture and its state.

Post-9/11 developments in hate and racial governance have had the effect of altering the meanings attached and attachable to race and rights in the United States. Change—and maybe even something more than change—has arisen with the emergence of two post-9/11 trends requiring us to rethink the racial binary that dominates U.S. civil rights discourse. First, the political mobilization of those targeted by post-9/11 haters has, first, formally introduced new voices into the larger rights discourse in the United States. For example, in Minnesota and North Dakota, U.S. rights claimants who have been constructed as "Muslim looking" or "Arab looking" make use of civic organizations such as the Islamic Society of Fargo-Moorhead in order to claim rights and react to state attempts to govern hate and "terrorism" by officially governing racial constructs. A significant development here has been that those constructed because they are "Muslim looking" or "Arab looking" has included Arab Americans and other Arabs, Muslim Americans and Muslim resident "aliens," Latinos and noncitizens from Latin America, South Asians who may or may not be Americans, Bosnian immigrants as white-"looking" Muslims, African Americans belonging to the Nation of Islam, and those with membership in First Nations, such as Sherman Alexie. As a result of the contours of the "look," discussions about racial profiling (as a mode of social construction and governance) and rights, for example, must include not only the day-to-day profiling of blacks and Latinos in states such as New Jersey and Texas but also the profiling and rights of the varied groupings with the "look." Those with the "look" have found themselves, after 9/11, making rights claims across ethno-racial and religious lines. As a result, crossing lines in a way tenuous at best within something like tort (as) structure, Somali rights claimants with the "look" have aligned themselves with claimants without the "look" who might come from El Salvador even as Somalis and Salvadorans do not necessarily find common political ground with, respectively, African Americans and Cubans. Somalis and Salvadorans have found themselves similarly situated as immigrants subjected to the post-9/11 immigration regulations of a state reluctant to take responsibility for its own racism as well as banal and xenophobic hate committed by those without the "look."

Second, beyond new rights claimants with the look, rights claims have started to function in a different register. Before 9/11, most rights talk revolving around racial profiling used to be about the aggressive "community" policing of black and Latino bodies in places such as former Mayor Rudolph Guilliani's New York City. After 9/11, the new conversation on racial profiling (as a mode of social construction and governance) and rights claiming has increasingly become a way to connect the wrongs of street cops who profile in a discriminatory way to the profiling practiced by airport security personnel, immigration officials, border vigilantes, murderers, and mosque vandals motivated by hate. Profiling debates after 9/11 have notably consisted of some consideration not just of how state and nonstate entities deprive blacks and Latinos of rights but how ordinary citizens without the look utter hateful racial slurs, helping to foster a culture of inequality in which employment discrimination directed toward those with the look occurs in the every day.

New rights claimants, with their new rights claims, have started to make civil rights claims that morph into human rights claims just as these new claimants with new claims transform the black-white civil rights binary predominant in the U.S. context—as if rights claimants with the look understand the changing racial formations and constructions shaping a "nonwhite" immigrant nation where the black-white binary is both increasingly less relevant *and* relevant in new ways. Aaron McGruder, the cartoonist and intellectual, and law professor Muneer Ahmad suggested as much. McGruder and Ahmad essentially considered Americans with the look to be new blacks, even *the* new blacks, along with blatinas such as Stacey Silvers and queer blacks like Stefan Chandler. Ahmad, for example, cognizant of "terrorist" as a code word given new meaning after 9/11, considered racial constructions of Muslim- and Arab-looking Americans and residents a mark of "the precariousness of citizenship for all people of color, immigrants and nonimmigrants alike," because the most dreaded racial "other" after 9/11 is constructed to be the Muslim- and Arab-looking terrorist (as "foreigner"), while the rest of "us" ("citizens") are constructed in degrees to be their innocent victims.[5] Elsewhere,

Ahmad directly related post-9/11 hate directed toward those with the look to hate historically directed toward African Americans.[6]

In the remainder of this chapter, I consider the post-9/11 role of the U.S. Commission on Civil Rights (USCCR). Specifically, I consider the state's response to hate claims after 9/11. I also think about how the USCCR has become an apparatus through which new rights claimants lodge new complaints against the state and society. Claims of the new U.S. rights claimants have the effect of starting to dislodge the state's legal and racial "science" and to make responsibility for racist hate less of an individual matter and more of a matter of collective concern.

Race, Rights, and Hate in the United States after 9/11

The United States Commission on Civil Rights

The United States Commission on Civil Rights came into being as a result of the Civil Rights Act of 1957.[7] On the heels of *Brown v. Board of Education* (1954) (347 U.S. 483), Congress gave the commission power to investigate rights violations. Protected bases, as specified in the legislation, were race, color, religion, and national origin, but they now also include sex, age, and disability. Authors of the 1957 legislation intended the independent and bipartisan commissioners to comprise a kind of information clearinghouse with little enforcement power. In lieu of enforcement power, Congress gave the commission limited power to issue subpoenas to complete investigations and to submit investigative findings to Congress, the executive branch, and the general public.

In order to extend its reach beyond the Washington beltway, the D.C.-based USCCR has used its state advisory committees in the fifty states and the District of Columbia. Together with the state advisory committees, USCCR commissioners have held multiple hearings around the United States to look at the ways that the rights of ethno-racial minorities have been apportioned since 9/11. (Advisory hearings addressed in this chapter primarily reflect hearings in the Midwest, but also New York, California, and Metropolitan Washington, D.C., between 9/11 and 2004.[8]) Topics of USCCR and advisory committee hearings have ranged from immigration and racial profiling to public housing and conflicts separating ethno-racial minorities and the dominant culture. State advisory hearings have been held to discuss the "issue of tolerance in light of the terrorist attacks" and to help promote the creation of the "Office of Rights and Liberties" in what was then only a proposed federal Department of Homeland Security.[9] Beyond hearings, and recommendations such as a rights office in the Department of Homeland Security, the commission has maintained a complaints hotline. Complaints have mostly led to referrals to the Department of Justice and the Equal Employment Opportunity Commission (EEOC).

Procedural State, Procedural Practices

Representatives from a variety of state agencies appeared at the USCCR and state advisory committee hearings on the post-9/11 backlash. The mayor of Fargo, North Dakota, spoke and took questions from a USCCR advisory committee, as did the chief of the Montgomery County Police in Maryland, subsequently more famous for his investigation of the Washington-area snipers. Commission hearings and advisory committee hearings also included state representatives from federal agencies such as the U.S. DOJ and the U.S. Department of Transportation (DOT).

In 2002, a representative of the DOJ participated in a special hearing that brought together the USCCR advisory committees from Maryland, Virginia, and Washington, D.C. The presentation made and questions fielded by the DOJ spokesperson at the hearings help illustrate the state's regulatory disposition after 9/11. At all levels, the state tended not just to disaggregate discrimination and hate from white supremacy but to render white supremacy invisible so that a more benign rhetoric of discrimination could be centered.

Before being riddled with somewhat hostile questions from those attending an advisory committee hearing in a D.C. suburb, the DOJ representative made a formal statement to the joint committee, the DOJ representative immediately declared "that this [backlash] is a problem that we take seriously in the Department of Justice."[10] Problematic in the mind of the representative and the DOJ were acts of hate committed by individuals or small groups deemed extremist by the state. These acts included "hate crimes and incidents of bias in other areas, including employment, housing, education, public accommodations, and air travel."[11] The Civil Rights Division (CRD) of the DOJ chiefly saw new immigrants as the targets of post-9/11 hate, and this hate was solely based on immigrant status. Unlike the argument recently made by Susan M. Akram and Kevin R. Johnson, however, immigration and citizenship status for the CRD of the DOJ proved not to be a "proxy for race."[12] In fact, race and racism were incidental to this CRD representative from the DOJ.

Attention to bureaucratic processes—and really procedural norms as justice—served as an important point of reference for the DOJ representative who made a presentation to the joint meeting of the D.C.-area advisory committees. For example, in response to a pointed and even hostile query about the state's complicity in post-9/11 hate,[13] the DOJ representative procedurally declared "that there is a—a receptacle in—in the federal government in—in every agency for filing complaints alleging civil rights violations by agency personnel."[14] The DOJ representative, seeking to simultaneously absolve the regulatory state of responsibility for hate and govern racism if not race itself out of existence, referred claims against the state to the Department's Office of the Inspector General and gave its 800 number and Web site where more information about the institutionalized process for complaints against the state can be found. The Civil Rights Unit of the FBI also received special treatment as a "receptacle" where complaints could be filed and complaints reviewed by the state. As recited by the DOJ representative, in a "legal science" tone,

> under Title VI, if a—a state or local agency receives Federal financial assistance, we can investigate allegations of civil rights violations by—by personnel in that agency. And as well, we can investigate allegations—of criminal violations in—in all cases by state—and local personnel. And finally, under—under Section 14141, we have the authority to investigate allegations of a pattern or practice of civil rights violations by state or local law enforcement. Is that—was that responsive to your question?[15]

An "objective" procedural tone also shaped the DOJ representative's defense of the agency's response to post-9/11 hate. The DOJ personnel "acted swiftly," according to the representative. Responding "swiftly" meant getting the head of the Civil Rights Division in front of cameras early and often, as well as meeting with communities with the look. It also comprised creating a National Origin Working Group within the CRD, which was headed by the representative that the DOJ's CRD sent to the Metropolitan Washington joint committee proceedings.

The state formed the National Origin Working Group in order to "combat discrimination in—in three ways," according to the representative who spoke with the D.C. advisory body in 2002. This included monitoring civil rights violations based on national origin, citizenship status, and religion, which was not forthrightly racial in the state's mentalité. Further, the group sought to strengthen the civil rights consciousness of the DOJ and other state agencies. Finally, it devised "outreach" efforts for itself and other state agencies.[16] Outreach for the state led to meetings with leaders of groups with the look serving as the "eyes and ears" of the state, because communities with the look did not trust the state. Further, in the name of outreach, the Community Relations Service of the DOJ offered training to state and local governments on hate and "preventing and resolving community conflict and violence" in a community policing vein akin to the policing of the Silvers-Hallowell case, the National Hate Crimes Training Curricula, and the Chicago Police Department's hate governance strategy developed in the 1980s and 1990s.[17] Prevention and resolution took place when, for example, school and university administrators knew "how to go about educating students with respect to the differences in culture." And this was to be done without infringing upon constitutional rights.[18]

New Complainants, New Complaints

Newly visible rights claimants understood hate, race, and the state in a different way than the federal government. Notably, in contrast to the Civil Rights Division of the U.S. DOJ, post-9/11 rights claimants reacted to the state's racial constructs and racial governance. New claimants making presentations included an array of Arab American and Muslim American groups. Ohio hearings, for example, featured the Council on American-Islamic Relations and the American-Arab Anti-Discrimination Committee. State advisory committee members in California looking into post-9/11 discriminatory forms in 2002, though, also heard from a San Diego representative of the NAACP. A hearing in New York on post-9/11 law enforcement included representatives from the American Civil Liberties Union and the New York Taxi Workers Alliance. New York's state advisory committee also received comments from linguist and progressive activist Noam Chomsky, as well as from an array of "Arab-looking" and "Muslim-looking" citizens and residents touched by post-9/11 hate and rights violations.

Complaints varied less than the backgrounds of the complainants. Concerns consistently turned on just a few issues: discrimination in the form of hate speech and hate crime, workplace discrimination, racial profiling "science," especially involving air travel, and immigration policies that often had a profiling "science" component. In terms of hate speech and hate crime, those making presentations before the USCCR and its state advisory committees recurrently referenced the racist lexicon gaining new meanings after 9/11. For example, in Michigan, "sand nigger" and "towelhead" as references for Arab Americans were not new, except that after 9/11 such hate slurs were accompanied by death threats made in more than a hoaxing vein.[19] Beyond the old slurs and new threats, haters introduced new slurs, as recounted by those testifying before the USCCR and its state advisory panels. Someone referred to an Indiana judge of Middle Eastern descent as "Taliban."[20] One person testifying before the Wisconsin Advisory Committee spoke of new slang coming into being where a "bin Laden" is someone hard to find, a messy room is "ground zero," and someone you do not like is a "terrorist."[21]

Hate speech, according to post-9/11 claimants birthed and aggravated the employment discrimination recounted by those with the look appearing before the USCCR and its state advisory committees. Most common, according to a representative of the Milwaukee Muslim Women's Coalition, was employment discrimination aimed at Muslim women. For example, one Wisconsin claimant told of Muslim women who conversed by phone with would-be employers brimming with excitement, only to find the same employers less than enthusiastic in person when they connected a Muslim name to the hijab. (One employer actually referred to the hijab worn by a job seeker as "the rag."[22]) A representative of Ohio's American-Arab Anti-Discrimination Committee described Muslim women fearful of wearing the hijab in public immediately after 9/11 as being under "house arrest," not free to work or even leave their homes.[23] Official bodies even in supposedly more liberal locales failed to make the workplace a less intimidating place for women and men with the look. For example, Bharavi Desai, a union representative from the Taxi Workers' Alliance of New York, claimed that the FBI arbitrarily checked fingerprints of taxi drivers kept by New York's Taxi and Limousine Commission. Official intimidation, according to Desai, caused drivers not to report incidents of physical and verbal hatred committed by private persons, because drivers actually feared the state that was to fight hate.[24]

Racial profiling "science" in airport security and immigration, as well as in secret detention and special registration, was the most common concern expressed by Americans with the post-9/11 look and their advocates. In the minds of new rights claimants, it seemed as if this concern with discriminatory practice was derived from white supremacy itself as hate form. And this was a white supremacy that was understood in historical terms when, for example, a presenter at the New York Advisory Committee hearings, traced profiling back to the enslavement of blacks and the social control of blacks that came with Jim Crow.[25] Two representatives of the Islamic Society of Milwaukee understood the discrimination faced by those with the look in binary terms, not unlike African American studies scholars thinking of the historical and contemporary basis of racism directed at African Americans. In fact, connecting the profiling of African Americans to the profiling of Americans with the look, one of the two representatives of the society specifically framed the matter in terms that took note of the structure of white supremacy's power. "You dehumanize people, you stereotype people, you make them feel low, then you punish them," testified the society representative. He continued, "That's where we are, all [of] us." The society representative contrasted the place of those with the look with the hierarchical position of "another group of people who are in control" and who want to "get rid of [those] dehumanized and stereotyped."[26]

New rights claimants asserted that the state helped foster a culture of hate by devising and implementing new border patrol practices. For example, the National Council of La Raza (NCLR), through a spokesperson testifying before the USCCR itself, expressed concern about local, state, and federal collaboration on immigration matters. Discomfort with this post-9/11 relationship increased as the scope of profiling and law enforcement expanded after 9/11 as federal authorities, for example, asked local authorities to participate in the roundup of foreign nationals mostly from predominantly Muslim nations.[27] With new tactics collapsing the boundary between local and federal authority, groups such as the NCLR feared that a routine traffic stop could potentially become an opportunity to harass someone with the look in the name of protecting "us" from "them."

Post-9/11, USCCR forum participants in New York brought another immigration concern to the forefront. Vive, Inc., a resource initially helping refugees from Central America to cross the border in western New York, sent a representative to the New York hearing in order to expound upon border control tactics. As relayed by the Vive representative, those in the United States with the Pakistani and Saudi look commenced an exodus toward the U.S.-Canada border in search of safe refuge from discrimination and hate with the arrival of "special registration." (The state ended special registration, a policy and practice requiring that males from many Muslim nations register with the state, in response to the protests of U.S. civil rights groups and U.S. allies abroad who were unhappy with the Bush administration's treatment of their nationals.) Vive's spokesperson described Vive's response to special registration as if the organization were the Red Cross. As a humanitarian agency run by religious women from Buffalo, New York, Vive aided whole families (including children with U.S. citizenship) in their attempt to safely reach the U.S.-Canada border. Vive helped shelter those fearing "incidents of border patrol [agents] knocking on the doors of hotel rooms at local hotels" near the border in intimidating ways.[28]

"Home"

Ideas of "home"—"home" here is both a familiar place, and a distant, alien place—shaped the post-9/11 existence of those in the United States with the look. For those with the look who are neither residents nor citizens, such as the Pakistani student who testified before the

Indiana State Advisory Committee, being away from the home country after 9/11 heightened feelings of vulnerability.[29] For those with U.S. citizenship, post-9/11 life was not without anxiety. Wisconsin's Advisory Committee, for example, heard from one lawyer who spoke of a client who even before 9/11 felt that he had few if any rights in a United States that was both home and not home.[30] This was especially the case for many older Arab American citizens who "simply view [inequality] as the price you pay for being Arab American and having feelings about the Middle East."[31]

Immigrants with the look who chose to become U.S. citizens also paid a price for having the look and being naturalized. Presenters at post-9/11 forums spoke of how new immigrants with the look understood rights. One presenter who addressed the state advisory committee in Indiana related how many Muslim immigrants come from nations where asserting individual or community rights led to violent retribution from irresponsible states.[32] One student at the University of Wisconsin's campus in Milwaukee told the Wisconsin committee that new citizens with the look who came from states with illiberal rights traditions "are fearful to basically fight for their rights on post-9/11] issues." The student said that Muslim and Arab Americans from authoritarian nations "fear that they will lose their standing here as American citizens" if they challenge the American state in any form.[33] The student leader related that Muslims "don't assume that they would just be able to have their rights taken care of."[34]

Discomfort at "home" extended to U.S. Muslims born in the United States. A representative of the Arab American Bar Association of Illinois, for example, constructed himself as the "all-American kind of guy," even as he was constructed by Americans without the look as the "other."[35] He frankly admitted to those at the Illinois hearings, "I'm frightened with the situation I see here in the United States." The representative of the association related how he never imagined that "one morning I would wake up and see this kind of thing in my own community."[36] At the Michigan hearings, an editor and a publisher of an Arab-American newspaper shared the sentiment of the Illinois lawyer who represented the state's Arab American Bar Association. The journalist asserted that, especially after 9/11, "to really get ahead in America, you need to bash Arabs." He asked, "Where are the civil rights?" According to the journalist, September 11 and the hate aftermath was "a disaster, *nakaba*, in Arabic, we say *nakaba*, it's a disaster."[37] While not having a problem with the state detaining those noncitizens with the look because of visa violations, the journalist noted that he feared for "people like us" born in the United States. He defiantly and vulnerably claimed the United States on behalf of Arab Americans, and the rights of American citizenship: "This is our country. Where are we to go?"[38]

The duality of "home" for those with the look helped underline the way that cross-national currents shape the rights claims of new rights claimants (as well as those fearful of claiming). Namely, Middle East conflicts frequently made their way into the post-9/11 forums sponsored by the USCCR. A Muslim chaplain listed struggles over the control of Palestine-Israel as one of the "underlying causes" preventing the construction of a "bridge of understanding of who America is, and what American is" to the Muslim diaspora.[39]

Prospects for the chaplain's "bridge" seemed distant if the thinking of one Indiana University academic is on the mark. Specifically, the academic, responding to a query from the Indiana State Advisory Committee, contrasted eschatological differences separating Islamic revivalists in the Islamic diaspora and Christian fundamentalists in the United States. Differences here depended on the Christian fundamentalist belief that Jews must control Jerusalem before the return of Jesus, and the revivalist view that there must be absolute "Muslim rights over [Jerusalem as] a holy place."[40] The president of the Islamic Medical Association (IMA) of Indiana put the eschatological differences in more blunt political terms. Differences, according to the IMA president, became a rights issue when Palestinians in general and Muslims in particular see a "lack of fairness," and this perception and reality produce mutual hate that crosses national and other borders. According to the IMA president, the United States had to acknowledge American complicity in state hate and terror "when the Palestinians see that their house is being demolished by the gunship and by the tanks given to [Israel] by [the] U.S.A."[41]

This new type of rights claiming by new rights claimants, where conceptualizations of rights travel across national borders, and where new claimants think of "home" in transnational terms, is not totally new. For example, African Americans have expressed their "linked fate" as well as their connection to other blacks in the United States and in the African diaspora.[42] Post-9/11 rights claims and rights claimants differ because claims and claimants, especially after 9/11, proximate Rita Kastoryano's "new global space" in Europe. "New global space," as conceptualized by Kastoryano, marks that place in Europe "where the cultural and political specificities of multiple national societies are combined with emerging multilevel and multinational activities."[43] In the U.S. context, a "new global space" emerges as those with the post-9/11 look find themselves engaged in associations that mark their national citizenship or residency, participation in things "Western" within and outside of the United States, as well as connections to points in, for example, the Middle East or

Central America. This space is ungovernable with the old tools, not unlike Stacey Silvers and Stefan Chandler, because racial lines are remade, national citizenship is recast, and communities are forced to engage the governmentalizing state in new ways.

New Constructions

One participant at the Wisconsin advisory hearings, looking back on his own racialization in the United States as a new immigrant from the Philippines, warned those with the look when he said that 9/11 was "going to change the color of your skin."[44] Witnesses testifying before the U.S. Commission on Civil Rights and its advisory committees character-ized the constructed look coming to the fore especially after 9/11. State and nonstate profilers racially constructed and governed those with the look by using several measures that are a part of the new phrenology. As an advisor to the Council on American Islamic Relations told the advi-sory committee in New York, language helped mark the post-9/11 look of visitors to the United States who not only flew as Arabs but spoke Arabic on an airplane.[45] Dress, too, as expounded upon by witnesses such as a representative of San Diego's Arab American community, aided in the construction of the look deemed "suspicious," especially after 9/11.[46] Items of dress included not only the hijab but the kafia and turban too. Naming contributed to the look, as in the name "Mohammed Ali." As communicated to the New York committee, a Mohammed Ali (not *the* Muhammad Ali) became the victim of "name profiling."[47] And, finally, a Koran visible through the rear window of a car warranted a police officer in Alexandria, Virginia, to construct a driver as a driving "other."[48]

A major problem with utilizing the aforementioned profiling measurements has been that they are not exactly scientific, or even pseudo-scientific, as the state might claim. That is, the measure has deprived the terrorist of rights as well as the person with the look who plays by the rules, displays the flag, pays his or her taxes, and who, as a result, becomes the victim of state and nonstate hate. Beyond this, measuring the look also has led to the profiling of those who are neither Muslim nor Arab.

This wide profiling net has created a general climate of xenophobic hate, leading some Latino activists to become very visible in the 9/11 discussions organized by the USCCR and its advisory committees. The post-9/11 response of a Latino organization such as the NCLR has been interesting, and perplexing. Its representatives, on the one hand, have endorsed security measures such as face recognition technology in order to more closely monitor the movement of bodies across and within the national borders of the United States.[49] The NCLR, on the other hand, has warned against monitoring too closely as it would, as stated in the council's written submission to the USCCR, be too hasty. Council representatives have warned that being too hasty and too aggressive "is a dangerous trend." And this has been a danger "not just for the Arab and Muslim communities, but for all Americans, including many Latinos." State actions after 9/11 have come to the attention of an interest group such as the NCLR because, as noted by the council's representative, Latinos in particular may be victimized as a result of "mistaken identity."[50]

State attempts to govern hate by governing race worried the NCLR in three ways. First, at the level of local law enforcement, council members thought that heightened security would offer state and local law enforcement officers a reason to "cross the line" between recognizing rights and not recognizing rights.[51] At a second level, the council cited incidents where agents of what used to be the Immigration and Naturalization Service seized property, diverted traffic, and made arrests in "roundup" form along the Mexican-United States border and in urban areas where informal laborers seek work. Using specific examples, including court actions as evidence, the NCLR bolstered its case by arguing that these officials primarily acted not on the basis of race and ethnicity but on the basis of "ethnic appearance."[52] Finally, outside and inside the realm of the state, the NCLR expressed concern about how a tone set at the federal level encouraged private citizens acting as border vigilantes and de facto agents of a governmentalizing state. The NCLR claimed that these new state agents "pose an equally dangerous threat to our fundamental values."[53]

The combination of the look and the policing of U.S. borders after 9/11 helped produce new political formations. Not only have the new formations generally linked Latino interests to the interests of those who are not Latino but who have the look, but they drew other groups into this new rights fold. For example, National Asian Pacific American Legal Consortium representatives sent a representative who warned of new "xenophobic instincts" that especially victimized Sikhs in a post-9/11 context.[54] The consortium representative, looking back and ahead, claimed the mantle of the old civil rights era by reminding the USCCR that Martin Luther King was dubbed a terrorist just as the representative reminded the commission of Japanese-American internment during World War II.[55] Blacks also entered the post-9/11 debate, in particular, immigrants from Africa who started their own advocacy organizations and formed alliances and coalitions with others with and without the look. In Minnesota and North Dakota hearings, Arabs made their cause a Somali and Sudanese cause, just as Africans in the United States embraced the cause of Arabs in the United States.[56] It was an ideal time for interracial alliances and coalitions for people of color as, for example, one Muslim activist from Wisconsin noted that, after 9/11, Muslims were "being treated like the African American community is being treated." The Wisconsin activist continued, "We're being looked at with suspicion."[57] Further, one community leader in metropolitan Washington, who is Sikh, suggested that many more South Asians linked their rights struggles to the struggles of blacks and Latinos. This activist understood South Asians, blacks, and Latinos to be in the "same boat."[58]

Interestingly, African American Muslims fit into this new rights mold even as, one Indiana professor noted, they tend to primarily bond to other African Americans.[59] The perspective of African American Muslims, post-9/11, came up elsewhere in a hearing of the Indiana committee. Specifically, an African American imam testified before the Indiana panel. A member of the committee asked the imam about the post-9/11 response of African American Christians to the discrimination faced by Americans with the look. The member said that in contrast to support from white Christians after 9/11, African American Christians consider African American Muslims "Mohamed Jihad."[60] Instead of the usual affinity for the larger African American community, in the post-9/11 world, African American Muslims felt a different affinity for Muslims who were not African Americans. For example, one African American Muslim leader in metropolitan Washington pointed out that Muslims who were not African American frequently turned to African American Muslims to mediate workplace discrimination. Interestingly, African American Muslims were "other" but not as "other" as Muslims without African American "privilege."[61]

The USCCR and state advisory committee members gathering information about 9/11 generally heard little from African Americans who were not Muslim. Queries regarding the interaction between African Americans and Muslims frequently surfaced in forum discussions. Usually these queries came from Muslims not African American or black American. For example, while a spokesperson for Michigan's American-Arab Anti-Discrimination Committee linked Arab American fate to Latinos and African Americans, among others,[62] one Arab American activist, who also proudly advised the San Diego Police Department (SDPD), bemoaned the lack of support from the African American community. This activist's tone was one of someone at his wit's end as to why there has been so much African American silence after 9/11.[63] Perhaps the testimony of the president of the NAACP's San Diego chapter best characterized the African American response to 9/11. A state advisory committee member asked the NAACP representative about the organization's response to post-9/11 discrimination. "In terms of effects of 9/11," according to the NAACP representative, who also was on the

SDPD African American advisory committee, "I haven't really thought about that." She finally said that 9/11 caused racial profiling to be taken to "another level."[64] While she could not articulate the concerns of African American Muslims in the area,[65] she confirmed that the NAACP had done nothing to build post-9/11 coalitions, because the racial "privacy" initiative in California was the NAACP's priority in 2002. And she immediately proceeded to talk about the initiative at length in this 9/11 hearing. [66] Here, old blacks in the United States contribute to the governance of new blacks by inaction and ignorance of a reality in the United States: If you are not white, you are black.

5

Complicating Identity, Naturalizing Equality

After 9/11, state actors in the United States downplayed the state's role in constructing race and making racist hate possible. After apartheid, state actors in South Africa sought to transform apartheid's racism and racial hatred by acknowledging the state's responsibility for both.

Undoing legal positivism has been critical to transformation in postapartheid South Africa.[1] Legal positivism—the intellectual basis upon which apartheid's judiciary functioned—helped the apartheid-era judiciary justify its ceding of its authority to apartheid's legislature and executive. Commenting on case and statutory law, John Dugard seminally contended that the apartheid judiciary's "allegiance to the positivist creed" produced a "statutory interpretation" that was "seen as a mechanical operation in which value judgments play no part." (Legal positivism was very much in the "legal science" tradition upon which tort and procedural notions of equality developed in the United States.) Dugard's understanding of "mechanical operation," which he traced back to nineteenth-century South African jurisprudence, produced a "rigid adherence" to legal forms and norms, making possible the apartheid judiciary's "neglect of considerations of human dignity, freedom of speech, freedom of movement, and assembly."[2] H. A. Strydom agreed with Dugard's critique, Strydom also drawing from his reading of cases and statutes. Strydom considered the apartheid judiciary's overemphasis of legislative supremacy in its decisions and judgments to be a sign of a "primitive" system in which bureaucratic judges with supposedly detached and scientific inclinations declined to exercise "the flexible and dynamic character of judicial interpretation."[3] According to Strydom, flexibility and dynamism preceded an advanced judiciary's ability to move beyond the plain-fact outlook in which the strictest statutory interpretation prevailed. Without this ability, Strydom thought that the apartheid judiciary allowed the security police to legally detain dissidents for ninety days without charge (as prescribed by legislation), formally release detainees, and then immediately redetain political opponents for another ninety days. This occurred, according to Strydom, because the apartheid judiciary only saw law as it is, not law as it ought to be.[4] In other words, there was no imagination, and, as a result, no room for value judgment.

Stephen Ellman rebutted the general argument presented by apartheid-era critics such as Dugard and Strydom, who stressed what they understood to be the fordist dimensions of apartheid judicial interpretation. Ellman did this by stating that he too had moral problems with the decisions and judgments reached by apartheid's bureaucratized courts, which mostly rubber-stamped government policies and practices. He emphasized the ways that liberal judges could curtail the prerogatives of the apartheid executive and legislative branches. Responding to the dominant critique of apartheid's judiciary during the 1980s, Ellman actually contemplated the correctness of Dugard's argument in particular. "Dugard may well be right" on the relationship between legal positivism as so-called legal science, legislative supremacy, and the denial of rights during apartheid, wrote Ellman.[5] But making use of case and statutory law, Ellman concluded that positivism also provided the interpretive "tools" important to "a rights-protective jurisprudence" manifested in the apartheid judiciary's "fondness for literalism, its refusal to consider the bulk of legislative history, and its array of canons of interpretation."[6]

The concerns of legal scholars such as Dugard, Strydom, and Ellman overlapped with the concerns of a sociolegal scholar such as Richard Abel. Abel, however, reaching beyond case law and statute, presented an account of the political that actually conditioned the judicial interpretation centered by Dugard, Strydom, and Ellman. The political, for Abel, helped to center apartheid as a white supremacist ideology challenged in multifaceted ways by those racially subjugated, whereas a South African legality without race, racism, *and* multiple strains of subaltern resistance prevailed amongst the 1980s critics primarily concerned with cases and statute. Abel's political, at the nexus of white domination and black resistance, reflected his concern not just with judicial interpretation of cases and statute alone but with the judiciary's acceptance of what Abel called "the last refuge of a scoundrel": the supposedly apolitical "science" used by apartheid bureaucrats in all branches of the state in order to make the indeterminate into something determinate.[7]

The sociolegal turn in scholarship on apartheid's judiciary, as exemplified in Abel's political, came to be when the would-be critics mostly working in South African law schools during the late 1980s stopped looking at the apartheid judiciary and understandably started contemplating postapartheid constitutionalism.[8] This led to the pronounced emergence of sociolegal scholars outside of or on the margins of the legal academy thinking of the colonial and apartheid judiciaries beyond cases and statute. For example, with historical perspective, sociolegal scholars brought to the fore nineteenth-century European missionaries that attempted to use the law to impose "technological innovations and a 'scientific' rationale" upon South Africa's Tswanas.[9] Racial governance through the linear knowledge systems of colonial "science" continued from 1948 with the "dispersal" of a bureaucratic "science" sprinkled "into everyday life."[10] South Africa's Department of Native Affairs (DNA), for instance, vigilantly enforced the Urban Areas Act (1923) and the Group Areas Act (1950) using an administrative "science" to limit the movement of black laboring bodies in the name of an efficient macroeconomic policy[11] and to reinforce a racial economy ("ethnos theory") where white supremacy and black inferiority were understood to be self-evident.[12] Apartheid's bureaucratic "science" shaped the legal and racial consciousness of apartheid magistrates (many of whom are still serving). This was a racial consciousness in which apartheid's racial economy of rights distribution was understood by apartheid magistrates to be "scientifically" just at the same time the state as a whole touted racial constructs in which white "superiority" and black "inferiority" were naturalized.[13]

Postapartheid actors have attempted to reconstruct and transform colonial and apartheid legal "science." This has entailed reconstructing and transforming colonial and apartheid policies and practices linked to the modern European medicine described by Foucault, where bodies were made "normal" and "abnormal," to modern literature on the racially "superior" colonizer and racially "inferior" colonized deconstructed by Gayatri Spivak,[14] as well as the modern judiciary problematized by 1980s critics and sociolegal scholars of the 1990s, mentioned earlier.

In order to start to reconstruct and transform the judiciary, and society, postapartheid actors wrote the Promotion of Equality and Prevention of Unfair Discrimination Act of 2000 (hereafter referred to using some combination of "equality" and "law"). With a significant hate speech component, the legislation has not only been used to further consciousness about race and gender, but the legislation is intended to reconstruct and transform the "scientific" processes particularly underlying apartheid's law. Postapartheid actors also have used the new legislation to underline the realness of white supremacist and patriarchal hate unique to the South African social context. This has been a social context where, for example, the institutionalization of material inequalities occurred through acts such as the Group Areas Act (1950), which depended on technocrats at the DNA as well as judges and magistrates charged with meticulously delineating apartheid's racial constructs as defined by the racial "science" of the Population Registration Act (1950). In short, the 2000 equality legislation has been used to try to create a racially "disoriented" South Africa, as Robert Chang might suggest,[15] to "ungovern" race and notions of racism as I think of it. The assumption of postapartheid actors has been that colonial and apartheid-era supremacies start to become undone with the undoing of the racial "science" of a justice system dependent upon legal "science."

There is a problem, though, with postapartheid equality regulations intended to reconstruct and transform the staid template of apartheid's judiciary and society, where the word "kaffir" ("nigger") is a weapon of hate. As Judith Butler suggested, thinking in comparative context:

> Antidiscrimination law has participated in the very practices it seeks to regulate; antidiscrimination law can become an instrument of discrimination in the sense that it must reiterate—and entrench—the stereotypical or discriminatory version of the social category it seeks to eliminate.[16]

Reiteration has tended to mean that, at points, the postapartheid state started to reinscribe apartheid's social constructs by reinscribing the "legal science" from which these constructs evolved. Reiteration and reinscription here have manifested themselves in, for example, the very "scientific" way in which a "person" is defined and constructed in the training documents designed to help judges and magistrates regulate hate as stipulated in the 2000 equality legislation. The "scientific" definition has been proposed by postapartheid rights bureaucrats, even as these administrators have complexly conceptualized a hate that is the product of complex constructions, formations, processes, and structures.

The remainder of this chapter is divided into two sections. The first analyzes the Promotion of Equality and Prevention of Unfair Discrimination Act of 2000. I argue here that, contrary to tendencies in the United States, developing hate regulations in postapartheid South Africa meant "ungoverning" race and staid notions of racism. I make use of legislative records that illustrate how hate regulation, within broader equality legislation, might be used to think about race and racial oppression in complex ways that reconstruct, and transform, even the apartheid state.

Legislating, though, is not implementing. The second section of this chapter addresses the Equality Court that is empowered to implement the hate and other provisions of the equality legislation of 2000. Training manuals for court officers show both the promise of the postapartheid state that attempts to interrogate "science" as well as the remnants of the state that preceded it.

Legislating Equality

Legislative Brief

Intended to enact the right to equality guaranteed in the South African Constitution, the Promotion of Equality and Prevention of Unfair Discrimination Act of 2000 was made possible by legislative routine. Charged with preparing drafts of the legislation, the Equality Legislation Drafting Unit (ELDU) held workshops bringing together those with an interest in equality issues, including bureaucrats and policy makers, as well as activists, NGO heads, academics, and intellectuals. (In South Africa, the participants in such a unit are quite interesting, given that, for example, policy makers readily move between NGOs and the academy, or from being activists to being civil servants.) Research and redrafting by the ELDU resulted in the legislative outline of the equality legislation presented to the minister of justice in June 1999. By October 1999, parliamentary leaders tabled the bill and appointed a parliamentary committee charged with guiding the legislation through the legislative process. The first meeting of the ad hoc joint committee considering the legislation brought together parliamentarians from the National Assembly (NA) and the National Council of Provinces (NCOP)—the two houses of the South African Parliament—in late October 1999. Public submissions and public hearings soon followed, as well as other open meetings of the ad hoc joint committee considering the legislation. After lively floor debates in the NA on January 26, 2000 and the NCOP on January 28, 2000, the bill passed. The state president assented on February 2, 2000, and the equality bill became law.

The equality law of 2000 is quite liberal in that it barely has a trace of the redistributive vigor marking the first two years of the postapartheid state. The content of the bill, nevertheless, has proven to be expansive, at points overlapping with other postapartheid legislation as varied as the Films and Publications Act of 1996 and the Employee Equity Act of 1998. Intended to bring about a substantive equality, the equality legislation has been intended to further the "consolidation of democracy,"[17] but with a gradualism ensuring that apartheid traces would not quickly disappear. As an early parliamentary press release dubbed the legislation, "This bill is a blueprint, and one of the main pillars of transformation in South Africa post 1994."[18] As a blueprint, the legislation is specifically intended "to prevent and prohibit unfair discrimination and harassment; to promote equality and eliminate unfair discrimination; to prevent and prohibit hate speech; and to provide for matters connected therewith."[19] Encoding constitutional provisions on hate speech into law, for example, the final version of the act reads, "No person may publish, propagate, advocate, or communicate words based on one or more of the prohibited grounds."[20] The hate speech provisions in the legislation have been expressly designed and interpreted to protect the hated from words that are "hurtful," "harmful or to incite harm," and "promote or propagate hatred."[21] The bill has empowered the director of public prosecutions to initiate criminal proceedings in cases where hate as discriminatory form is deemed to be actionable. Provisions of the general legislation are expressly used to cover individuals and groups on the following grounds: race, gender, sex, pregnancy, marital status, ethnic or social origin, color, sexual orientation, age, disability, conscience, belief, culture, language, and birth.[22]

As for enforcement, special equality courts are increasingly being used to enforce the provisions of the 2000 legislation. Selected officers of the equality courts, drawn from sitting magistrate and high court officers, have started to undergo special training as sanctioned by the minister of justice. As the legislation reads, equality court officers are "designated, by reason of his or her training, experience, expertise, and suitability in the field of equality and human rights."[23] Training for court officers has proved to be a crucial part of the 2000 legislation. As a result, only the minister of justice initially had the power to declare a court an equality court if and when there were judges or magistrates with adequate qualifications.[24] And, as specified in the implementation provisions of the 2000 act, the minister of justice, the Judicial Service Commission, and the Magistrates Commission became responsible for creating manuals "establishing uniform norms, standards, and procedures to be observed by presiding officers and clerks in the performance of their functions and duties and in the exercise of their powers."[25]

The official opposition in Parliament, the Democrats, protested the 2000 provisions dealing with the naming and training of equality court officers. Democrats charged that the training provision was a power grab by the ruling African National Congress (ANC), which would institutionalize forms and norms of equality, especially those promoting substantive equality over formal equality. Because of a perceived threat to judicial independence, the protocol used to establish the Equality Court and to train court officers was changed with a recent amendment to the legislation. This 2002 amendment took power away from the ministry of justice with regard to the naming and training of officers of the Equality Court. In order to strengthen the judiciary's independence from the legislative and executive branches, and to enhance democracy, the Judicial Service Commission and the Magistrates Commission received more authority to devise the means to train court officers.[26] The change was intended to let judges and magistrates have more authority to define equality.

History

Historicizing race and racism was important for actors shaping the 2000 equality legislation and its hate regulation component. The primary drafters of the equality legislation noted early in the committee phase that many contemporary forms of discrimination are connected in some way to apartheid and colonialism, and the racial pseudoscience of both of these political systems.[27] As a result, those drafting the equality legislation thought that a discriminatory practice such as hate speech was, historically, something essential to the maintenance of hierarchies sustaining white supremacy. One ANC member suggested on the floor of Parliament that discriminatory practices are "a necessary adjunct of the capitalist system built on the back of colonial conquest."[28] And, as emphasized in the public submission of the Congress of South African Trade Unions (COSATU), an imbricated capitalism and colonialism shaped discriminatory material inequalities that persist in systemic ways long after the formal end of apartheid.[29] A member of the drafting team actually suggested that the phrase "suffered in the past" in an early draft be changed to "suffers" to accentuate the historic and ongoing nature of colonial and apartheid discrimination.[30]

On the verge of constructing themselves as racial "other," some white South Africans challenged the historical basis of contemporary discrimination. Big business and the predominantly white political parties tended to pointedly contest the way that the past was privileged by the drafting team and the ANC members of Parliament who controlled the committee hearings and floor debate on the 2000 legislation. For example, as recorded in the minutes of the parliamentary committee considering the legislation, a spokesperson for the South African Council of Businesses (SACOB) flatly stated that he did not care about the past. Not unlike many white South Africans unwilling to take responsibility for the colonial and apartheid past, the SACOB representative urged the committee considering the legislation to move beyond the past, since, in his opinion, all South Africans are now equal in the eyes of the law.[31] Also considering inequality a thing of the past, the major opposition party, then called the Democratic Party (DP), criticized the hate speech provision in the equality legislation. The DP representatives viewed the hate speech provisions of the 2000 bill as unnecessary and going beyond what was constitutionally required.[32] Beyond their hesitance to regulate hate speech, the DP particularly reacted against the racial constructions used to ground the legislation as a whole. For example, its lead spokesperson on the 2000 equality legislation had problems with the way the term "colonial settlers" was used to construct whiteness in the draft legislation.[33] In fact, based on the tenor of the official opposition's lead parliamentarian on the equality legislation, "colonial settlers" was a kind of hateful racial slur when uttered as a code word for whites in general and Afrikaners in particular. The official opposition's lead parliamentarian on the equality bill further objected to the way that the privileging of white supremacy downplayed what the legislator depicted as racial discrimination faced by whites at the hands of blacks.[34]

In the final draft of the equality legislation of 2000, the prevailing governmental notions of race and racism in South African history stood out even more. The preamble of the equality legislation, with its hate components, became a succinct summation of the prevailing notion of discrimination. As one of the drafters pointed out, the preamble set the historical context against which the legislation is to be understood and applied.[35] Parliamentarians used the preamble to state that

> the consolidation of democracy in our country requires the eradication of social and economic inequalities, especially those that are systemic in nature, which were generated in our history by colonialism, apartheid, and patriarchy, and which brought pain and suffering to the great majority of our people.[36]

Less sentimental than some of the earliest drafts of the legislation read in Parliament and debated in committee, the final version of the preamble named race and racism as well as gender and patriarchy as particular targets of the legislation. Legislators used the preamble in the final draft to acknowledge past wrongs and to assume responsibility for transforming these wrongs.

Identities and Intersections

While it was hard for different political interests to come to a consensus on the historical function of racism in South Africa, it was as difficult for divergent interests to agree on how race and racism should be used to ground the equality legislation of 2000. For example, driven by a liberal embrace of free speech ideals, the Freedom of Expression Institute's (FXI) submission to the parliamentary committee considering the 2000 bill focused on the hate speech provisions of the equality legislation. Its thinking on equality recurrently pointed to the antiregulation arguments made in the constitutional debates on hate speech, briefly mentioned in chapter 1 of this book. At no point in the FXI's written submission to Parliament were free speech arguments placed in relation to the need to be responsive to those who are hated based on race, gender, sexuality, and their intersections.[37] (This thinking resembled the "talk" that Phyllis Pease

Chock pinpointed in U.S. legislative contexts. In the U.S. contexts, race and especially the salience of racism were not forthrightly addressed. Instead, race and racism, in public discourse, only existed in the margins.[38])

In contrast, for another organized interest such as the South African Institute of Race Relations (SAIRR), race was not everything; it was the only thing. The SAIRR, in its public submission and testimony, wanted an equality bill just dealing with race and racism. Including other categories of discrimination and categories of affected persons only distracted from what it depicted as the real problem at hand—the legacy of apartheid, apartheid's racial constructs, and the racism that apartheid produced. After some gentle prodding, an ANC parliamentarian directly asked the SAIRR representative testifying before the ad hoc committee to define race, which the SAIRR representative conveniently declined to do, citing time constraints.

Different than the FXI and SAIRR submissions, some historical and contemporary ideas about race and racism came across in more nuanced ways. The minister of justice actually named whiteness as an invisible but ever-present identity construct when leading the parliamentary floor debate preceding the final passage of the equality legislation.[39] Naming whiteness and its associated privileges, not unlike whiteness studies scholars working on the U.S. case,[40] had the effect of problematizing race. This forced race, but also other social constructs such as gender and sexuality, out of the biological domain where race and the hate that is white supremacy, as well as gender and patriarchy, could be maintained as natural phenomena. Along these lines, Kevin Durrheim played with constructs of whiteness in particular but also race in general. Durrheim, a psychology professor, insisted not only upon the constructedness of race but also its fluidity. He noted that early drafts of the equality legislation presented race as a constant with distinct categories. This postapartheid racial "science" perplexed Durrheim, "as if," stated Durrheim, "the apartheid government did not have enough trouble assigning people to these categories on any objective or defensible basis."[41]

More noteworthy than the casual way in which race was generally understood as social construct was the debate about other social constructs such as sexuality, ability, class, and, especially, gender. The emphasis on gender as construct was more evident in the written and oral input of nongovernmental organizations and independent state agencies with a gender research and advocacy focus. For example, the Commission on Gender Equality (CGE) made a public submission that problematized the way that early drafts of the equality legislation conflated sex and gender. (The CGE is an independent state body created as a result of section 187 of the South African Constitution of 1996.) The public submission of the CGE was used to point out that sex is generally understood in new scholarship to be a biological denotation, while gender is understood to be a socially constructed identity in academic and intellectual circles. According to the CGE, making the distinction between the biological and the social meant better preparing judges and magistrates for cases where sex discrimination might be easily understood, but where gender discrimination might be submerged within layers of heteromasculinist norms deeply rooted in cultures of hate.[42]

Beyond pointing to the constructed nature of identities and the realness of supremacist forms, nongovernmental organizations and state organs such as the CGE stressed the intersectionality that characterized that place where race and gender constructs meet. This line of argument seemingly referenced the critical race theorizing of a U.S. legal scholar such as Kimberlé Crenshaw who, as noted in chapter 3 of this book, wrote of the ways in which intersections work in misogynist hate speech.[43] (In fact, Crenshaw is frequently cited in equality legislation and Equality Court discussions of intersectionality.) The emphasis on intersectionality became most evident in the way that race and gender were articulated in the committee hearings on the equality legislation in order to point out that apartheid was harshest for rural black women whose identity and relation to oppression had been conditioned by race and gender, racism and patriarchy, and place and space.[44]

This tendency to connect social constructs and supremacist forms of discrimination did not stop with the intersecting of race and gender. As the CGE's submission read, "In South Africa, the deepest forms of disadvantage are experienced as a result of a confluence of factors such as race, gender, illiteracy, lack of income, resources, and opportunities."[45] In the course of the legislative process, where undoing hate was linked to realizing equality, this type of thinking was readily related to other intersections. For example, the Deaf Federation of South Africa (DEAFSA) voiced its concern about coverage for those with multiple disabilities.[46] Similarly and even more practical concerns received voice from the Equality Alliance with regard to the gay, lesbian, bisexual, transgendered, and transsexual (GLBT) communities.[47] Specifically, the alliance's major concern was to ensure that identities and discriminatory forms could be understood to intersect and to interlock so that, for example, GLBT communities could be protected from hate on the basis of sexuality as well as "family responsibility" and "family status."[48] Such a proposal had a dual purpose. First, it protected sexual minorities along family responsibility and family status lines in the event that the sexual minority provisions of the equality legislation were discounted in regulatory practice. Second, and very much related to the first point, the alliance's proposal had the effect of expanding the predominant conceptualizations of family that tend to be framed in fixed heterosexual and heterosexist terms.

As with the contest over historicizing colonialism and apartheid in the equality legislation, as well as disagreement about how race and racism should inflect the equality legislation, those most directly engaged in assembling the equality legislation disagreed about whether or not identities existed as complex and intersecting constructs. While disagreement about the historical significance of apartheid and colonialism largely fell along the postapartheid racial lines that differentiate South African political parties and interest groups, disagreement about the bounds of race as construct mostly broke along gender and cultural lines dividing South African political parties and organized interest groups lobbying Parliament. For example, one of the lead spokespersons for the Inkatha Freedom Party (IFP) insisted that homosexuality had nothing to do with gender, and that homosexuality was an urban (i.e., white) thing that rural black women do not necessarily understand or find moral.[49] In a similar vein, maintaining the social constructs making hate possible, the Institute for Democracy in South Africa (IDASA) made a submission rejecting the way that gender identity and sexual orientation condition and inflect each other. The institute's written submission actually provided an example

> where a male employs a homosexual male, and upon discovering his employee's homosexuality, fires him. This unfair discrimination has nothing to do with the employee's gender, his being male. Similarly, a lesbian woman who faces unfair discrimination on the basis of being in a same-sex relationship, is suffering this discrimination, not because she is a woman, but because she is a lesbian.[50]

Here gender and sex are conflated, leading IDASA to ignore the ways that gay or lesbian gender identities might inflect sexuality and how sexuality might inflect gender. In addition, the sexual and gender identities of those subjected to hate speech and other forms of hate were the "problem," and not the sexual and gender identities of those doing the discriminating.

The written record revealed a few other places where identity constructs conceptualized by those involved in the legislative process resembled the fixed constructs upon which the hate that was apartheid depended. For example, one member of the Pan African Congress (PAC) questioned why the legislation bundled patriarchy in particular with "more serious" issues such as colonialism and apartheid.[51] Here the member overlooked the ways by which the *swart gevaar* ("black peril") rhetoric recurrent in South Africa history has been used in state discourse and the popular imaginary in order to construct black men as "beasts" lusting after "good" white women in need of "protection." As the historian of the U.S. South, Jacquelyn Dowd Hall, convincingly demonstrated twenty-five years ago, contrary to the view held by at least one PAC member of Parliament, white supremacy and patriarchy have depended upon each other, keeping inferior constructions of black men and white women in place in order to simultaneously perpetuate the supremacy of white men.[52]

As drafts of the equality legislation were reworked, those understanding identity as intersecting social constructs won a legislative victory. The South African Parliament basically accepted what an organized interest group like Black Sash proposed in its public submission, whereas protections against hate speech, for example, were extended based on "one or more of the prohibited grounds."[53] The final version of the legislation did two things to improve upon the legislation with identity constructs and intersections in mind. First, the final draft of the legislation included a more open definition of discrimination that understood the ways that identities could intersect and discriminatory forms could interlock. Second, the final version of the act protected "any person on one or more of the prohibited grounds."[54] On a practical level, this more fluid understanding of identity and supremacy prevented the eventual scenario where an equality court judge would have to choose which measure of discriminatory hate should be used in a given case, the racial hate and discrimination measure, for example, or the gender hate and discrimination measure. These victories came even as the final version of a key section of the legislation listing prohibitions against unfair gender discrimination contained jumbled language that seemingly equated gender with being female and a woman.[55]

Though reconstruction and transformation have been the desired end of the equality legislation, with the end of hate speech being the enumerated goal, postapartheid legislation failed to extinguish apartheid-era values. As mentioned earlier, those opposed to the legislation understood history in quite a different way than most of those who supported the legislation. Perhaps this led to the opposition's resistance to reconstructive and transformative remedies in the equality legislation that, for example, placed the burden of proof on those accused of discrimination. Similar views were apparent even amongst those in the opposition who eventually supported the equality legislation. For example, one IFP member of the ad hoc committee considering the legislation asked the representative of the National Coalition for Gay and Lesbian Equality (NCGLE) testifying before the committee whether there was such a thing as "occasional gays." An ANC member responded that sexuality was not a lifestyle choice but a part of a gay person's "core identity."[56] Not satisfied with this explanation, the IFP member asked the

ANC member to explain exactly what homosexuals do sexually. Here the IFP member who conflated sex and sexuality did not see the connection between gender and sexuality.

Second Nature

During the debates on the equality legislation, at least up until passage, postapartheid actors offered many insightful assessments of the status of postapartheid democracy and many proposals to further the democratic project. For example, the IDASA proposed the creation of equality tribunals or juries that would institutionalize the more populist legality favored by those against magisterial courts that alienate people from justice. An "equality jury" was envisioned to spark conversations not just about the law but about the nature of equality and reconstruction.[57] Such a jury was seen as a mechanism that would institutionalize—and even naturalize—equality in ways not unlike the equality proffered by the deputy minister of justice. The deputy minister used floor debate on the equality bill in the National Council of Provinces in order to articulate how the government intended to displace supremacist forms such as homophobia and ableism as natural, and thus invisible, forms of discrimination. The minister stated, "Every decision that we take in policy formulation, legislation, implementation, and in our day-to-day lives should be guided and informed by the substance of this Bill."[58] The minister continued, "It (equality as envisioned in the equality legislation) should and must become second nature to us, a natural human instinct."[59] According to the minister,

> This bill will be our conscience, our guide, and our mentor. It will form and shape the way we think and behave. No person or entity will remain untouched by this enactment, whether it be in the way we conduct ourselves in business or in our daily lives, whether it be in religious organizations or traditional systems of belief.[60]

Questions remain as the postapartheid state has involved itself in the undoing of the past through pieces of legislation such as the Promotion of Equality and the Prevention of Unfair Discrimination Act of 2000. Namely, what does it matter that in the development of the hate policies and practices state actors and organized interests are thinking about race, gender, and their intersection in new ways? If postmodern theorists like Jacques Derrida (who wrote on South Africa) are correct, then the racial constructions of the postapartheid state matter quite a bit.[61] If supremacist hate forms are built on binaries and fixed ideas about identity and supremacy, then interrogating these binaries and fixities theoretically leads to undoing systems like apartheid that depended on the relative fixity of certain identity constructs. But it is important to point out that, in the making of the hate policies and practices in South Africa, those involved in shaping the equality legislation were pragmatic in their work. That is, first, the legislation reflects an understanding that, at a certain level, we need categories, such as race, gender, and so on, in order to help us understand our world. Second, legislative pragmatism has meant tempering a reconstruction and transformation agenda intended to reconstruct and transform both identity constructs and material inequalities in radical ways.

If the implementation of the act is any indication, then the path from theory to practice has its own set of problems. In addition to the institutionalization of a new, unproblematized "natural," the legislation is used to call for more than 350 years of colonialism and apartheid to be undone with inadequate resources, at all levels of government. For example, section 187 agencies such as the South African Human Rights Commission (SAHRC) and the Commission on Gender Equality (CGE) have broad legislative and constitutional mandates without having the budgets to adequately monitor, advise, and advocate. Further, with regard to the monitoring provisions of the equality legislation, the SAHRC and CGE have a conflicting relationship especially with the state agencies they are supposed to monitor. For example, intellectual and activist Rhoda Khadali questioned the independence of the section 187 agencies. As mentioned earlier, individuals move with relative ease between government departments, NGOs, positions in the governing party apparatus, and independent state agencies. In addition to these hurdles and political compromises, reports recurrently emerge through the grapevine about ethno-racial and sex-gender tensions within the sectors crucial to processes of reconstruction and transformation, including government departments and section 187 bodies. That is, the bodies charged with reconstruction and transformation have problems reconstructing and transforming themselves.

Considering the aforementioned, where will South Africa be ten years from now with a state that has forthrightly attempted to complicate identity and naturalize equality through legislation like the equality bill? Will we look back twenty years from now and say that the state, in response to those engaged in struggle, initiated regulatory state practices that subvert white supremacy's racial binaries in ways that resemble Pierre Bourdieu's "symbolic subversion" used to undo "masculine domination"?[62]

Equality Courts

Training

The success of the equality legislation largely depends on the success of the new equality courts. The *Bench Book for Equality Courts* and the *Resource Book for Equality Courts* are critical to this success.[63] The *Bench Book* contains guidelines for the judges and magistrates presiding over the equality courts, while the *Resource Book* is for clerks who administer the new courts. Three themes stand out in these two instruments intended to spur social transformation in and through law: the significance of the judiciary's grasp of South Africa's social context; the need to tailor substantive legal forms and norms for a South African context where apartheid's bureaucratic constructs of race and gender made apartheid oppressions possible; and the importance of rethinking identity and oppression as understood by courts and court officers.

Social Context

Attention to "social context" drives both the *Bench Book* and *Resource Book* and sets the tone for a postapartheid departure from the bureaucratic forms and norms of apartheid's judiciary. In fact, social context training for presiding officers and clerks is required with the passage of a 2002 amendment to the 2000 equality legislation.[64] The *Bench Book* contains a twofold understanding of the importance of social context giving rise to, for example, hate speech. First, social context in the manual for judges and magistrates "refers to the broad social and economic inequalities in society that exist between groups, such as black and white people, or women and men." Second, "social context illustrates that there are multiple viewpoints and perspectives on any particular matter that are shaped by people's different experiences and opportunities." Understanding the social context of hate within the purview of the 2002 amendment to the 2000 equality legislation becomes essential not just to equalizing relations between individuals and groups but also calling "attention to the biases and stereotypes that can operate in the process of judicial decision making."[65] Comparative references to social context help the authors of the guide for judges and magistrates make their point by calling upon court officers to "become sensitive to differences not only between themselves and litigants, but also among litigants" coming from different backgrounds. Pointing to bench books in Australia and the United Kingdom as models,[66] composers of the bench book for judges and magistrates write that "those who dispense justice must be aware of diversity, including disparities within society as a whole."[67]

History is critical to the social context conveyed in the manuals for equality court officers. The authors of the clerk's handbook, not unlike those legislating equality via the 2000 equality legislation, understand the past in simple but not at all simplistic ways. "In the past," reads the clerk's handbook, "those in positions of power and with control of resources, used this power and control to treat people unequally, thereby keeping power and wealth for themselves."[68] In the clerk's handbook, this difference in treatment is primarily based upon racial difference, but also based upon gender, language, and sexual orientation, among other measures. The judge and magistrate's bench book has additional material on social context for discriminatory forms such as hate, but in a more legalistic tone, reflecting the professionalization increasingly narrowing the qualifications gap separating judges and magistrates. Authors of the bench book for judges and magistrates state that "apartheid was a system of legal discrimination."[69] The guide for judges and magistrates contains multiple references to specific laws used by the colonial and apartheid states, such as the Native Land Act (1913), the Group Areas Act (1950), and the Separate Amenities Act (1953), which by promoting and using particular social constructs reproducing hate, "entrenched the racist policies and patterns of life in the past." The authors take into account that "to a large degree, state institutions, including the courts, enforced these laws willingly." It follows that the embodiment of hate that was the apartheid state, as understood in the guide for judges and magistrates, concretized racial divisions—"African, Colored and Indian and White." Authors of the bench book for judges and magistrates also understand racial divisions to be conditioned by "ethnicity, language, culture, and religion."[70]

Conscious of the way that social constructs intersect and hate-enabling oppressions interlock, those who composed the bench book for judges and magistrates contextualize the effect of African customary law and Muslim personal law under apartheid. Specifically, the authors of the juridical template for equality judges and magistrates point out that in the South African social context, apartheid's bureaucracy helped construct these black cultural and legal forms to be something less than white cultural and legal forms. The authors of the bench book for judges and magistrates assert that women were oppressed under African customary law and Muslim personal law. Bench book authors distribute responsibility for this misogynous oppression between the racist apartheid state as well as patriarchal forms and norms underlying African customary law and Muslim personal law as applied. Drafters of the bench book for judges and magistrates contend that white supremacists and patriarchs of color perpetuated particular hardships for women of color. This "confluence," according to the authors of the bench book, helps illustrate "the linkages between gender, race, and class in constituting the social and economic position of women in South Africa."[71]

Both the *Bench Book* for judges and magistrates and the *Resource Book* for clerks contain forceful language used to recognize the lingering effects of colonialism and apartheid. Authors of the guide for judges and magistrates refer to contemporary remnants of apartheid as "deep scars."[72] Characteristically, to remedy the "deep scars" of hate, those drafting the bench book for judges and magistrates reference South African Constitutional Court jurisprudence that has "explicitly underlined poverty and social inequalities as serious trademarks of South African society that must be taken into account in interpreting rights and freedoms and providing remedies."[73] The authors of the *Resource Book* for clerks also acknowledge that apartheid's "deep scars" led to the South African Constitutional Assembly to draft a constitution that "put the rights to equality and human dignity at the very top of the list." As if it needed to be said, drafters of the clerk's resource admit that "even with these rights protected in the Bill of Rights, we need only look around to see that people in South Africa are nowhere near equal as yet."[74]

Court Practices

With a particular notion of social context and its impact on discriminatory forms such as hate, officers of the Equality Court supposedly start to depart from colonial and apartheid forms and norms. Both the *Bench Book* for judges and magistrates as well as the *Resource Book* for clerks describe the "substance" of the Equality Act as the procedures and concepts guiding court officers and helping to make the courts vital organs of justice. For example, "the clerks of these equality courts," as the *Resource Book* reads, "will have an important role to play in making real the promises of the Equality Act." According to the drafters of the resource for clerks, "Equality court clerks should therefore not only know the Equality Act, but should treat individuals in a way that the principles of equality are made visible." Consistent with the intent of the parliamentary committee considering the legislation in its bill form, authors of the handbook for court clerks stress that clerks are key to "creating a user friendly environment which provides access to justice."[75] As the authors of the clerk's handbook concede, "Despite the fact that presiding officers will receive training to sensitize them to the social context of cases and complaints, presiding officers of the equality courts to some extent remain members of a particular class."[76]

Authors of the resource for equality court clerks call for a number of court technologies to bridge difference, as difference might play out in a courtroom where a hate case might be heard. For example, the authors of the clerk's handbook give a role to specially trained assessors able to navigate class separating a black female judge from a black female complainant who works as a cashier in a shop.[77] To make the process less intimidating, those assembling the clerk's handbook advocate a departure from the "'accusatorial approach'" common in other courts, "where each party brings their own evidence and presents their case to an impartial presiding officer."[78] The intent is to level the playing field, where a white and working class complainant will not have the same access to a lawyer as a black empowerment company listed on the Johannesburg Stock Exchange, even when the white worker brings her or his white privilege to court. The "new approach" of the equality courts also includes a courtroom geography that lessens courtroom hierarchies, rules of evidence for civil procedures that are less stringent, clerks and presiding officers who become advocates for complainants, and presiding officers who may prescribe alternative options for dispute resolution.[79]

Apartheid ways die hard, though, even as the postapartheid state veers from the relatively static forms and norms of old that helped perpetuate hate and other forms of discrimination. This becomes clear as the architects of both the *Bench Book* for magistrates and judges as well as the *Resource Book* for clerks seek to establish new procedures and processes for the new equality courts. Authors of the *Bench Book* for judges and magistrates define just what the Equality Court is, as well as who officiates in the courts and the professional qualifications of court officials.[80] Beyond this, complainants in the courts receive definition right down to what the definition of a "person" is. ("'Person'" is defined in section 1(1)(xviii) of the act as including "any juristic person, a nonjuristic entity, a group or category of persons."[81] "Person" here encompasses a notion of personhood, where personhood is constructed by the person and others.) Direction to the clerks, as noted in the *Resource Book* for clerks, is even more fordist, just as the state is directed to overcome the bureaucratic identity constructs upon which the hate that was apartheid depended. Fordisms within the new forms and norms are outlined using bureaucratic flowcharts, for example, for pre-hearings. The *Resource Book* for clerks reads:

> Step 1: Person bringing a case notifies the Clerk of the Equality Court, in writing, using form 2. Step 2: Clerk notifies respondent (using form 3) within 7 days. Step 3: Respondent has 10 days from date of receipt to reply. If the respondent replies, Clerk must give a copy of this to the complainant within 7 days of receiving it.[82]

Understandably, courts need regularized forms and norms in order to function. But at what point do the regulatory forms and norms of the judiciary start to govern the social constructs that are supposed to be transformed in and through the new equality courts? At what point should it be emphasized that the flowchart is a rough guide and not a way of thinking? At what point do the guides start to function like tort (as) structure?

Both the *Bench Book* for magistrates and judges and the *Resource Book* for clerks embrace a rather sophisticated understanding of equality and difference not necessarily reflecting the pre-hearing procedure in the *Resource Book* for clerks. For example, the legislation requires equality courts to work toward substantive equality, as opposed to formal equality. A fundamental assumption of states working toward substantive equality is that "treating all people the same is not necessarily equal," as the *Resource Book* for clerks reads, because "men and women have not been treated identically historically."[83] As understood by Parliament and the authors of the manuals legislating and training against hate, South Africa's social context, where apartheid identity constructs continue to yield inequalities, requires the state to treat individuals and groups differently in order to achieve social reconstruction and transformation. Authors of the *Bench Book* for judges and magistrates recall the words of a South African Constitutional Court justice who wrote in a decision that "the desire for equality is not a hope for the elimination of all differences."[84] *Bench Book* authors relate this in another place by offering a particular conceptualization of difference that underlies

> the idea that difference is not intrinsic, but relational. The differential treatment of a person should not be judged according to an abstract norm (usually determined by the more powerful groups in society), but in terms of the relationship between individuals and groups.[85]

New understandings of equality and difference change the understanding of that which constitutes discrimination and what needs to be done to remedy discrimination. The *Resource Book* definition of "discrimination" means "to treat them unequally for no good reason."[86] But this definition, which obviously pertains to acts of hate, not unlike the prescribed bureaucratic procedure for pre-hearings listed earlier, has to be a guide, not an absolute. After all, conceptualizing difference as relational cannot necessarily be reduced to a checklist; it requires a different level of thinking more accurately measured on a written exam than an exam given by a nameless professor in a large lecture hall using an exam for which responses are to be graded by machine.

Identities and Oppressions

Drafters of the *Bench Book* for presiding officers and the *Resource Book* for clerks articulate an understanding of identity and oppression reflecting both the nimble yet focused understanding of South Africa's social context. The drafters also, at points, tend to advocate a postapartheid form of apartheid's legal and racial "science." The authors of both the *Bench Book* and *Resource Book* transmit an understanding of identity through the listed grounds enumerated in the Equality Act. Identity in both manuals exists in relation to oppressions. For example, in the clerk's handbook, the drafters decipher age as construct in relation to discrimination faced by "persons based on their age, especially advanced age." "This definition," as relayed in the resource for clerks, "does not mean that young people do not have a claim in terms of the Act, however." But age, and more particularly aging as construct, creates situations where "many elderly people are subjected to discrimination on a regular basis, especially in the area of employment and violence against them," which may indeed be motivated by a particular form of hate and not merely bias or prejudice.[87]

The importance of an articulated identity and oppression becomes clearer when the listed grounds are placed next to the prohibited grounds. For example, authors conceptualizing the prohibited grounds in the training handbook for clerks clearly link discrimination against the disabled to binary constructs where the disabled are constructed as "abnormal" and those with able bodies are constructed as "normal."[88] Beyond understanding the binary constructs underlying ableism, drafters of the *Resource Book* for clerks typically relay the power dimensions connected to social constructs in a way that would be understandable even to those outside of the legal profession. "Those in positions of power and with control of resources [have] used this power and control to treat people unequally thereby keeping power and wealth for themselves," according to the authors of the resource material for clerks. As stated in this resource for clerks, discriminatory forms such as hate result from the unequal distribution of power made possible by stereotyping, which is "where we take a characteristic of an individual or individuals and turn [it] into a generalization." "Stereotyping," which is in boldfaced type as if to be a part of the vocabulary of equality and inequality regulation of which hate acts are a part, leads us "to see ourselves as belonging to a group (the 'in-group') while the groups of people different to us are known as 'out-groups.'" This, according to the drafters of the clerk's handbook, makes possible binary constructions of, for example, class so that the poor are constructed and blamed for their status because they supposedly have many children as opposed to the rich who are perceived to have fewer children.[89] Though not explicitly mentioned in the clerk's handbook, this particular construct contains racial as well as sexual overtones linking the supposed sexual licentiousness of "nonwhites" to poverty as opposed to the supposed superiority of whites able to control their sexual urges.

Race as construct in the *Bench Book* for judges and magistrates is even more demonstrative of the identity logic (and, at points, illogic) of those who designed manuals that could become governance tools. Once again, characteristic of the *Bench Book* for presiding officers, race as construct operates in legalese. As the *Bench Book* reads, "Race discrimination involves treating people unfairly because of their actual or perceived membership of (sic) a racial group."[90] Immediately afterward the authors of the guide for judges and magistrates refer to apartheid-era laws restricting black ownership of land, and apartheid laws limiting where people could live based on race. South African legal history, as understood in the *Bench Book* for judges and magistrates, "has also generated divisions between disadvantaged race groups in our country."[91] Taking note of socially ascribed values attached to skin color, the authors refer to the "preferential treatment of coloured over African people in the Western Cape," which "has led to people in some cases judging each other according to the lightness or darkness of skin."[92] This racism, or colorism, not only leads to hate between groups but to self-hate, where racism is internalized.

At other points, however, the authors of the *Bench Book* for judges and magistrates convey an understanding of ethnicity, social origin, birth, and nationality used not so much to show the way that these constructs inflect each other but to parse individuals and groups with the supposed precision of apartheid's governance technologies. And this understanding of ethnicity, social origin, birth, and nationality takes on a bureaucratic quality in which people and groups must be neatly assigned to the racial equivalent of Linnaeus's species, families, and groups so that a discriminatory form such as hate speech can be regulated. For example, the guide for clerks contains the following understanding of "ethnic or social origin or birth" under listed grounds:

"Ethnic or social origin" relates to the tribe or group or social group that you belong to: whether you are Tswana or Afrikaner or Jew, to which caste you belong; on which side of the tracks you live. Birth links closely with "ethnic or social origin."[93]

This view of "culture"—that word Raymond Williams described as the most problematic word in the English language[94]—reflects an understanding of ethnicity that resembles the ethnos theory problematized by

Ivan Evans in *Bureaucracy and Race: Native Administration in South Africa.*[95] According to Evans, ethnicity, when theorized, regulates and governs people by parsing identity into what were thought to be neatly discernible groups whose origins could be traced with the disciplinary exactitude of the human and social "science" being "perfected" early in the last century.

The authors of the guide for judges and magistrates have an understanding of "ethnic and social origin" that is even more problematic and even contradictory when placed next to the drafters' more complex understanding of sex and gender. Specifically, as judges and magistrates are trained to regulate hate and hate speech, the *Bench Book* drafters think that "ethnic origin implies membership of a biological group with common descendants, cultural heritage, and possibly a territorial area."[96] When the ethnos theory of the manuals is understood within the South African social context as well as comparatively, both guidebooks for presiding officers and clerks seem to ironically reproduce the regulatory form and norm if not the substance and intended outcomes of apartheid's legal and racial "science." This does not at all diminish the realness of supremacies based upon socially constructed categories and the need to remedy apartheid hate by readily recognizing the connection between supremacies and categories. But at what point does the new postapartheid bureaucratic "science" become the old apartheid bureaucratic "science," but in "drag."

While race as construct might be reductionist in the manuals for presiding officers and clerks, the complexity of identity in both documents primarily comes across in the way that the documents are used to position gender. According to the drafters of the *Resource Book* for clerks, "at first sight it appears strange that the drafters of the Act refer to both sex and gender." Sex in the *Resource Book* refers to "the biological differences between males and females—in other words discrimination based on differences between the bodies of males and females." (Pregnancy is the example provided by the drafters.) Gender, on the other hand, "relates to social and cultural roles for men and women." For example, social and cultural norms might be used to argue that women are better at childbearing and, as a result, should not be employed outside of the home. The drafting team responsible for the resource for clerks emphatically states that "there is no difference between men and women that make women better biological caregivers than men."[97]

In a more academic voice, the *Bench Book* for judges and magistrates has much the same understanding of sex and gender as the resource for clerks. "The difference between gender and sex is based on a distinction between maleness and femaleness arising from biological and social characteristics." Drafters of the *Bench Book* continue, "Gender refers to socially constructed aspects of maleness and femaleness."[98] Significantly, the Bench Book for judges and magistrates includes an added point to stress that sex and gender "in the main applies to women because of their disadvantaged position in society, although it could also affect men."[99] Adding complexity to sex and gender discrimination, drafters of the judge and magistrate's book characteristically reference an appellate case, *Brink v. Kushoff* (1996),[100] where a South African Constitutional Court judge remarked that "patterns of disadvantage are particularly acute in the case of black women, as race and gender discrimination overlap."[101] Not unlike those who assembled the training modules for clerks, the *Bench Book* authors merely borrow the wording of the final draft of the 2000 legislation, which states that "one or more of the listed grounds"[102] may be the basis of hate as a form of discrimination.

A question remains, however: Just how far will the Equality Act of 2000 and the training mechanisms stipulated by the act reconstruct and transform South African law and society by reconstructing and transforming the social constructs underlying hate and hate speech? Further, will the act and its regulatory mechanisms be able to counteract the tendencies of an apartheid state that, with a vast bureaucracy, governed inequality by fastidiously attempting to govern race and other social constructs with "scientific" precision? (This was a "precision" that enabled the apartheid state to call itself democratic and accept no responsibility for apartheid inequalities, because, procedurally, state bodies followed the letter of apartheid law.) Yes, the authors of the *Bench Book* for judges and magistrates strongly convey a sense of the intersections differentiating postapartheid legality from the relative stasis characterizing apartheid social constructs. For example, in a section on prohibited grounds, drafters of the *Bench Book* impart an intersectional analysis when referring to a constitutional court case, *National Coalition for Gay and Lesbian Equality v. Minister of Home Affairs* (1998),[103] used to recognize "overlapping discrimination" on the grounds of sexual orientation and marital status.[104] But in terms of mapping hate policies and practices, the manuals still ultimately center one intersection over others: the intersection of race and gender. At what point does thinking about intersectionality become bureaucratic and constitutive of a new legal and racial "science"?

6

Can Racism Burn?

Mbongeni Ngema has used his art to make other South Africans uneasy. During the 1970s, he took to the stage as an actor confronting apartheid. In the early 1980s, he cofounded Committed Artists, a theater company, for which he wrote and directed antiapartheid dramas such as *Asinamali!*, first performed in South Africa in 1983 and in the United States in 1986, and *Sarafina!*, a musical debuting in 1987 in South Africa and the United States. *Asinamali!* related the experiences of five activists imprisoned for their 1980s politics and earned Ngema a 1987 Tony nomination for directing. *Sarafina!* recounted the 1976 student uprisings in Soweto, earned Ngema three Tony nominations in 1988, and was turned into a 1992 film starring Whoopi Goldberg.

By 2002, after the formal end of apartheid, the broadcast and distribution of a single song defined Ngema. The song "AmaNdiya" ("The Indians" in Zulu) represented a troubling flash point in the history of conflict between South Africa's Zulus and Afro-Indians. Ngema used his song to initiate what he called a "constructive discussion" about conflicts separating Zulus and Afro-Indians. "AmaNdiya" became a tool used to accuse Afro-Indians of slyly taking advantage of postapartheid efforts to redistribute power, while, according to the lyrics, "Zulus do not have money and are squatting in shacks as chattels of Indians." As the lyrics of "AmaNdiya" assert, Afro-Indian businesspersons used their economic and political clout to prevent Zulus from opening shops in the best business districts of Durban, South Africa. Ngema even said things were "better with whites [in power because Zulus] knew then it was a racial conflict." Perceptions of Afro-Indian power and privilege led Ngema to present Afro-Indians in postapartheid South Africa as foreign "others" bent on Zulu subservience and slavery. This was the representation presented by Ngema, even though Afro-Indians, too, were exploited colonial and apartheid laborers. The lyrics of Ngema's "AmaNdiya" noted that Zulus do not move en masse to Bombay; "yet, Indians arrive every day in Durban—they are packing the airport full."[1]

This final chapter considers hate, race, and the popular culture. Two forms of hate and racial governance are compared and contrasted in this chapter. In many respects, the two types of hate regulation highlighted in this chapter point to change as well as a kind of continuity between apartheid and postapartheid regulatory state practices. This change and continuity moot the transformation intended by those passing and implementing the 2000 equality legislation that was the subject of this book's previous chapter.

The first section of this chapter explores the bounds of permissible hate in postapartheid broadcasting, where the state's gradual withdrawal from regulatory processes leads to the private regulation of the Broadcasting Complaints Commission of South Africa in a case like the Ngema one.

In a genealogical vein, the second section of this chapter compares the regulation of film and video distribution during late apartheid. Regulatory processes at the apartheid-era Publications Appeal Board and the postapartheid regulation at the Film and Publication Board are compared.

Governing Sounds

Responses to "AmaNdiya"

Reactions to Ngema and "AmaNdiya" were largely divided along ethno-racial lines. Afro-Indians, for example, understood the song to incite hatred toward Afro-Indians. A newspaper columnist, describing himself as an African who happens to be Indian, wrote that "instead of awakening [the Afro-Indian] community to its shortcomings, the song's fundamentally racist character has increased fear and anger."[2] Zulus and other blacks speaking African languages mostly agreed with the song's sentiments and defended Ngema's constitutional right to express what many consider seldom-spoken truths. During the winter of 2002, I spent three months in South Africa listening to radio talk shows and frequently heard blacks who speak an African language describe Afro-Indians in ways similar to how some African Americans speak of Korean American shopkeepers, or how anti-Semites refer to the "Jew banker." In contrast, many if not most African-speaking intellectuals and politicians (most notably, Mandela) quickly distanced themselves from Ngema and the song. White and Afro-colored South Africans tended to echo the concerns of the Afro-

Indian community while simultaneously calling for the dignity of the
Afro-Indian community to be protected, even if that meant limiting artistic
expression. Supporting limits on expression, for example, Bronwyn Harris
of the Center for the Study of Violence and Reconciliation labeled Ngema's
song "a divisive trick" that threatened Afro-Indians, who constitute 2.5
percent of the South African population. "Not only does it [Ngema's song]
challenge the idea of racial inclusiveness and unity, it also suggests that
South African identity is racially exclusive."[3]

Official responses to Ngema's song primarily came in three legal
forms. First, after receiving a complaint from the South African Human
Rights Commission and a complaint from a private citizen, the
Broadcasting Complaints Commission of South Africa (BCCSA), a
"private" industry body with the statutory power to regulate public
airwaves, limited the broadcast of Ngema's song to radio and television
programs where the song would explicitly be used to stimulate "public"
debate. A second agency, the Film and Publication Board (FPB), of South
Africa, concerned itself with the commercial distribution of the song. The
FPB, wholly a state agency and a unit of the South African Ministry of
Home Affairs, received complaints from "consumers" (an FPB term)
leading it to review the "AmaNdiya" lyrics in view of legal prohibitions
against hate expression. The FPB officials eventually limited who could
buy the recording in stores by imposing an age restriction of eighteen.
Finally, controversy surrounding Ngema's song led to court action; a
temporary interdict was requested by a citizen and granted by a high
court in Durban. The same high court subsequently declined to issue a
permanent interdict, however, which would have completely prohibited
the marketing and distribution of "AmaNdiya" in South Africa.

The research in this half of the chapter focuses on the first of the official responses to Ngema's "AmaNdiya"—that of the BCCSA, a
self-regulatory body financed and operated by South Africa's broadcasting industry. The BCCSA action in the Ngema case represented the
most problematic form of media regulation in a South Africa trying to
remake itself as a postapartheid society. The BCCSA response to
"AmaNdiya," and its responses in the ten other hate cases preceding the
Ngema case understood by the BCCSA to involve hate, reflected a negative effect of the state's privatization of a "public" regulatory function.
("Hate" and forms of "hate" referenced here specifically refer to
postapartheid cases in which, according to the BCCSA, a speech act's hate
content is at issue. [4] The effect manifested itself most clearly when an
industry body with public regulatory functions, such as the BCCSA,
responded to what it considered actionable hate by governing racial
constructs and notions of racism in ways that contradict the predominant trajectory of South Africa's transition from an apartheid dictatorship

to a multicultural democracy. Specifically, BCCSA commissioners failed to situate "AmaNdiya" within the South African "social context." State bodies, in contrast, such as the South African Parliament and South African Ministry of Justice units charged with shaping and implementing the equality legislation of 2000, tend to pay close attention to social context. Race and racism, as understood by Parliament and the Ministry of Justice, must be considered within a South African social context inextricably molded by the white supremacy of European colonialism and apartheid.

Legal Basis of Governance

South Africa's 1996 constitution contains a bill of rights readily referenced as the BCCSA governed Ngema's "AmaNdiya" and apportioned racial responsibility. Freedom of expression is a primary right. Section 16(1) guarantees that

> everyone has the right to freedom of expression which includes—(a) freedom of the press and other media; (b) freedom to receive or impart information or ideas; (c) freedom of artistic creativity; and (d) academic freedom and freedom of scientific research.[5]

Whereas some liberal constitutions stop here, such as the U.S. Constitution, section 16(2) of the South African Bill of Rights limits these rights, as mentioned in chapter 1. South Africa's internal limitation makes it possible for the state to bound expression when expression amounts to

> propaganda for war; incitement of imminent violence; or advocacy of hatred that is based on race, ethnicity, gender or religion, and that constitutes incitement to cause harm.[6]

In addition to the constitutional provisions, two pieces of post-apartheid legislation helped texture BCCSA governance of "AmaNdiya" in foundational ways—the Independent Broadcasting Authority Act of 1993 and the Independent Communications Authority of South Africa Act of 2000. Passage of the Independent Broadcasting Authority Act led to the creation of the Independent Broadcasting Authority (IBA). Sensitive to state censorship during apartheid, the IBA was "to function wholly independent of state, governmental, and party political influences and free from political or other bias or interference."[7] The IBA regulated broadcasts by, for example, licensing broadcasters and settling "public" complaints against broadcasters.

In 2000, the IBA was disbanded and its authority was assumed by the new Independent Communications Authority of South Africa (ICASA). Still sensitive to the role of apartheid censorship and capital's self-interest, the South African Parliament stipulated that the ICASA be an "independent" agency "subject only to the Constitution and the law"[8] and "without any political or commercial interference."[9] Parliament passed the ICASA Act with the intent of spurring technological integration and innovation within and between the broadcasting and telecommunications industries. Largely leaving IBA forms and norms in place, members of Parliament apparently assumed the ICASA would make broadcast and telecommunications regulation more effective and efficient.

In terms of reach, the ICASA ceded some of its power to the BCCSA, a commission created in 1993 by the National Association of Broadcasters (NAB). The ICASA partially handed over its power to the NAB's BCCSA, because the ICASA endorsed the BCCSA's Code of Conduct. The code of conduct of an industry body such as the BCCSA was understood to be consistent with standards of state agencies such as the IBA and ICASA. The code also committed the BCCSA signatories to a set of professional standards, community standards, and a BCCSA constitution consistent with South Africa's 1996 constitution. All of the major radio and television broadcasters in South Africa—"public" and "private," not that this distinction has been easy to make in broadcasting and broadcast regulation—became the BCCSA signatories. The BCCSA signatories agreed to abide by the BCCSA's Adjudication Committee in response to a complaint.[10] In many respects, and not unlike the rating system of self-regulatory entities such as the Motion Picture Association of America, South Africa's National Association of Broadcasters created the BCCSA to avoid more direct state regulation of broadcasting that might be more onerous.

The BCCSA officials received two "AmaNdiya" complaints. Both came after Ngema's song was aired on a public affairs program of the South African Broadcasting Corporation (SABC), the state-owned broadcaster. In response to a listener's complaint, the "private" BCCSA was charged with regulating the "public" SABC. (The BCCSA's Adjudication Committee only acts in response to listener or viewer complaints.[11]) One complaint came from the South African Human Rights Commission (an independent state agency) on behalf of a class of citizens (Afro-Indians), and the other from an individual the BCCSA does not name, because it is a "private" corporation with "public" regulatory functions. (The Commission does not accept information requests made under South Africa's Promotion of Access to Information Act of 2000.) Both "AmaNdiya" complainants made reference to a provision of the BCCSA

Code requiring that member broadcasters not air material detrimental to the "feelings of a section of the population," or "which is likely to harm relations between sections of the population or is likely to prejudice the safety of the state of the public order."[12]

The Ngema case proceeded according to the BCCSA's own regularized procedures: the BCCSA administrators accepted the "AmaNdiya" complaint within thirty days of the broadcast and determined that it was a legitimate complaint, one involving a BCCSA signatory. Ukhozi FM, the state's SABC affiliate that broadcast the song, formally received official notice from the BCCSA that the Ngema complaint would be brought forward. Ukhozi then gave the BCCSA a copy of the program in question as required by the BCCSA Code. Kobus van Rooyen—head of the BCCSA and former head, from 1980 to 1990, of a censorship agency of the apartheid state—then appointed a tribunal consisting of himself and two other BCCSA commissioners to hear the case.

Governing Hate and Governing Race

Shortly before the Ngema case was heard by the BCCSA tribunal, South Africa's Constitutional Court judges handed down a decision refining the constitutional and statutory limits of free expression. The decision significantly changed the way the Ngema case was judged by the BCCSA. The decision in *Islamic Unity Convention v. the Independent Broadcasting Authority and Others* (2002)[13] moved beyond the usual case law cited in hate expression decisions. Such case law, as found in, for example, *State v. Mamobolo* (2001),[14] merely reiterated sections 16(1) and 16(2) of the Bill of Rights. In *Islamic Unity Convention*, South Africa's Constitutional Court, not unlike the BCCSA commissioners who would hear the "AmaNdiya" case, noted the importance of free expression, especially considering the apartheid past, but also mentioned necessary limitations to this right. In *Islamic Unity Convention*, Constitutional Court justices agreed that "pluralism and broadmindedness ... central to an open and democratic society can ... be undermined by speech which seriously threatens democratic pluralism itself." And threats to "an open and democratic society" needed to be limited. Addressing the hate expression limits in section 16(2) of the South African Bill of Rights, the Constitutional Court unequivocally stated in *Islamic Unity Convention*—a case the BCCSA had to follow in the "AmaNdiya" case as a private body with a "public" regulatory function—that "what is not protected by the Constitution is expression or speech that amounts to 'advocacy of hatred.'" Significantly, and pivotal to the Ngema case, the Court added that postapartheid hate acts outside of constitutional bounds had to be motivated by identity.[15]

Before *Islamic Unity Convention*, the BCCSA and other entities "objectively" deployed the law to determine hatefulness based on whether or not
an expressive act harmed relations between South African groups. A
remnant of apartheid censorship legislation,[16] apartheid "conservatives"
at the Directorate of Publications used the "harmed relations" measure to
censor and ban material, while apartheid "liberals" at the Publications
Appeal Board, such as Kobus van Rooyen, a lawyer, used the measure to
take the regulatory onus and responsibility from the state and supposedly
give it to self-governing individuals. This apartheid-era measure of hate
made its way into postapartheid judgments of the BCCSA such as
Myburgh v. Radio 702 (2001) and *Fouche v. 94.7 Highveld Stereo* (2000).[17] In
Islamic Unity Convention, however, South Africa's Constitutional Court
considered the old "harmed relations" measure to be too broad: "Not
every expression or speech that is likely to prejudice relations between
sections of the population would be 'propaganda for war,' or 'incitement
of imminent violence,' or 'advocacy of hatred.'" The Court, in *Islamic Unity
Convention*, decided that hate expression could only be constitutionally
limited when it is narrowly "based on race, ethnicity, gender or religion" to
the point that it "'constitutes incitement to cause harm.'"[18]

After *Islamic Unity Convention*, in cases such as Ngemas and *Clarke and
Others v. East Coast Radio* (2003),[19] the BCCSA still projected itself as an
"objective" adjudicator interpreting the law without needing to consider
"subjective" dimensions that social context injects into a given case.[20] After
Islamic Unity Convention, however, Kobus van Rooyen and other BCCSA
commissioners had to refine their modernist and positivist "objectivity" by
dissecting the new directions of the constitutional court into a series of
fixed tests. Clarification of the old "objective" measure, as it applied to
"AmaNdiya," involved asking the following five questions: (1) "whether
the song amounts to 'advocacy of hatred'"; (2) whether or not "'the hatred
is based on race in terms of the [BCCSA] Code'"; (3) whether or not "'the
words are also inflammatory'"; (4) whether or not the song "'incites to
harm'"; (5) whether or not "'there is harm.'"[21] Commissioners, beyond
responding to these questions, started to tie a closer reading of the limits
on expression in section 16(2) of the bill of rights to a closer reading of the
relationship between speech rights and social constructs such as race and
gender. This was the strategy in the Ngema case, *Prinsloo and Venter v.
Rippel 90.5 fm* (2002),[22] and *Clarke* (2003). The need to consider closely
social constructs such as race and gender grew from the *Islamic Unity
Convention* standard, in which hate "based on race, ethnicity, gender or
religion" and hate that" 'constitutes incitement to cause harm'" were found
not to be constitutionally protected.[23]

Connecting the limits to expression in section 16(2) of the South
African Constitution and social constructs such as race was not an easy

thing for BCCSA commissioners. Before *Islamic Unity Convention*, BCCSA judgments contained no consideration of basic yet complex questions, such as what is race, and, further, the relationship between race and racism. To determine whether a postapartheid expression of hate was "racial" in a case like the Ngema one, BCCSA commissioners, in their very legalistic way, apparently felt compelled to have some "objective" and static understanding of race (as construct), and a notion of racism that could be made to fit multiple cases. This was an "objective" and linear understanding that followed the relatively fixed forms and norms of the modernist and positivist apartheid judiciary.

Grappling with social constructs such as race and gender was difficult for the BCCSA unless social constructs fell within the racial bounds that the apartheid state tried to normalize through classification. For example, BCCSA officials had no problem articulating a narrative of race as construct, or the realness of racism, when hate was clearly scripted as white-on-black, as in a case such as *Fouche v. 94.7 Highfeld Stereo* (2000).[24] When the BCCSA sought to understand and assess hate expression outside of the white-on-black binary, or the masculine-feminine binary, however, BCCSA conceptualizations of race, gender, and sexuality appeared awkward and antiquated. For example, in *Johnson v. 94.7 Highveld Stereo* (2002),[25] a case heard shortly after *Islamic Unity Convention*, BCCSA commissioners relied on the authority of a dictionary in order to conclude that "chink" was derogatory when used by a white person to describe someone of Chinese descent. Likewise, *Prinsloo and Venter v. Rippel 90.5 fm* (2002) exemplified how sexuality and gender confounded the commissioners then trying to determine whether or not calling a "drag" queen a *dit* (Afrikaans for "it") contravened the commission's code on hate. The BCCSA commissioners seemingly reached their judgment in *Prinsloo* (2002) as a result of the Commission's conflation of not only gender with female and feminine but also of gender with sexuality. So, essentially, commissioners concluded that "drag" had nothing to do with gender, because *Prinsloo*'s "drag" performers were male. This led the Commission to miss the contingencies within and between these categories as well as to misperceive the power plays inextricably connected to gender and sexuality in a patriarchal and heterosexist society in transition from apartheid forms and norms to postapartheid's democratic multiculturalism. In *Clarke* (2003), the BCCSA tried to discern "race" and "racial" from a comment made by a white radio announcer who referred to Sri Lanka's national cricket team as "horrible little people" with "stupid names that no one can pronounce" and "willies [that] rattle in our African condoms."[26] The announcer's words did not necessarily amount to hate expression under the BCCSA Code and South African Constitution, but the commission puzzlingly concluded that the comments were not racial because "the accent was on the team and their unsporting behavior, not on their race or ethnicity."[27]

The BCCSA commissioners similarly reckoned with race as construct and racism as oppression in the Ngema case. They judged "AmaNdiya" to be "hatred" that "is based on race." The BCCSA measures, however, were neither scientific nor sophisticated enough to transform an apartheid society built on apartheid's static cultural and legal boundaries. According to the commissioners, "AmaNdiya" conveyed racial hate because "not only is the name of the song *AmaNdiya*, but the *Indians*, by way of generalization, are blamed [for Zulu suffering]."[28] With no more social context than a general history of censorship where the centrality of race and racism was omitted, the commission considered the mere utterance of the word "AmaNdiya" to constitute "race" and to be "racial."

The BCCSA's thinking in the remainder of the "AmaNdiya" judgment ironically reads somewhat like a postcolonial critique of white supremacy offered by Steve Biko in *I Write What I Like* or Edward Said in *Orientalism*,[29] except that the BCCSA commissioners turn Zulus into the colonizer and Afro-Indians into the colonized. Along these lines, the BCCSA concluded that Ngema's "song polarizes"[30] and presents "a clear polarization"[31] so as to, basically, binarize two ethno-racial communities. Ngema's song consisted of "generalization,"[32] "sweeping generalizations,"[33] and "politically loaded generalizations,"[34] according to the Commission. The BCCSA understood these constructs to depict Zulus, on the one hand, with an "accent on poverty, [as] chattels, clowns, fools, deprivation and oppression [as] an effective instrument in conveying such hate."[35] On the other hand, according to the Commission, Ngema constructed the Afro-Indian community to be "a cause of poverty of Zulus," "worse than the Whites were," as the group that "turned an important clan into clowns, have disposed them, have suppressed them and play the fool with them."[36]

But the centering of what the BCCSA considered the racial binaries in Ngema's song meant that the Commission slighted the central binary in South African history. Specifically, looking at Ngema's binary construction of Afro-Indians as "bad" and villainous, as opposed to Zulus who were constructed as "good" and victimized, ignored how colonial and apartheid constructions of race conditioned the material inequalities underlying both apartheid and the Zulu and Afro-Indian conflict. These inequalities received material grounding through apartheid's racial hierarchy, a hierarchy that afforded Afro-Indians apartheid "privileges" because Afro-Indians outranked Zulus in the apartheid state's social order.

"Sweeping generalizations" in "AmaNdiya" led the BCCSA to label the song inflammatory enough to incite harm. Specifically, "AmaNdiya" proved inflammatory enough, according to the BCCSA, to make South

Africa's Afro-Indian community feel as if it might be targeted for harm.[37] "Whether there is a likelihood of real attack is irrelevant," according to the BCCSA in its judgment. The Commission continued: "There would, in our opinion, be a likelihood of fear—a fear based on reasonable inference, in the light of the emotionally laden language employed" in Ngema's "AmaNdiya."[38] The BCCSA concluded, largely relying upon what it presented as binary constructs showing a "clear polarization," that

> the broadcast of the song constitutes incitement to cause harm, in the sense that it violates dignity and places the constitutional right to security of Indians at risk—even if it is limited, as we find, to a distinct sense of fear among a substantial number of Indians.[39]

The Politics of Responsibility

South African satirist Peter-Dirk Uys presented a cheeky but frank statement pointing to the importance of the politics of responsibility in postapartheid South Africa. Through the persona he created and performs on stage—Evita Buizedenhout, popularly understood to be the most famous white woman in South Africa—Uys said that, among white South Africans, the future is certain. It is the past, and who is responsible for the past, that is uncertain.

Debates about the past, especially those about how to transform the racial past, persist in South Africa. In many respects, an important function of the BCCSA has been "negotiating the past,"[40] especially who is responsible for the apartheid past and how the past can be collectively righted. Long after controversies such as the "AmaNdiya" controversy have been forgotten, the lasting influence of entities such as the Commission and the FPB comes not so much from their power to ban, or to classify and certify, their real power has grown out of their ability to remember the past and consider the present. This occurs when the BCCSA and the FPB accept "consumer" complaints, react to the media frenzy immediately following the release of a cultural artifact such as Ngema's "AmaNdiya," and generally react to the mood of the South African "street." As barometers of the pace of transformation, organizations such as the BCCSA and FPB have the power to record, reaffirm, redirect, and reorder the past and present.

Not unlike the BCCSA and the FPB, scholars studying governance in Foucouldian ways, have the power to record, reaffirm, redirect, and reorder academic discourse in advanced liberalism. A transformative intervention by governance scholars, however, is impossible when governance scholars redistribute responsibility by sidelining racial context as social context. Without race as a critical dimension of social context, governance scholars fall into the same predicament as the BCCSA and FPB.

Governing Images

Apartheid Censorship

The governance of hate and race in the "AmaNdiya" case has a more specific genealogy with traces located in late apartheid regulation. This past started during the 1970s and 1980s, as opponents of the apartheid state intensified their resistance to the regime. This resistance occurred in the form of strikes, unsanctioned mass rallies, direct confrontations with apartheid security forces, and covert military and political operations by the banned African National Congress, as well as international boycotts and sanctions. South African censors responded to the new challenges in two ways unaddressed by scholars writing on apartheid censorship.[41] First, the censors reformed the way they regulated film and video distribution. Second, and connected to the reform measures, censors strategically adjusted their understanding of race and notions of racism instrumental to the regulation of film and video distribution.

This politicization of race and racism during the 1980s is not surprising, given South Africa's colonial and apartheid history, and the ethno-racial hatred that colonialism and apartheid generated. Beyond the obvious, though, late apartheid censorship illustrated how and why a budding form of governance came into existence in order to govern hate by governing racial constructs. Specifically, those charged with regulating film and video distribution in South Africa subtly started to govern the way the state visualized, understood, and talked about whites and "nonwhites." These "liberal" South African censors significantly helped soften the binary tenor of apartheid's racial template, where whites historically used discourse to construct themselves as "civilized" and "nonwhites" as "savage." Furthermore, these "liberal" censors—or, really, neoliberal censors—also sought to direct responsibility for the 1980s political conflict and correction of these conflicts away from the apartheid state and toward individuals and groups that were to increasingly govern themselves. Indicative of what neoliberal critic Pierre Bourdieu called an "ethos of deregulation,"[42] and what Foucault called "governmentality," this redirecting of responsibility, in addition to neutering the state as a force for good, made it possible for apartheid censors to talk about race without really talking about race and especially without forthrightly talking about apartheid as racist ideology. From the censor's perspective, circumventing discussions of race and racism removed politics from film and video distribution.

Problematically, the regulatory form adopted and deployed by the late apartheid censorship apparatus has survived apartheid as the postapartheid state has sought to govern hate as well as control other media deemed by the state to be counter to the state's interests. Of course, the face of the South African state has dramatically changed since the establishment of a multiracial democracy in 1994, even if, as one Nigerian commentator derisively suggested, South Africa is a white country with a black president. There exists, though, a kind of continuity between the old and new states, specifically between the late apartheid and the postapartheid forms of film and video regulation. This continuity in the regulation, understood in this chapter in neoliberal terms, has hindered the transformation of apartheid's regulatory state practices because the role of the state has been marginalized and the public sphere eroded in the name of a private and individual "freedom." Continuity in the regulation of film and video distribution also has stymied the transformation of race and the destruction of racism in postapartheid South Africa because not unlike the regulatory order in late apartheid censorship, a postapartheid reckoning with race as construct and racism as reality is deferred.

Mapantsula *as Image*

Official response to the film *Mapantsula* (1988) exemplifies the problematic continuity in South African media regulation before and after apartheid. Shot entirely in South Africa, *Mapantsula* is the work of two South Africans, Thomas Mogotlane, who is black, and Oliver Schmitz, who is white. Shot during the third state of emergency, and set in Soweto and Pretoria during the Soweto rent strikes of the mid-1980s, *Mapantsula* chronicles the day-to-day life and political coming-of-age of Panic (Thomas Mogotlane), a small-time gangster and thief.

Early in the film, Panic, the gangster and thief, accidentally ends up in the middle of a political protest that lands him in jail. Using the tactics of the apartheid security apparatus, apartheid authorities attempt to get Panic to identify protesters he does not know (because he was not a protester), and in exchange they will release him. The past grounds the present as the filmmakers use flashbacks to gradually reveal what would become Panic's antiapartheid defiance. From a rather memorable scene where Panic picks the pocket of a helpless white businessman to the chronicling of the growing consciousness and activism of Panic's girlfriend Pat (Thembi Mtshali), the film captures the multiple dimensions of apartheid repression as well as the way blacks from the townships coped with and resisted the state.

The film is important because, among other things, it presents racial constructs of blacks that countered the constructs normally sanctioned and promoted by the apartheid state. Whereas many feature films classified and certified (and even subsidized) by the apartheid state fell into the "buddy" genre, *Mapantsula* rejects the racial reconciliation themes of films such as *Cry Freedom* (1987) and *The Power of One* (1992), where the "good" white guy allies himself with a black junior partner in order to redeem South Africa. *Mapantsula* marks a break not only with the "buddy" films but also with the "structured integration" films (e.g., *Way of Life*, 1981; *Will to Win*, 1982), the "back-to-homeland" films (e.g., *Maloyi*, 1978; *Isivileo* 1979), and the gangster films (e.g., *Phindesela*, 1979; *Ukuhlupheka*, 1982).

Instead of operating within apartheid's preferred film genres, *Mapantsula* features oppositional racial constructs. For example, apartheid exists in the film as a wholly illegitimate social, political, and economic system. Whites benefiting from this illegitimate system exist as either maniacal, as in the character of the policeman (Marcel van Heerden), who violently interrogates Panic, or clueless and self-absorbed, as Mrs. Bentley (Vanessa Cooke), for whom Panic's girlfriend, Pat, does domestic work. In contrast, constructions of blacks in the film are empowering, as when Panic, in the movie's last word, decisively says "No!" to both his white police interrogator and the white police interrogator's black "buddy" (Magic Hlatswayo) who not only demand that Panic inform on activists but also that he implicate a union leader in "terrorist" acts. Constructions of "uncivilized" whites and their black collaborators rest alongside black racial constructs where race and class lead Panic's girlfriend and the union leader mentioned earlier, Duma (Peter Sephuma), to organize not only against the apartheid state but also against the subdominant class of black municipal leaders that helps administer apartheid in the townships. While "good" blacks and "bad" blacks are contrasted here, the world that is *Mapantsula* has only "bad" whites.

When Whites Were the "Likely Viewer"

The distributor of *Mapantsula*, One Look Productions, submitted the video version of the film for classification and certification on May 7, 1988. Two publications committees of the Directorate of Publications considered the video version. The committees, like all Directorate committees involved in the classification and certification process, left a record outlining the rationale for their decision. This record, form DP 2F, was the "Film Working Document." This form, filled out by each member of the committee, had blocks in which each committee member recorded his or her name, telephone number, the name of the film being considered, its running time, and the case number. In addition, each member was to check the box indicating whether the film was "not undesirable" and "unconditionally approved," "undesirable" and "rejected," or "conditionally approved." Conditions included restrictions (mainly age restrictions) on who could and could not view the film, on where the film could and could not be screened, and on which parts of the film could and could not be screened. The latter restriction required that specific reference be made to what needed to be excised for classification *and* certification to occur. In addition to dating and signing the form, each member was to record in prose form the reasons he or she made the particular decision.

After meeting on June 3, 1988, the first classification hearing for the video version of *Mapantsula* resulted in an age restriction of two to eighteen, but there was some disagreement on how the film should be classified. The publications committee member least concerned with the political content of the film noted that the film has "a strong colloquial flavor," providing insight into the daily life of a small-time gangster. This member seemed less concerned with Panic's activism than with the racial consciousness emerging from the way the police mistreated him. This led to concern about how the mistreatment of Panic might figure when placed next to antiapartheid chants used at demonstrations depicted in *Mapantsula*. The member continued, "My feeling is that although the actual chanting and meaning of the words used are not understood, the film could have an emotive effect on the viewer but does not present a clear and present danger to the safety of the state" as underlined in 47(2)(e) of the Publications Act or in 1983 guidelines set out by the Publications Appeal Board.[43] A second member of the publications committee had a similar concern, which led this member to recommend cutting the chanting of struggle slogans, the cursing, and some of the scenes depicting police violence directed toward Panic, which were understood to foment racial hatred between racial groupings.[44] A third member considered the video version of the film undesirable. This member wrote that "the security authorities, white housewives, or to be more accurate whites in general, and the black township authorities are shown in an unfavorable though not exaggerated light." This concern about the stirring of hatred between racial groups prompted this member to label the video version of *Mapantsula* "a borderline case" that needed to be screened by the security committee.[45]

Likely due to both its subject matter *Mapantsula* and to the divisions among the members of the first committee, the video version of

Mapantsula was reviewed by a second publications committee on June 22, 1988, which unanimously classified the video version as "not undesirable" and "unconditionally approved." This second publications committee had fewer security concerns. In fact, its rationale was in line with the later *Mapantsula* decision rendered by the more liberal Publications Appeal Board (PAB), headed by Kobus van Rooyen. For example, the chair of the second committee wrote, "The film does not incite or harm racial relationships—in fact, it has very little impact—even on black viewers."[46] Writing in Afrikaans, another committee member used the words "weak" and "fragmented" to characterize the artistic merit of *Mapantsula* before writing that it "poses no threat to the security of the state."[47] This second committee typically characterized the video version as containing a "few violent scenes" that are not "unusual."[48] In fact, in summarizing the panel's deliberations, the chair of the second committee asserted that "everything shown is known to all South Africans and in particular to blacks who experience these things daily."[49]

Cry Freedom and Mapantsula

Chronology became important at this point. The first two reviews of *Mapantsula*, which were classification and certification deliberations for the video version of the film, occurred in June 1988. On July 5, 1988, the producers of *Mapantsula*, through their attorneys, submitted an application for the general theatrical release of the film.[50] Directorate of Publications officials formally issued a certificate of classification for the video version of *Mapantsula* on July 21, 1988 with the special proviso that "the theatrical version must be submitted de novo to a Committee of Publications for a decision."[51] On August 15, 1988, seventeen days after the general release of the theatrical version of *Cry Freedom*, organizers of the Weekly Mail Film Festival sought classification and certification for *Mapantsula* screenings in a Johannesburg theatre, listing "township gangster" in the "subject" box of the "Application for Approval/Review Form," the organizers clearly trying to deflect attention from the film's political content, for the gangster genre usually was viewed by the state as benign.[52]

That the *Mapantsula* request for theatrical classification and certification came seventeen days after *Cry Freedom* opened, and closed, in South Africa was important. *Cry Freedom*, about the politics and state murder of black consciousness movement leader Steve Biko, was distributed in South Africa in 1988 and then quickly withdrawn by the distributor on opening day after bomb threats and an actual bomb disrupted the Durban and Johannesburg openings. (It was later revealed that state security was responsible for the terror around the South African opening of *Cry Freedom* in the name of squelching black resistance, fed by, in the mentalité of the censors, the stirring of blacks' hatred of whites.)

The controversy surrounding *Cry Freedom* and *Mapantsula* came at a time when political troubles were severely disrupting the apartheid order. The year before, the ruling National Party had convincingly won a whites-only election. Outside of South Africa, states and international organizations tightened sanctions against the regime, precipitating capital flight from the country. At the same time, in 1988, the liberal guardians of the apartheid state began to have a marked impact on the political scene. For example, at the highest levels of government, liberal apartheid guardian F. W. de Klerk suddenly replaced P. W. Botha as head of the National Party in February 1989, after Botha suffered a nondebilitating stroke. By August 1989, apartheid liberals forced Botha to resign as state president and quickly replaced him with de Klerk, whose "liberalism" was described by Mandela as being bent on one thing: "to ensure power for the Afrikaner in the new dispensation."[53]

When Blacks Were the "Likely Viewer"

A new publications committee met to consider *Mapantsula* for general theatrical release on August 15, 1988, the same day the application for theatrical release arrived at the Directorate of Publications. The committee rejected the application for general release and approved just three screenings at the Market Theatre in Johannesburg as part of the Weekly Mail Film Festival, largely because blacks were much more likely to view the film in general release than in video release.[54] Justifying the committee's decision, the chair warned of how, unlike video, "the large screen amplifies the dangerous political effects the film could have on probable viewers in this country," and these "effects" were black resistance, which was understood to be hatred of whites for keeping blacks, within the apartheid rationale, in their rightful place.[55] Basically constructing the black "likely viewer" in savage terms, several of the committee's main points touched upon how "the film has the power to *incite* probable viewers to act violently."[56]

Directly connected to concerns about violence committed by the "savage" who was, of course, black, the publications committee considering *Mapantsula* for general theatrical release decisively expressed its concerns about the "propagandistic tendencies" of the film.[57] Specifically, the committee pointed to the "*one-sidedness*"[58] of the film. "Although one-sidedness is not sufficient to find a film undesirable," committee members noted that "the blatancy with which this line is followed in *Mapantsula* is an aggravating factor."[59] Publications committee members suggested that the filmmakers should have made some attempt to relay an understanding of why the rent increases were "inevitable."[60] In the committee's reading, the protests documented in the film are about rent, not really about an apartheid loathed by blacks, about the system of racial constructs used to justify white privilege protected through "emergency regulations" that "have to be enforced."[61]

Members of the publications committee considering *Mapantsula* for general theatrical release were concerned with the maintenance of a particular order that was upset when South Africans of color sought to racially construct themselves and the white minority. The place for whites was historically constructed in order to naturalize white supremacy, where whites were subjects and people of color but objects. South Africa's racial order, as suggested in the committee's rationale, was upset with "the involvement of the *trade union* in addressing the problem"[62] that was apartheid. When race and class as empowering social constructs and realities intersect on film, "*friction* between *blacks and whites* (employer and employee)" was understood to follow.[63] Racial order, according to the committee's reasoning, was disturbed even further when the filmmakers constructed the police as an oppressive force defending the interests of the white minority, creating hatred in the black body politic, which apartheid functionaries seemed to read as unmediated hatred directed toward whites. The police perspective, according to the committee, was "conveniently set aside."[64] The committee then mentioned the last scene and word of the film when, increasingly conscious of his blackness, Panic says "No!" to his police interrogators. The committee concluded that "the effective closing scene communicates a clear message to the viewer: Refuse cooperation with the authorities and side with the rebellious elements in black society."[65] In other words, "good" and more "civilized" blacks cooperated with the state on film and in real life, while "bad" and "savage" blacks not only "side with the rebellious element in black society" but constitute "bad" itself.

One Look Productions, the distributor of *Mapantsula*, formally appealed the general release decision to the PAB, in writing, on September 16, 1988. The distributor rejected both the age restriction (no one between two and eighteen years old) and the certification for just three screenings at the Weekly Mail Film Festival. One Look made its case on the basis of the film's "charismatic and artistic merits," which it felt had been ignored by the publications committee considering the film for general release. Responding to the claim that the film was "dangerous," the distributor contended that this finding is at odds with precedents of the Publications Appeal Board whereby more stringent conditions are placed on videos while films shown in theaters are more likely to draw their true likely audiences than are videos shown in private homes.[66]

In its appeal, One Look pointed to the language used by the publications committee, which was unusually harsh for a film with conditional certification. The distributor argued that the claims of the committee classifying the theatrical version were irrational, the distributors likely playing to the modernist governance rationale of the PAB, headed by the liberal Kobus van Rooyen.

Arranging and Rearranging the "Likely Viewer"

Though he does not center race, J. M. Coetzee, the 2003 Nobel Laureate, used his scholarship to start to understand Kobus van Rooyen's liberal censorship practices at the PAB. Coetzee specifically asserted that van Rooyen implemented a system based on "objective" classification and certification of media, in contrast to the more subjective and outright state censorship preferred by apartheid conservatives. Coetzee argued that van Rooyen's PAB applied a "standard of impersonality" in classification and certification that is "not to be confused with objectivity" devoid of political motives.[67] Van Rooyen's "objective" classification and certification of media, however, as I contend in this chapter, was not merely lacking in "objectivity," as Coetzee argued; van Rooyen's regulation was first and foremost a different system of racial control packaged in "objective" and liberal garb.

Van Rooyen used a handbook of sorts, *Censorship in South Africa*, to outline the regulatory system used by the PAB in late apartheid. This system excluded van Rooyen's "ideal" but untenable "form of control": "self-control" (or self-governance).[68] Although van Rooyen liked "self-control" because it minimized overt state interference, he ultimately thought it was not realistic. Another regulatory alternative for van Rooyen was "direct control by way of criminal law,"[69] but he considered this to be "rather slow, and as a result of the nature of criminal sanctions, the courts are reluctant to pass a judgment of guilty."[70] He eventually stated his and the PAB's preference for control through "administrative process,"[71] concluding that administrative control "tends to be more impersonal and is, in any case, more effective."[72] (Van Rooyen considered "publications control" "a science and not merely a hit or miss game of darts."[73]) This impersonality came when experts oversaw a process that was not unlike an assembly line:

A person who applies for approval of any film submits such an application.... The applicant must at his own expense make arrangements to exhibit the film to the committee.... The director informs the applicant of the committee's decision.... The applicant may appeal to the PAB.... Any person may.[74]

Fordist regularity supposedly produced a fairness that van Rooyen understood in terms of "objectivity" and "balance." By the 1980s, van Rooyen and the PAB viewed their role as that of "an objective and independent arbiter, not a persecutor on behalf of sectional interests."[75] The PAB's status as an "independent arbiter" resulted from its "balancing of interests," as if all interests had equal power in political practice. This was the kind of arbitration where "general or sectional interests are continually weighed against minority interests." But van Rooyen denied the centrality of race; for him, "interests" were primarily "dramatic, artistic, and literary interests as well as the interests of likely viewers and readers"[76] who might, of course, be "nonwhite." Van Rooyen explicitly spoke of racial "interests" only when, for example, the Board called on black academics for their opinions about the racial "other," [77] or Desmond Tutu, who became the Board's expert on black reception of "kaffir," the hateful racial slur.[78]

Summarizing the thinking of the PAB in what was presented as a systematically reasoned legal judgment without a racial tinge, van Rooyen set out the main issues of the *Mapantsula* case.[79] He forthrightly stated that the Board did not understand why the video version was approved and the theatrical version not approved. Trying both to understand the thinking of the publications committees and set its own regulatory course, the PAB used its judgment to establish its own authority as an honest broker whose sole purpose was to maintain "peace and order" by asking and establishing "whether the screening of this film is likely to provide or contribute to sedition."[80] The central question in this case, according to the PAB, claiming a politic brand of authority, led to what was presented as a corollary question. The corollary revolved around the likelihood of seditious acts by the "likely viewer" who might be moved by a "provocative" scene in a film such as *Mapantsula*.

Parties to this case used "likely viewer" or sometimes "probable viewer" as a code word with formal and informal application. "Likely viewer" as concept, for example, had a formal history. Specifically, after the passage of the Publications Act of 1974, regulators used the "average decent-minded, law-abiding, modern and enlightened citizen with Christian principles" who was "a man of balance" to determine if a work was "undesirable" or "not undesirable."[81] By the late 1970s, this yardstick changed to the "reasonable reader/viewer" not "hyper-critical or over-sensitive," who contemplates "all relevant factors including the standards of likely reader and the merits of the work into consideration."[82]

Informally, however, "likely viewer" had a hidden history that allowed the apartheid state to talk about race without talking about race. That is, when the Directorate's publications committees in particular but also the PAB had racial concerns, Directorate and PAB personnel raised the specter of the "likely viewer," about whom certain racial assumptions were made. When a film was considered for video classification and certification, and most of its "likely viewers" were white, the decision of apartheid censors was not unlike the decision reached by the second publications committee considering *Mapantsula* for video release. Apartheid guardians tended to react with greater caution, however, when, as in the hearing for the theatrical version, the "likely viewer" was mostly "nonwhite." Clearly, apartheid censors had concerns about the way that blacks in particular would react to certain films in certain mediums. Censors seemingly assumed that when blacks were the "likely viewers," and when the content was provocative, as in *Mapantsula*, blacks would react in a violent, and hateful, way. This unsurprisingly fell within stereotypes of blacks as "savages," incapable of reason.

The PAB adopted relatively liberal constructions of the "likely viewer" living in the township, in stark contrast to the constructions of the publications committee reviewing *Mapantsula* for theatrical release, which largely constructed blacks as the *swaart gevaar*, "black peril" or "black threat," ready to wreak racial havoc after viewing *Mapantsula* in theaters. The PAB's constructions of blacks reflected a supposedly objective and race neutral method of classifying and certifying films. Positioning themselves as disinterested adjudicators, Board members tried to understand the context producing *Mapantsula* characters such as Panic as well as blacks who actually protested on the streets. Van Rooyen, writing for the Board, used the *Mapantsula* judgment to try to come to terms with the "realities of township life" shaping Panic, and the "realities of the domestic relationship" shaping Pat's political consciousness.[83] The PAB found that these cinematic constructions did not contravene the provisions of the Publications Act of 1974.

Pathologizing blacks, and not the system that created the harsh conditions under which blacks lived, the PAB failed to scrutinize apartheid itself as a political system. As the Board deferred reckoning with apartheid as the underlying cause of black unrest, a subtle change in state discourse streamed into regulatory practice. Significantly, another reality of township life received acknowledgment when van Rooyen pointed to the reality of police violence and its effects on blacks.[84] The Board explicitly offered an understanding of the effects of police action, though it did not explicitly recognize that apartheid was the problem, and that the police (or rather the "deviant" apartheid police officer acting indiscriminately) merely enforced that system.

The PAB's concern with "race relations" (i.e., the circulation of racial hatred) in the *Mapantsula* case, especially between politically conscious blacks and the largely white police force, had a statutory grounding. Board concerns revolved around the enforcement of section 47(2)(c-e) of the Publications Act of 1974, which enabled the Board to justify excisions when particular scenes "[brought] any section of the population of the Republic into ridicule and contempt," or when scenes were judged injurious to state security (47(2)(e)). In essence, the Board concerned itself with media representations of hate that might spawn hate speech or other forms of hate. Van Rooyen had communicated his particular understanding of section 47 in his *Censorship in South Africa* (1987). Here, van Rooyen, while head of the PAB, acknowledged that "relations between sections of the population, especially between black and white, are at the very basis of South African politics."[85] Along these lines, he applauded an unnamed state that made "it an offence to harm these relations" between South Africans and between South Africans and the state. This was the case even though, as he hesitantly admitted, this unnamed state "has through some of its own legislation and the application thereof given cause for deterioration in these relations."[86]

Bound by the system whose name it did not mention in its *Mapantsula* judgment, PAB maintenance of good "relations" required reform of what it considered the overly regulated "relations" of the more conservative publications committees. The PAB regulations, using a particular governing rationale, stressed the maintenance of individual boundaries on-screen and off so that the state could seemingly remove itself from what might appear to be excessive regulation. "Bounds are overstepped" in *Mapantsula*, warned the PAB in its judgment. Basically, racial constructions projected by the makers of *Mapantsula* were, at the very least, problematic for the state. Speaking as a supposedly neutral arbiter, the Board thought the filmmakers needed to act responsibly and respect the bounds of existing apartheid law (e.g., 47(2)), which supposedly protected the interests of blacks. For example, in the *Mapantsula* judgment, Board members wrote that the repetition of struggle slogans threatened "relations" between blacks and whites.[87] The offending chants, in Zulu, which were used on-screen and off so that blacks could construct and empower themselves, called on ANC leader Oliver Tambo to tell P. W. Botha to release Nelson Mandela, urged blacks to march to Pretoria, and encouraged blacks to continue the armed struggle.[88]

Similarly, PAB regulators thought police officers had to stay in bounds on-screen and off, so that a state desiring a diminished regulatory role could emerge. More self-governance—or "self-control," as van

Rooyen put it in *Censorship in South Africa*—would make it possible to move toward a seemingly more benign, more objective, and more balanced system of classification and certification. For the Board, that meant projecting itself as race neutral; those posed by the depiction of chanting black activists were similar to the problems posed by the depiction of security personnel as violent—as in the interrogation scene in *Mapantsula*. Board members specifically thought that "aspects of interrogation as well as the obvious third-degree are not undesirable."[89] It was not as if the Board "denies that these scenes could take place in real life," but the Board concluded that subjective moralizing was "not our task."[90] "We believe," though, the Board continued, "that the relations between black and white would be affected detrimentally when the bounds are overstepped by the Police and Panic is held out the window."[91]

Seeking to maintain good "relations," the PAB set two conditions and requested four cuts before *Mapantsula* could be classified and certified for general theatrical release. First, the Zulu call-and-response "Amandla" ("the power")—"Awethu" ("is ours") chanted twice at a public meeting, had to be removed.[92] Second, the scene where the police interrogator threatens to throw Panic out of a window had to be removed.[93] Third, the word "kak" ("shit") and the shot of Panic squatting while naked had to be deleted.[94] Fourth, scenes of the police firing a gun while in a van and scenes of the police wielding whips had to be removed.[95] In addition, the PAB required a two to eighteen age restriction be set and also that the film not be screened before more than 200 people. But this victory of sorts for One Look and the filmmakers became moot when Ster-Kinekor, a major film chain in South Africa, declined to screen the film in theaters.

Postapartheid's Changing Same

In 1991, after the rise of F. W. de Klerk and other apartheid liberals was complete, the distributor of *Mapantsula* asked for and received a new hearing before a publications committee of the Directorate of Publications. It wanted general theatrical release without restrictions. Most notably, the security concerns evident in the 1988 regulation of *Mapantsula* were understandably less urgent. With different security concerns, members of the 1991 publications committee tended to use their standardized forms to summarize the film's story line, with little or no comment on or discussion of section 47(2) and its treatment of "race relations" and state security.

The 1991 committee saw *Mapantsula* the film as representative of a racial past that was no more. The chair of the 1991 committee wrote that "the film is history."[96] He continued, "1985: State of Emergency: Amandla.... The *toitoing* [and] chanting has become less 'threatening' since February 1990."[97] (Mandela was released from prison on February 11, 1990.) "History" here has more than one meaning. It means that the moment represented in *Mapantsula* had passed, that the tension born of the initial transition was decreasing. "History" also means that *toitoing*, as African protest dance, is now "less threatening" to whites. The reference to "history" also obscures the racial politics of the past as if this politics is a thing of the past. Viewing apartheid as history, the 1991 committee imposed a two to eighteen age restriction and requested two excisions: the word "kak" ("used in its primary sense") and a scene of "policemen firing indiscriminately with their rifles (implying that a live ammunition was used) with apparent intent to kill."[98]

Moving beyond the 1991 classification and certification of *Mapantsula*, and moving even farther toward the self-governance as "self-control" idealized by van Rooyen in late apartheid, postapartheid regulation of film started to crystallize in December 1994, eight months after the election of South Africa's first democratic government, when a special task group presented its report to the Minister of Home Affairs, the minister being directly responsible for the regulation of film before and after apartheid. The task group, chaired by the same Kobus van Rooyen, who headed apartheid's PAB, scrutinized apartheid's Publications Act of 1974 in light of the interim South African constitution of 1994 and formally presented the framework for a postapartheid regulatory agency that would succeed the apartheid-era Directorate of Publications and PAB.[99] After reviewing the 1974 legislation and its amendments, the task group concluded "that a new Publications Act is necessary."[100] In presenting this conclusion, the group adopted many of the arguments used by the reformers of film and video distribution in Britain during the late 1970s and early 1980s.[101]

The administrative recommendations of the task group reflected, not unlike British reformers, the late apartheid tendency to move even farther away from outright censorship, and toward a system of classification and certification understood to be politically neutral and objective. The task group rejected "a censorship body, in view of all the implications carried by the word 'censorship.'"[102] Instead it recommended that the postapartheid film and publication legislation establish "an administrative board with appeal to a quasi-judicial review aboard," which, in form, was not unlike the apartheid state's Directorate of Publications and PAB.[103] Further, not unlike the old censorship apparatus, the task group recommended preclassification of publications and then certification of films[104] using "objective" and "neutral" criteria. Supposedly race neutral and apolitical, this preclassification would primarily focus on age restrictions (mostly based on language and violent content) and on prohibiting child pornography and other images understood to degrade "human dignity." Most significant in this regard, the task group members chose an approach in which the state tepidly wielded its power through "consumer advice," especially advice to parents. The business cards of the postapartheid agency that the task force helped create—the Film and Publication Board (FPB)—captured the regulatory disposition of a late apartheid official like van Rooyen and the postapartheid regulators at the FPB: "We [the FPB] classify," you [the 'consumer'] decide."

In its final report, van Rooyen's task group recommended that when classifying and certifying "the emphasis should, as far as possible, be on regulation and management of the problem, and not on prohibition."[105] "Management," leaving room for self-governance as self-control, set the tone for South African film and video regulation after apartheid, along the lines of the British model. For example, the British Board of Film Censors changed its name in 1985 to the British Board of Film Classification to reflect its new preclassification and certification orientation. Further, in 1995, the Board—a private industry body with public regulatory functions—started to use its consumer advice box.[106]

By the end of 1999, a second postapartheid government had been inaugurated. A second microeconomic plan had been put into place as well, the neoliberal GEAR (Growth Employment and Redistribution, 1996) economic program, which replaced the more social democratic RDP (Redistribution and Development Program, 1994–1996).

Regulation of *Mapantsula* in 1999, after GEAR, illustrated the regulatory form recommended by van Rooyen's task group. By 1999, gone was the flowery language reflecting the unfettered optimism of the 1991 hearing for classification and certification. In its place, members of the 1999 publications committee considered *Mapantsula*, both the film and video, based on the following supposedly apolitical categories: "violence," "language," "criminality," and "prejudice." Referring to the language in *Mapantsula*, one reviewer wrote that the "language use is typically South African, including 'fuck' and 'kak.' "[107] Language concerned the examiner who deemed "criminality" in *Mapantsula* "potentially problematic—though these 'techniques' probably are broadly known."[108] Publications committee members decided upon a 10LP classification and certification for *Mapantsula*, with no child under ten allowed because of profane language and "prejudice." "Prejudice" appears to be a part of the new race talk used in order to mute talk of racism, with "prejudice" being a euphemism for racism as well as other oppressions such as patriarchy and heterosexism. It was not clear, though, who in *Mapantsula* exhibited this "prejudice" or whether or not the film required, as some multiculturalists in the United States might claim, "prejudice reduction." By the time a senior officer at the FPB saw the comments of the examiners and the report of the chief examiner, the film had been assigned a 10L classification and certification for no viewer under ten and strong language. Even mention of "prejudice" disappeared.

Ungoverning Images

The South African case is instructive, suggesting that—and this is not necessarily a characteristic of neoliberalism—relatively peaceful political transition means that there is an interstitial period where the regulatory disposition of the outgoing regime shapes the regulatory disposition of the regime that follows. Apartheid's PAB dominated this interstitial period and, as a result, remnants of apartheid's regulatory state practices have survived apartheid, even as the old governors keep their heads but lose their jobs or, in the case of van Rooyen, get new jobs.

This is the regulatory disposition in which the FPB finds itself, and this disposition makes it possible to wonder how transformative the FPB can be. Considering that South Africans continue to suffer because apartheid's racial constructs and racism survive every day, does transformation at the FPB mean that the state should be as invisible as possible in order to allow the so-called free market and the marketplace of ideas to determine the shape of constructions of race, gender, and sexuality on-screen and off? Does transformation mean that a forceful but nonrepressive state should encourage and empower individuals and groups to construct themselves through subsidies to local filmmakers and video makers? Or does transformation of film and video regulation mean something new and different that goes beyond either of these possibilities?

Make no mistake the FPB is not the Directorate of Publications or the PAB. That said, it is easy for liberals to say that less regulation means less state censorship and more freedom. Angst, though, easily grows from a concern with a receding state power, especially the power of a state organ such as the FPB, which is uniquely positioned to redistribute rights denied during apartheid. Bodies such as the FPB, in addition to offering "consumer advice," have the power to take sum of, for example, religious bigotry in South Africa as weighed against the South African constitution. State agencies such as the FPB also have the power to synthesize public opinion and constitutional guidelines into a moral vision, so that leaving some without a protective and responsible state will never be seen as moral. This is not a neutral, objective moral vision but a moral vision helping to ungovern images and to direct a multicultural society toward a multicultural, egalitarian future without hate.

Postscript

This book is not intended in any way to suggest that state agents stop using police reports in order to avoid particular representations of individuals or groups, or that the state stop considering "race" in appellate court decisions that are really about race and racism, nor does it call upon legislatures to make difference less visible and central. Instead, I hope it suggests something else, namely, that those governed by states must continue to act up, act out of prescribed racial bounds, and force the state to be more holistic in its regulatory practices, to not leave the hated in any degree of statelessness.

Reconstructive and transformative change would mean that a new kind of state emerges, and this state must not only stop promoting the responsibilization of society, it must use what Richard Delgado once called the "teaching function of law"[1] to undo what, in many instances, the state has helped bring about and perpetuate: race as construct and the racial hatred made possible by particular racial constructs.

Starting to undo particular constructs and "-isms" with legality itself as a pedagogical instrument would not just mean reconsidering and rethinking the form of practices. Social reconstruction and transformation would also mean making state agencies and agents themselves more aware of the ways in which their banal acts affect the ways agencies and agents govern hate and race, and, by extension, racism. If I had my druthers, state agents and agencies would not only be "sensitive" to difference but sophisticated enough to sense the cultural dynamics of hate and race, sophisticated enough to understand the flow of power in the broadest sense, producing and reproducing racism. This sophistication would include state recognition of its own position within the flow of power, a position grounded in supremacist forms and norms directly and indirectly in the service of various supremacies. This would mean moving beyond the thoughtlessness of the South African law professor who, in a positivist vein, insists that we be more sympathetic to police practices with problematic genealogies. (Just imagine if the state and its agents acted with cultural studies sensibilities, if the state and its agents were trained by scholar-intellectual-activists who think like Kimberlé Crenshaw or Bonaventura de Sousa Santos.[2]) Above all, law and legality as teacher would mean remembering what was, and is, so as never to devalue the force of oppressions, past and present.

Some will be unhappy with my call to relinquish some old ways of thinking. Straying from Marxist conventions in particular, the state visualized in this book is not simply a tool of the ruling class. In globalizing societies, where capital and cultural flow means that "robber barons" ride to work on bicycles and drink double decaf lattes with skim milk (also known as "why bothers") at Starbucks in a historically "other" (black, Jewish, Asian, and Latino) neighborhood such as Seattle's Central District, finding an identifiable ruling class can prove elusive anyway. (Try demonizing the World Trade Organization, if you can find it.) That said, the state understood and envisioned here—not unlike the race understood and envisioned here—is not indeterminate, and impotent. In fact, the state here proves to be a state capable of bad, and good.

As I have thought about hate and racial governance in the United States and South Africa, Stuart Hall, the cultural studies scholar, has never been far from my mind. Hall has offered new insight into the work of Antonio Gramsci, the Italian communist. In fact, Gramsci is never really far from Hall's thinking. Hall's Gramsci is used to rethink the state in conventional Marxism, where class is centered. Rereading Marx via Gramsci, Hall's Gramsci is more open, not so dependent upon class, but instead with a class articulated to other identities. Hall has dubbed Gramsci's Marxism a "Marxism without guarantees,"[1] where the position of class in social relations is not assured. In a different article, Hall used this Gramsci to rethink race, beyond the ethnic studies models that, after the fall of the Berlin Wall, still survive. (These are ethnic studies models implicitly contested in this book, which also is about new iterations of postindustrial blackness. Call what is going on here "transethnic studies," "postethnic studies," or whatever.) Whereas Gramsci saw a class that is not unitary, Hall's race and racism have defied unitary constructions.[4] Though Hall did not necessarily label his race in the way he labeled Gramsci's Marxism, he easily could have referred to a race and racism *without the old guarantees*, or even a race and racism without guarantees at all.

This book proposes that race and racism without the old guarantees would become a central element in regulatory state practices. This was the intent of the 2000 equality legislation, which, several years after its implication, has had mixed results.[5] Here, race and racism without the old guarantees mean many things, as they pertain to the possibility of a new kind of state, primarily, a race and racism that should ultimately be understood in more provisional terms to capture the changing constructs and material inequalities characterizing race and racism in new times. It is through different notions and practices that state agents and agencies might contribute to the reconstruction and transformation of societies. State practices may be used to serve supremacist ends, but they also can be remade to split supremacies into smaller and smaller parts, and inequalities into smaller and smaller bits.

Notes

Chapter 1

1. See, for example, Ian Haney-Lopez, *White by Law: The Legal Construction of Race* (New York: New York University Press, 1996). Also see Gabriel Gutierrez, "Affirmative Action of the First Kind: Social and Legal Constructions of Whiteness and White . . . Male Privilege in Nineteenth Century California," *Latino Studies Journal* 11 (2000): 14–48; Natsu Taylor Saito, "Symbolism under Siege: Japanese American Redress and the 'Racing' of Arab Americans as 'Terrorists,' " *Asian Law Journal* 8 (2001): 1–29; Frank H. Wu, *Yellow: Race in America Beyond Black and White* (New York: Basic Books, 2001); Susan D. Carle, "Theoretical Agency," *American University Law Review* 55 (2005): 307–93; Nicholas DeGenova, *Working the Boundaries: Race, Space, and "Illegality" in Mexican Chicago* (Durham, NC: Duke University Press, 2005); Mary L. Dudziak and Leti Volpp, *Legal Borderlands: Law and the Construction of American Borders* (Baltimore, MD: Johns Hopkins University Press, 2006). This work inflects and is inflected by the mid-1990s emerging interest in whiteness—whiteness studies. See Noel Ignatiev, *How the Irish Became White* (New York: Routledge, 1996); Annalee Newitz, ed., *White Trash: Race and Class in America* (New York: Routledge, 1997); Ruth Frankenberg, *Displacing Whiteness: Essays in Social and Cultural Criticism* (Durham, NC: Duke University Press, 1997); David R. Roediger, *The Wages of Whiteness: Race and the Making of the American Working Class* (New York: Verso, 1999).
2. Hall identified eight characteristics of the postindustrial change: 1) the rise of information technologies; (2) new organization of work and the accompanying decline in the manufacturing of the "old economy"; (3) outsourcing of labor functions; (4) consumption of goods that inflects and shapes identity; (5) decline in mostly male working class and rise of differently gendered service and white-collar workers; (6) proliferation of multinational corporations; (7) globalization of financial markets; and (8) new social divisions, such as between public and private, increase in subdivisions of those formally dubbed "rich" and "poor." See Stuart Hall,

"The Meaning of New Times," in *New Times: The Changing Face of Politics in the 1990s*, ed. Stuart Hall and Martin Jacques, 116–19 (London: Lawrence & Wishart, 1989).

3. Manning Marable, *Beyond Black and White: Transforming African-American Politics* (London: Verso, 1995), 120.

4. Cynthia Kros, "Secularity in a World 'Torn by Difference': A Consideration of the French Headscarf Affair from South Africa," *Politikon: South African Journal of Political Studies* (2005): 1–16.

5. See, for example, U.S. scholarship such as Mari Matsuda et al., *Words That Wound: Critical Race Theory, Assaultive Speech, and the First Amendment* (Boulder, CO: Westview Press, 1994); Richard Delgado and David Yun, "The Neo-Conservative Case against Hate Speech Regulation—Lively, D'Souza, Gates, Carter, and the Toughlove Crowd," *Vanderbilt Law Review* 47 (1994): 1807–25; Richard Delgado and Jean Stefancic, *Must We Defend Nazis?: Hate Speech, Pornography, and the New First Amendment* (New York: New York University Press, 1997); Alexander Tsesis, *Destructive Messages: How Hate Speech Paves the Way for Harmful Social Movements* (New York: New York University Press, 2002); Anthony Cortese, *Opposing Hate Speech* (Westport, CT: Praeger, 2005). Though not nearly as voluminous as the U.S. debate, see South African scholarship such as Shadrack B. Gutto, "The Criminalization of Hate Speech?," in *Between Speech and Silence: Hate Speech, Pornography, and the New South Africa*, ed. Jane Duncan, 103–27(Cape Town: Idasa, 1995).

6. See, for example, Edward J. Eberle, "Hate Speech, Offensive Speech, and Public Discourse in America," *Wake Forest Law Review* 29 (1994): 1135–1213; Henry Louis Gates Jr., "War of Words: Critical Race Theory and the First Amendment," in *Speaking of Race, Speaking of Sex: Hate Speech, Civil Rights, and Civil Liberties*, ed. Gates et al. (New York: New York University Press, 1994); James B. Jacobs and Kimberly Potter, *Hate Crimes: Criminal Law and Identity Politics* (New York: Oxford University Press, 1998); James Weinstein, *Hate Speech, Pornography, and the Racial Attack on Free Speech Doctrine* (Boulder, CO: Westview Press, 1999). Positions shift, though, over time, as has been the case with Eberle, but not completely. For example, see Eberle, "Cross Burning, Hate Speech, and Free Speech in America," *Arizona State Law Journal* 36 (2004): 953–1001. In South Africa, see Gilbert Marcus, "Racial Hostility: The South African Experience," in *Striking a Balance: Hate Speech, Freedom of Expression, and Non-Discrimination*, ed. Sandra Coliver, 208–22 (London: University of Essex Press, 1992); Marcus, "Incitement to Hatred: A Southern African Perspective," *Media Law and Practice in Southern Africa* (February 1998): 11–19.

7. See Judith Butler, *Excitable Speech: A Politics of the Performative* (New York: Routledge, 1997). Butler's position is rather unique, but not totally unique, among queer theorists and activists. See, for example, "Kiss & Tell," *Her Tongue on My Theory: Images, Essays, and Fantasies* (Vancouver, BC: Press Gang Publishers, 1994).

8. See, for example, Lene Johannessen, "A Critical View of the Constitutional Hate Speech Provision," *South African Journal on Human Rights* 13 (1997): 135–50.

9. See Lynn Adelman and Pamela Moorshead, "Bad Laws Make Hard Cases: Hate Crime Laws and the Supreme Court's Opinion in *Wisconsin v. Mitchell*," *Gonzaga Law Review* 30 (1995): 1–27; Steven G. Gey, "What if *Wisconsin v. Mitchell* Had Involved Martin Luther King Jr?: The Constitutional Flaws of Hate Crime Enhancement Statutes," *George Washington Law Review* 65 (1997): 1014–70; E. M. Read, "Put to the Proof: Evidentiary Considerations in Wisconsin Hate Crime Prosecutions," *Marquette Law Review* 89 (2005): 453–74.

10. See Valerie Jenness and Ryken Grattet, *Making Hate a Crime: From Social Movement Concept to Law Enforcement Practice* (New York: Russell Sage Foundation, 2001); Jeannine Bell, *Policing Hatred: Law Enforcement, Civil Rights, and Hate Crime* (New York: New York University Press, 2002); Jon B. Gould, *Speak No Evil: The Triumph of Hate Speech Regulation* (Chicago: University of Chicago Press, 2005). Also see Laura Beth Nielsen, *License to Harass: Law, Hierarchy, and Offensive Public Speech* (Princeton, NJ: Princeton University Press, 2004).

11. Richard Schur, "The Dialogic Criticism of Richard Delgado: Chicano/a Literature, Equality, and the Rhetoric of Form," *Law and Inequality* 19 (2001): 151.

12. Paul du Gay et al., *Doing Cultural Studies: The Story of the Sony Walkman* (London: Sage Publications, 1997), 11.

13. Jacobs and Potter, *Hate Crimes*, 95–96.

14. Ian Haney-Lopez, *Racism on Trial: The Chicano Fight for Justice* (Cambridge, MA: Harvard University Press, 2003), 6–8, 109–33.

15. Lisa Frohmann, "Convictability and Discordant Locales: Reproducing Race, Class, and Gender Ideologies in Prosecuting Decision Making," *Law and Society Review* 31 (1997): 531–56.

16. Stuart Hall, "The Spectacle of the 'Other,'" in *Representation: Cultural Representations and Signifying Practices*, ed. Stuart Hall et al., 257–59 (London: Sage Publications, 1997).

17. Paul Gready and Lazarus Kgalema, "Magistrates under Apartheid: A Case Study of the Politicization of Justice and Complicity in Human Rights Abuses," *South African Journal on Human Rights* 19 (2003): 150.

18. Gready and Kgalema, "Magistrates," 147–50.

19. Peter Fitzpatrick, "Racism and the Innocence of Law," in *Critical Legal Studies*, ed. Peter Fitzpatrick and Alan Hunt, 119–20 (London: Blackwell, 1987). In the case of the police officers in South Africa, reminders of this infamous past are reenforced when artifacts such as police uniforms jog the historical imagination while walking in Cape Town's central business district. Police officers in postapartheid South Africa wear the same uniforms of police during apartheid.

20. Patricia Williams, *The Alchemy of Race and Rights* (Cambridge, MA: Harvard University Press, 1991), 150–53. Williams continued, "Rights imply a respect that places one in the referential range of self and others, that elevates one's status from human body to social being. For blacks, then, the attainment of rights signifies the respectful behaviour, the collective responsibility, properly owed by a society to one of its own" (153).

21. See, e.g., Herbert Kitschelt, "Linkages between Citizens and Politicians in Democratic Polities," *Comparative Political Studies* 33 (2000): 845–79; David Lublin, "Racial Redistricting and African-American

Representation: A Critique of 'Do Majority-Minority Districts Maximize Substantive Black Representation in Congress?,'" *American Political Science Review* 93 (1999): 183–86; James Stinson, "Opinion and Representation," *American Political Science Review* 89 (1995): 179–83; Arend Lijphart, "The Political Consequences of Electoral Laws, 1945–1985," *American Political Science Review* 84 (1990): 481–96; Charles S. Bullock III and Susan A. MacManus, "Staggererd Terms and Black Representation," *Journal of Politics* 49 (1987): 543–52.

22. See, e.g., Stuart Hall, "The Whites of Their Eyes," in *Silver Linings*, ed. R. Brunt, 89–93 (London: Lawrence and Wishart, 1981).

23. Hall, "The Spectacle," 245.

24. Vine Deloria, *Red Earth, White Lies: Native Americans and the Myth of Scientific Fact* (New York: Scribners, 1995); Gayatri Chakravorty Spivak, *The Post-colonial Critic: Interviews, Strategies, Dialogues* (New York: Routledge, 1990); Michelle Habell-Pallan, *Loca Motion: The Travels of Chicana and Latina Popular Culture* (New York: New York University Press, 2005); Dwight A. McBride, *Why I Hate Abercrombie & Fitch: Essays on Race and Sexuality* (New York: New York University Press, 2005); Charles W. Mills, *The Racial Construct* (Ithaca, NY: Cornell University Press, 1997); Paul C. Taylor, *Race: A Philosophical Introduction* (Cambridge: Polity Press, 2004).

25. Michael Hardt and Antonio Negri, *Empire* (Cambridge, MA: Harvard University Press, 2000), 138.

26. See George M. Fredrickson, *White Supremacy: A Comparative Study in American and South African History* (New York: Oxford University Press, 1981); Fredrickson, *Black Liberation: A Comparative History of Black Ideologies in the United States and South Africa* (New York: Oxford University Press, 1995); Anthony W. Marx, *Making Race and Nation: A Comparison of the United States, South Africa, and Brazil* (New York: Cambridge University Press, 1998). Fredrickson also wrote a useful monograph on comparative method. See Fredrickson, *The Comparative Imagination: On the History of Racism, Nationalism, and Social Movements* (Berkeley: University of California Press, 1997).

Chapter 2

1. Foucault, "Governmentality," in *The Foucault Effect: Studies in Governmentality*, ed. Graham Burchell et al., 102 (Chicago: University of Chicago Press, 1991).

2. Foucault, "Governmentality," 92–94.

3. Foucault, "Governmentality," 101.

4. Foucault, "Governmentality," 95.

5. Michel Foucault, *Discipline and Punish: The Birth of the Prison* (New York: Pantheon, 1977).

6. Foucault, "Governmentality," 102.

7. See, e.g., Malcolm Voyce, "The Privatization of Public Property: The Development of a Shopping Mall in Sydney and Its Implications for

Governance through Spatial Practices," *Urban Policy & Research* 21 (2003): 249–62.

8. James W. Williams and Randy Lippert, "Governing on the Margins: Exploring the Contributions of Governmentality Studies to Critical Criminology of Canada," *Criminology & Criminal Justice* 48 (2006): 703–19; Kevin Stenson, "Sovereignty, Biopolitics, and the Local Government of Crime in Britain," *Theoretical Criminology* 9 (2005): 265–87; Steven Robins, "At the Limits of Spatial Governmentality: A Message from the Tip of Africa," *Third World Quarterly* 23 (2002): 665–89; M. O'Brien, "Governing Risk and Drug Use in Juvenile Justice Settings," *Contemporary Drug Problems* 28 (2001): 625–49; John Braithwaite, "The New Regulatory State and the Transformation of Criminology," *British Journal of Criminology* 40 (2000): 222–38; Russell Smandych, ed., *Governable Places: Readings on Governmentality and Crime Control* (Aldershot, England: Ashgate, 1999).

9. Paul Joyce, "Governmentality and Risk: Setting Priorities in the New NHS," *Sociology of Health and Illness* 23 (2001): 594–615; Rob Flynt, "Clinical Governance and Governmentality," *Health, Risk & Society* 4 (2002): 155–73; Ing-Britt Trankell and Jan Ovesen, "French Colonial Medicine in Cambodia: Reflections of Governmentality," *Anthropology & Medicine* 11 (2004): 91–105; Russell Prince et al., "Governmentality, Discourse, and Space in the New Zealand Health Care System, 1991–2003," *Health & Place* 12 (2006): 253–66; Patrick O'Byrne, "The Micro-fascism of Plato's Good Citizens: Producing (Dis)order through the Construction of Risk," *Nursing Philosophy* 8 (2007): 92–101.

10. Katherine Rankin, "Governing Development: Neo-liberalism, Microcredit, and Rational Economic Woman," *Economy & Society* 30 (2001): 18–37.

11. Michael P. Brown and Paul Boyle, "National Closets: Governmentality, Sexuality, and the Census," in *Closet Space: Geographies of Metaphor from the Body to the Globe*, ed. Michael P. Brown, 88–115 (New York: Routledge, 2000); T. Brown, "AIDS, Risk, and Social Governance," *Social Science & Medicine* 50 (2000): 1273–84; Moira Carmody, "Sexual Ethics and Violence Prevention," *Social & Legal Studies* 12 (2003): 199–216; Anita Harris, "Discourses of Desire as Governmentality: Young Women, Sexuality, and the Significance of Safe Spaces," *Feminism & Psychology* 15 (2005): 39–43; Damien Riggs, "Locating Control: Psychology and the Cultural Production of 'Health Subject Positions,'" *Culture, Health & Sexuality* 7 (2005): 87–100.

12. Foucault, "Governmentality," 101.

13. Foucault, "Governmentality," 95.

14. Burchell et al., eds., *The Foucault Effect*; A. Barry et al., eds., *Foucault and Political Reason: Liberalism, Neo-liberalism, and Political Reason* (Chicago: University of Chicago Press, 1996); Mitchell Dean and Barry Hindess, eds., *Governing Australia: Studies in Contemporary Rationalities of Government* (Cambridge, MA: Cambridge University Press, 1998); "Special Section," *Social & Legal Studies* 7 (1998): 539–76; Russell Smandych, ed., *Governable Places: Readings on Governmentality and Crime Control* (Aldershot, Engand: Ashgate, 1999); Jack Bratich et al., eds.,

Foucault, Cultural Studies, and Governmentality (Albany: State University of New York Press, 2003).

15. Pat O'Malley, "Indigenous Governance," in *Governing Australia: Studies in Contemporary Rationalities of Government*, ed. M. Dean and B. Hindess, 156–72 (Cambridge, MA: Cambridge University Press, 1998).

16. U. Kalpagam, "Colonial Governmentality and the 'Economy,'" *Economy & Society* 23 (2000): 418–38.

17. Giorgio Agamben, *Homo Sacer: Sovereign Power and Bare Life*, trans. Daniel Heller-Roazen (Stanford, CA: Stanford University Press, 1998); Agamben, *State of Exception*, trans. Kevin Attell (Chicago: University of Chicago Press, 2005); Miriam Ticktin, "Policing and Humanitarianism in France: Immigration and the Turn to Law as State of Exception," *Interactions* 7 (2005): 347–68; Ben Chappell, "States of Exception and Threat Governmentality," *Cultural Dynamics* 18 (2006): 313–34; Andrew N. Neale, "Foucault in Guantánamo: Towards an Archaeology of the Exception," *Security Dialogue* 37 (2006): 31–46. Judith Butler, *Precarious Life: The Powers of Mourning and Violence* (New York: Verso, 2006), 50–100.

18. Ann Stoler, *Race and the Education of Desire: Foucault's History of Sexuality and the Colonial Order of Things* (Durham, NC: Duke University Press, 1995).

19. See, e.g., Martin Gilens, *Why Americans Hate Welfare: Race, Media, and the Politics of Anti-Poverty Policy* (Chicago: University of Chicago Press, 2000).

20. Sally Engle Merry, "Spatial Governmentality and the New Urban Social Order: Controlling Gender Violence through Law," *American Anthropologist* 103 (2001): 16–29; Katherine Rankin, "Governing Development: Neo-liberlism, Microcredit, and Rational Economic Woman," *Economy & Society* 30 (2001): 18–37; Samantha J. King, "Doing Good by Running Well: Breast Cancer, the Race for the Cure, and New Technologies of Ethnical Citizenship," in *Foucault, Cultural Studies, and Governmentality*, ed. Jack Z. Bratich et al., 295–316 (Albany: State University of New York Press, 2003); Lisa King, "Subjectivity as Identity: Gender through the Lens of Foucault," in *Foucault*, 337–52; Valerie Hey and Simon Bradford, "The Return of the Repressed?: The Gender Politics of Emergent Forms of Professionalism in Education," *Journal of Education Policy* 19 (2004): 691–713; Suzan Ilcan et al., "Spaces of Governance: Gender and Public Sector Restructuring in Canada," *Gender, Place, & Culture: A Journal of Feminist Geography* 14 (2007): 75–92.

21. Augusta Police Department (APD), APD-Form 1, 1996, Case #9622395. Note: Police forms in this case were directly obtained from the Augusta Police Department.

22. See *Maine Revised Statutes Annotated 1997* (St. Paul, MN: West Publishing, 1997), 17A.S210.

23. APD, APD-Form 1.

24. APD, APD-Form 1.

25. APD, APD-Form 1.

26. Augusta Police Department, APD-Form 2, 1996. The Memorandum of Law submitted to state court by the Maine Department of the Attorney General acknowledged that Silvers "is biracial (of Puerto Rican and Caucasian origin); she has two biracial children whose father is African

American." Memorandum of Law in Support of Request for Temporary
Restraining Order (without notice), 1996, Case #CV-96-282.
Note: Memoranda submitted by the Maine Department of the Attorney
General were directly obtained from the court.

27. Stacey Silvers, Affidavit, Kennebec County Superior Court, 1996, Case
#CV-96-282. Note: This affidavit, collected by the Augusta Police
Department, was directly obtained from the Kennebec County Superior
Court.

28. Silvers, affidavit.

29. Silvers, quoted in Paul Carrier, "Augusta Tries to Heal Recent Wounds of
Racism," *Portland Press Herald*, July 7, 1996, pp. 1A, 12A.

30. See, e.g., Office of Management and Budget, *Race and Ethnic Standards for
Federal Statistics and Administrative Reporting* (Washington, DC: Office of
Management and Budget, 1977); Office of Management and Budget,
Statistics Policy Directive No. 15 (Washington, DC: Office of Management
and Budget, 1977). Also see Norma Rodriguez, *Changing Race: Latinos, the
Census, and the History of Ethnicity in the United States* (New York: New
York University Press, 2000); Sylvia A. Marotta and Jorge G. Garcia,
"Latinos in the United States in 2000," *Hispanic Journal of Behavioral
Sciences* 25 (2003): 13–34; Rogelio Saenz, *Latinos and the Changing Face of
America* (New York: Russell Sage Foundation, 2004).

31. Juan Flores, "'Que Assimilated, Brother, Yo Soy Asimilao': The
Structuring of Puerto Rican Identity," in *Divided Borders: Essays on Puerto
Rican Identity*, ed. Juan Flores, 184 (Houston, TX: Arte Publico Press,
1993).

32. Most actions initiated by the attorney general have come as a result of
referrals from law enforcement officers in local jurisdictions, usually officers trained by the Department of the Attorney General. The assistant
attorney general responsible for hate cases has tended to conduct a separate investigation in conjunction with local authorities, usually with the
designated civil rights officer as the liaison between the state and the
local law enforcement agency. The state has routinely acted with great
haste in hate cases, requesting restraining orders. Once approved, the
superior court justice's order is delivered by hand to the defendant.
Violation of the permanent order can result in criminal charges and a
penalty of up to $5,000, as well as up to a year in jail.

33. *Maine Revised*, 285.

34. The "Complaint (Injunctive Relief Requested)" produced by the attorney
general reiterated the intent of the Civil Rights Act, 5 M.R.S.A., section
4684-A, which "provides that a person has the right to engage in lawful
activities without being subject to physical force or violence, damage or
destruction of property, trespass on property or the threat of physical
force of violence motivated by reason of race, color, religion, ancestry,
sex, national origin, physical or mental disability, or sexual orientation."
Mediating constructed differences that lead to socioeconomic inequality
was a secondary concern. See Kennebec County Superior Court,
Complaint (Injunctive Relief Requested), 1996, Case #CV-96-282. Note: A
copy of this complaint was directly obtained from the Kennebec County
Superior Court.

35. See, e.g., Richard Bernstein, "First Amendment Limits on Tort Liability for Words Intended to Inflict Severe Emotional Distress," *Columbia Law Review* 85 (1985): 1749–85.
36. *Maine Revised*, 290.
37. U.S. DOJ, "Student Manual: National Hate Crimes Training Curricula," 1998, 1.
38. U.S. DOJ, "Student Manual," 1.
39. U.S. DOJ, "Student Manual," 2.
40. U.S. DOJ, "Student Manual," 9.
41. U.S. DOJ, "Student Manual," 9.
42. U.S. DOJ, "Student Manual," 9.
43. U.S. DOJ, "Student Manual," 10.
44. U.S. DOJ, "Student Manual," 10.
45. U.S. DOJ, "Student Manual," 20.
46. U.S. DOJ, "Student Manual," 19.
47. U.S. DOJ, "Student Manual," 20.
48. U.S. DOJ, "Student Manual," 22.
49. U.S. DOJ, "Student Manual," 13.
50. U.S. DOJ, "Student Manual," 12.
51. U.S. DOJ, "Student Manual," 12–13.
52. U.S. DOJ, "Student Manual," 3.
53. U.S. DOJ, "Student Manual," 3.
54. U.S. DOJ, "Student Manual," 18. The authors continue: "Often the victims search for other reasons to explain the attack because their group membership represents an aspect of themselves which is not generally possible to change; they will forever be identified as a member of that group and therefore vulnerable to attack."
55. U.S. DOJ, "Student Manual," 4.
56. U.S. DOJ, "Student Manual," 71.
57. U.S. DOJ, "Student Manual," 60.
58. U.S. DOJ, "Student Manual," 59.
59. U.S. DOJ, "Student Manual," 51.
60. U.S. DOJ, "Student Manual," 51.
61. U.S. DOJ, "Student Manual," 60. In many respects, this remedy resembles medical treatment of those who complain of physical ailments but whose symptoms, after multiple attempts at diagnosis, do not add up to an illness by medical measures. The "medicine," in such cases, becomes a kind of placebo in which something that will not necessarily do harm to the patient (such as vitamins) is prescribed. Prescriptions, like vitamins, publicly acknowledge the pain felt by the patient, but with a wink. Winking here happens as an aside, as medicine privately considers the illness to be in the patient's mind. Medical professionals, not unlike law enforcement officers responding to hate, think of themselves as avoiding "secondary injury" with such tactics.
62. Stephen Wessler, *Promising Practices against Hate Crimes: Five State and Local Demonstration Projects* (Washington, DC: U.S. Department of Justice, Office of Justice Programs, Bureau of Justice Assistance, 2000), 11, 14. Also see Wessler, *Addressing Hate Crimes: Six Initiatives That Are*

Enhancing the Efforts of Criminal Justice Practices (Washington, DC: U.S. Department of Justice, Office of Justice Programs, Bureau of Justice Assistance, 2000); Wessler and Margaret Moss, *Hate Crimes on Campus: The Problem and Efforts to Confront It* (Washington, DC: U.S. Department of Justice, Office of Justice Programs, Bureau of Justice Assistance, 2001).

63. Jack Levin and Jack McDevitt, *Hate Crimes: The Rising Tide of Bigotry and Bloodshed* (Boulder, CO: Westview Press, 2001); Levin and McDevitt, *Hate Crimes Revised: America's War on Those Who are Different* (Boulder, CO: Westview Press, 2002). Russell W. Glen et al., *Training the 21st Century Officer: Redefining Police Professionalism for the Los Angeles Police Department* (Santa Monica, CA: Rand Corporation, 2003), 93.

64. See Samuel P. Huntington, *The Soldier and the State: The Theory and Politics of Civil-Military Relations* (Cambridge, MA: Harvard University Press, 1957); Huntington, "The Hispanic Challenge," *Foreign Policy* 141 (2004): 30–45; Huntington, *Who Are We?: The Challenges to America's National Identity* (New York: Simon & Schuster, 2004).

65. According to the department's own institutional memory, "established in 1948 as the Human Relations Section, the Civil Rights Unit is primarily responsible for affirming the Department's policy to observe, uphold, and enforce all laws relating to individual rights without regard to race, gender, color, religion, national origin, marital status, disability, age, or economic status." See Chicago Police Department (CPD), "Hate Crime," *Training Bulletin* 35 (November 28, 1994): 3.

66. William Julius Wilson, *When Work Disappears: The World of the New Urban Poor* (New York: Knopf, 1996).

67. CPD, "Hate Crime," 3.

68. CPD, "Hate Crime," 3.

69. See *Chicago Lawyers' Committee et al. v. City of Chicago et al.*, 74 C 1982 (1982); *Alliance to End Repression et al. v. City of Chicago et al.*, 74 C 3268 (1988); *American Civil Liberties Union et al. v. City of Chicago et al.*, 75 C 3295 (1988). Also see Chicago Police Department, "Amendment Investigations," General Order 88–17, September 8, 1988. In 2002, the Alliance against Repression won modifications to the 1982 and 1988 actions that required the department to audit its own practices involving hate policing and the First Amendment.

70. See *Alliance to End Repression v. City of Chicago*, 237 F. 3d 799 (2001). Also see Chicago Police Department, "The First Amendment and Police Actions," General Order 02-10, October 11, 2002.

71. On the "culture wars," see Ronald Takaki, *From Different Shores: Perspectives on Race and Ethnicity in America* (New York: Oxford University Press, 1994); Chip Berlet, ed., *Eyes Right: Challenging the Right Wing Backlash* (Boston, MA: South End Press, 1995); Robin D. G. Kelly, *Yo' Mama's Disfunktional: Fighting the Culture Wars in Urban America* (Boston, MA: Beacon Press, 1997); Gary B. Nash, *History on Trial: Culture Wars and the Teaching of the Past* (New York: Knopf, 1997).

72. Chicago Police Department, "Human Rights and Human Resources," General Order 92-1, July 3, 1992, 1.

73. Chicago Police Department, "Hate Crimes/Criminal and Noncriminal Incidents Motivated by Hate," General Order 92–1, Addendum 4, July 3, 1992. Two years later, in 1994, the department's *Training Bulletin* was

released, in which hate was deplored and legally defined, and reporting procedures were outlined. These definitions and procedures simply reinforced the policy objectives outlined in the department's own 1992 general order on human rights and hate. See CPD, "Hate Crime."

74. Chicago Police Department, "Hate Crimes/Criminal and Non-Criminal Incidents Motivated by Hate."

75. Chicago Police Department, "What Is CAPS?," cite http://www.gov.city-ofchicago.org/city/webportal/portalContentItemAction.do?blockName =Police%2fHow+CAPS+Works%2fI+Want+To&deptMainCategoryOID=-9965&channelId=-536879037&programId=536879161&entityName=Polic e&topChannelName=Dept&contentOID=10912&Failed_Reason=Invalid+ timestamp,+engine+has+been+restarted&contentTypeName=COC_EDIT ORIAL&com.broadvision.session.new.new=Yes&Failed_Page=%2f webportal%2fportalContentItemAction.do&Context=dept (accessed January 4, 2008).

76. Chicago Police Department, "What Is CAPS?"

77. Chicago Police Department, "CAPS at 5: A Report on the Progress of Community Policing in Chicago, 1993–1998," 7.

78. See John Conroy, "Police Torture in Chicago," *Chicago Reader* (weekly), February 4, 2005, http://www.chicagoreader.com/policetorture/050402 (accessed June 4, 2007); Human Rights Watch, "Chicago Torture," undated, http://www.hrw.org/reports98/police/uspo53htm (accessed June 4, 2007); Fran Spielman, "Council to Hold Hearings on Alleged Police Torture," Chicago Sun-Times (daily), March 24, 2007, http:// www.suntimes.com/news/politics/398398,23burge.article (accessed June 4, 2007).

Chapter 3

1. Ernest Weinrib, "The Case for a Duty to Rescue," *Yale Law Journal* 90 (1990): 247–93; Jules Coleman, *Risks and Wrongs* (New York: Cambridge University Press, 1992).

2. Martha Chamallas, "Questioning the Use of Race-Specific and Gender-Specific Economic Data in Tort Litigation: A Constitutional Argument," *Fordham Law Review* 63 (1994): 73–124. Chamallas, e.g., cites *Stanton v. Stanton*, 421 U.S. 7, 16 (1975). Also see Equal Pay Act, 29 U.S.C., section 623 (1994).

3. See Chamallas, "The September 11th Victim Compensation Fund: Rethinking the Damages Element in Injury Law," *Tennessee Law Review* 71 (2003): 51–79.

4. Chamallas, "Civil Rights in Ordinary Tort Cases: Race, Gender, and the Calculation of Economic Loss," *Loyola of Los Angeles Law Review* 38 (2005): 1435–68. Quote from Chamallas, 1467–68.

5. See, e.g., Audrey Chin and Mark Peterson, *Deep Pockets, Empty Pockets: Who Wins in Cook County Jury Trials* (Santa Monica, CA: Rand Corporation, 1985); New York State Judicial Commission, *Report of the New York State Commission on Minorities* (New York: The Commission,

1991); Oregon Supreme Court Task Force, "Report of the Oregon Supreme Court Task Force on Racial/Ethnic Issues in the Judicial System," *Oregon Law Review* 73 (1994): 823–942.

6. Chin and Peterson, *Deep Pockets*, 5.

7. Jody Armour, "Race *Ipsa Loquitir*: Of Reasonable Racists, Intelligent Bayesians, and Involuntary Negrophobes," *Stanford Law Review* 46 (1994): 789.

8. Armour, "Race *Ipsa*," 786. Armour, e.g., cites *Palmore v. Sidoti*, 466 U.S. 429 (1984). Also see Armour, *Negrophobia and Reasonable Racism: The Hidden Costs of Being Black in America* (New York: New York University Press, 1997).

9. U.S. Constitution, amendment 14, section 1.

10. Jennifer B. Wriggins, "Torts, Race, and the Value of Injury, 1900–1949," *Howard Law Journal* 49 (2005): 99–138.

11. Victor M. Goode and Conrad A. Johnson, "Emotional Harm in Housing Discrimination Cases: A New Look at a Lingering Problem," *Fordham Urban Law Journal* 30 (2003): 1143–1214.

12. Frank M. McClellan, "The Dark Side of Tort Reform: Searching for Racial Justice," *Rutgers Law Review* 48 (1996): 767.

13. McClellan, "The Dark Side," 782.

14. Martha Chamallas, "The Architecture of Bias: Deep Structures in Tort Law," *University of Pennsylvania Law Review* 146 (1998): 463–531.

15. Armour, "Race *Ipsa*," 1994, 786.

16. Chamallas, "The Architecture," 466. Chamallas cites, e.g., *Payton v. Abbot Labs*, 437 N.E. 2d 171 (1982).

17. Martha Chamallas and Linda Kerber, "Women, Mothers, and the Law of Fright: A History," *Michigan Law Review* 88 (1990): 814. Chamallas and Kerber cite, e.g., *Dillon v. Legg* as the case where the analogue starts to bend. See *Dillon*, 68 Cal. 2d 728, 441 P. 2d 912, 69 Cal. Rptr. 72 (1968).

18. Leslie Bender, "Is Tort Law Male?: Foreseeability Analysis and Property Managers' Liability for Third Party Rapes of Residents," *Chicago-Kent Law Review* 69 (1993): 313–43. Bender primarily works with *Doe v. Linder Construction Company*, 845 S.W. 2d 173 (1992).

19. Jennifer B. Wriggins, "Toward a Feminist Revision of Torts," *American University Journal of Gender, Social Policy, and the Law* 13 (2005): 139–59.

20. Linda Hamilton Krieger, "The Content of Our Categories: A Cognitive Bias Approach to Discrimination and Equal Opportunity," *Stanford Law Review* 47 (1995): 1161–1248; Charles R. Lawrence III, "The Id, the Ego, and Equal Protection: Reckoning with Unconscious Racism," *Stanford Law Review* 39 (1987): 317–88.

21. See Paul Sniderman et al., "The New Racism," *American Journal of Political Science* 35 (1991): 423–48; Amy Elizabeth Ansell, *New Right, New Racism: Race and Reaction in the United States and Britain* (New York: New York University Press, 1997); Simon V. Virtanent and Leonie Haddy, "Old-Fashioned Racism and New Forms of Racial Prejudice," *Journal of Politics* 60 (1998): 311–32.

22. Krieger, "The Content," 1165–68. Krieger, e.g., cites *Equal Employment Opportunity Commission v. Flasher Co.*, 986 F. 2d 1312 (1992); *Warren v. Halstead Industries, Inc.*, 802 F. 2d 746, 752–753 (1986). Title VII of the 1964

Civil Rights Act, which is central to Krieger, provides protection from employment discrimination. On Title VII, see 42 U.S.C., sections 2000e-2000e-17; also see Judith Winston, "Mirror, Mirror on the Wall: Title VII, Section 1981, and the Intersection of Race, Sex, Gender, and the Civil Rights Act of 1990," *California Law Review* 179 (1991): 75–82; Marvin Jones, "No Time for Trumpets: Title VII, Equality, and the *Fin De Siecle*," *Michigan Law Review* 92 (1994): 2311–69; Barbara J. Flagg, "Fashioning a Title VII Remedy for Transparently White Subjective Decision Making," *Yale Law Journal* 104 (1996): 535–40.

23. Lawrence, "The Id," 322. Lawrence, e.g., cites *Gomillion v. Lightfoot*, 364 U.S. 339 (1960); *Village of Arlington Heights v. Metropolitan Housing Development Corp.*, 429 U.S. 252 (1977); *Memphis v. Greene*, 451 U.S. 100 (1981).

24. Herbert Marcuse, *One-Dimensional Man: Studies in the Ideology of Advanced Industrial Society* (Boston, MA: Beacon Press, 1964).

25. Marcuse, *One-Dimensional Man*, 252.

26. For Crenshaw see Matsuda et al., *Words*, 114. Also see Sherri Sharma, "Beyond 'Driving While Black' and 'Flying While Brown': Using Intersectionality to Uncover the Gendered Aspects of Racial Profiling," *Columbia Journal of Gender and Law* 12 (2003): 275–309; Angela Hooton, "A Broader Vision of the Reproductive Rights Movement: Fusing Mainstream and Latina Feminism," *American University Journal of Gender, Social Policy, and the Law* 13 (2005): 59–86.

27. Matsuda, *Words*, 114.

28. Crenshaw cites, e.g., *DeGraffenreid v. General Motors*, 413 F. Supp. 142 (1976).

29. Emily Grabham, "Taxonomies of Inequality: Lawyers, Maps, and the Challenge of Hybridity," *Social and Legal Studies* 15 (2006): 5–23.

30. See, e.g., Pamela J. Conover and Stanley Feldman, "How People Organize the Political World: A Schematic Model," *American Journal of Political Science* 28 (1984): 95–126; Conover and Feldman, "The Role of Inference in the Perception of Political Candidates," in *Political Cognition*, ed. Richard Lau et al., 127–58 (Hillsdale, NJ: Erlbaum, 1986); Conover and Feldman, "Candidate Perception in an Ambiguous World: Campaigns, Cues, and Inference Processes," *American Journal of Political Science* 33 (1989): 912–40.

31. Judith Butler, *Gender Trouble: Feminism and the Subversion of Identity* (New York: Routledge, 1990), 139. Also see Butler, *Undoing Gender* (New York: Routledge, 2004).

32. See, e.g., Michael Omi and Howard Winant, *Racial Formation in the United States: From the 1960s to the 1980s* (New York: Routledge, 1986); James A. Geschwender, "Ethnicity and the Social Construction of Gender in the Chinese Diaspora," *Gender and Society* 6 (1992): 480–507; Ruth Frankenburg, *White Women, Race Matters: The Social Construction of Whiteness* (Minneapolis: University of Minnesota Press, 1993); Laura Desimone, "Racial Discourse in a Community: Language and the Social Construction of Race," *Journal of Negro Education* 62 (1993): 414–18; Norberto Valdez and Janice Valdez, "The Pot That Called the Kettle White: Changing Racial Identities and U.S. Social Construction of Race," *Identities* 5 (1998): 379–413.

33. See, e.g., Neil Gotanda, "A Critique of 'Our Constitution is Color-Blind,'"
    Stanford Law Review 44 (1991): 1–68; Ian Haney-Lopez, "The Social
    Construction of Race: Some Observations on Illusion, Fabrication, and
    Choice," *Harvard Civil Rights-Civil Liberties Law Review* 29 (1994): 1–62;
    Martha Mahoney, "Segregation, Whiteness, and Transformation,"
    University of Pennsylvania Law Review 143 (1995): 1659–84; Haney-Lopez,
    White; Carrie Lynn H. Okizaki, "'What Are You?': Hapa Girl and
    Multiracial Identity," *University of Colorado Law Review* 71 (2000): 463–94.

34. Haney-Lopez, *White*, 13. Haney-Lopez cites, e.g., *In re Ah Yup*, 1 F. Cas.
    223 (1878); *Ex parte Shahid*, 205 F. 812 (1913).

35. Mahoney, "Segregation," 1662, 1659.

36. Mahoney, "Segregation," 1659.

37. For examples of "QueerCrit," see Francisco Valdes, "Beyond Sexual
    Orientation in Queer Legal Theory: Majoritarianism,
    Multidimensionality, and Responsibility in Social Justice Scholarship or
    Legal Scholars as Cultural Warriors," *Denver University Law Review* 75
    (1998): 1409–64; Adele M. Morrison, "Queering Domestic Violence to
    'Straighten Out' Criminal Law: What Might Happen When Queer Theory
    and Practice Meet Criminal Law's Conventional Responses to Domestic
    Violence," *Southern California Review of Law and Women's Studies* 13 (2003):
    81–160.

38. Natsu Taylor Saito, "Model Minority, Yellow Peril: Functions of
    'Foreignness' in the Construction of Asian American Legal Identity,"
    Asian Law Journal 4 (1997): 71–95.

39. Neil Gotanda, "'Other Non-Whites' in American Legal History: A
    Review of Justice at War," *Columbia Law Review* 85 (1985): 1186–92.

40. Saito, in "Model," cites, e.g., *In re Takuji Yamashita*, 30 Wash. 234 (1902);
    Cal. Gov't. Code 53069.65 (1997).

41. Kevin R. Johnson, "'Aliens' and the U.S. Immigration Laws: The Social
    and Legal Construction of Nonpersons," *University of Miami Inter-
    American Law Review* 28 (1998): 263–92. Johnson cites, e.g., *Mathews v.
    Diaz*, 426 U.S. 67 (1976).

42. Susan M. Akram and Kevin R. Johnson, "Race, Civil Rights, and
    Immigration Law after September 11, 2001: The Targeting of Arabs and
    Muslims," *New York University Annual Survey of American Law* 58 (2002):
    295–355; Natsu Taylor Saito, "Symbolism under Siege: Japanese
    American Redress and the 'Racing' of Arab Americans as 'Terrorists,'"
    Asian Law Journal 8 (2001): 1–29.

43. See, e.g., Marion Crain and Ken Matheny, "'Labor's Divided Ranks':
    Privilege and the United Front Ideology," *Cornell Law Review* 84 (1999):
    1542–1625; Nancy Levit, "Critical Race Theory: Race, Reason, Merit, and
    Civility," *Georgetown Law Journal* 87 (1999): 795–822.

44. See, e.g., McClellan, "The Dark Side," Chamallas, "The Architecture."

45. Matsuda et al., *Words*.

46. *R.A.V. v. St. Paul*, 505 U.S. 377 (1992).

47. Matsuda et al., *Words*, 96.

48. See, e.g., Jack M. Battaglia, "Regulation of Hate Speech by Educational
    Institutions: A Proposed Policy," *Santa Clara Law Review* 31 (1991):
    345–92; Jean C. Love, "Tort Actions for Hate Speech and the First

Amendment: Reconceptualizing the Competing Interests," *Law and Sexuality* 2 (1992): 29–35; Frederick Schauer, "Uncoupling Free Speech," *Columbia Law Review* 92 (1992): 1321–57.

49. American Law Institute, *Restatement (Second) of Torts* (St. Paul, MN: America Law Institute, 1965).

50. Matsuda et al., *Words*, 109.

51. Matsuda et al., *Words*, 97.

52. See Dominick Vetri, *Tort Law and Practice* (New York: Matthew Bender and Company, 1998), 590–91.

53. G. Edward White, *Tort Law in America: An Intellectual History* (New York: Oxford University Press, 1980), 20–62.

54. Holmes, quoted in David Rosenberg, *The Hidden Holmes: His Theory of Torts in History* (Cambridge, MA: Harvard University Press, 1995), 14.

55. Christopher Columbus Langdell, quoted in White, *Tort Law*, 27.

56. Mary Louise Pratt, *Imperial Eyes: Travel Writing and Transculturation* (New York: Routledge, 1992), 24–37. Also see Nancy Stepan, *The Idea of Race* (London: Macmillan, 1982); David Theo Goldberg, *Anatomy of Racism* (Minneapolis: University of Minnesota Press, 1990); Jennifer Terry and Jacqueline Urla, *Deviant Bodies: Critical Perspectives on Difference in Science and Popular Culture* (Bloomington: Indiana University Press, 1995); Michael L. Blakey, "Scientific Racism and the Biological Concept of Race," *Literature and Psychology* 45 (1999): 29–54; Waltraud Ernst and Bernard Harris, eds., *Race, Science, and Medicine, 1700–1960* (New York: Routledge, 1999).

57. Howard Schweber, "The 'Science' of Legal Science: The Model of Natural Sciences in Nineteenth-Century American Legal Education," *Law and History Review* 17 (1999): 423.

58. G. Edward White, "The American Law Institute and the Triumph of Modernist Jurisprudence," *Law and History Review* 15 (1997): 3–4.

59. Matsuda et al., *Words*, 109–110.

60. Matsuda et al., *Words*, 110.

61. Matsuda et al., *Words*, 103–106.

62. Matsuda et al., *Words*, 99. Delgado cites, e.g., *Irving v. J. C. Marsh*, 46 Ill. App. 3d 162, 360 N.E. 2d (1977). Irving lost because the case did not fit into recognized defamation categories.

63. Matsuda et al., *Words*, 90–96. Delgado, e.g., cites Kenneth B. Clark, *Dark Ghetto: Dilemmas of Social Power* (New York: Harper and Row, 1965).

64. Ernesto Laclau and Chantal Mouffe, *Hegemony and Socialist Strategy: Towards a Radical Politics* (London: Verso, 1985).

Chapter 4

1. Angelo Ancheta, *Race, Rights, and the Asian American Experience* (New Brunswick, NJ: Rutgers University Press, 1998); Juan F. Perea, "The Black and White Binary Paradigm of Race: Exploring the 'Normal Science'" of American Racial Thought," *California Law Review* 85 (1997): 1213–58; Eric K. Yamamoto, "Critical Race Praxis: Race, Theory, and Political

Lawyering Practice in Post-Civil Rights America," *Michigan Law Review* 95 (1997): 821–99; Michael Omi and Dana Takagi, "Situating Asian Americans in Political Discourse on Affirmative Action," in *Race and Representation*, eds. Robert Post and Michael Rogin, 271–81 (Boston, MA: MIT Press, 1998). Perea wrote of a key civil rights casebook like Geoffrey Stone's *Constitutional Law*, in which Stone excluded cases such as *Hernandez v. Texas*, 347 U.S. 475 (1954), in which Mexicanos took white supremacy's segregated schools to court. Perea used Thomas Kuhn's *Structure of Scientific Revolutions* to understand civil rights in the United States as reproduced in an important casebook by Geoffrey Stone, as well as in books by Andrew Hacker and Cornell West. See Kuhn, *Structure of Scientific Revolutions* (Chicago: University of Chicago Press, 1962); Geoffrey Stone, *Constitutional Law* (Boston, MA: Little, Brown, 1991); Andrew Hacker, *Two Nations: Black and White, Separate, Hostile, Unequal* (New York: Scribner's, 1992); Cornell West, *Race Matters* (Boston, MA: Beacon Press, 1993).

2. Robert Chang, Disoriented: Asian Americans, Law, and the Nation-State (New York: New York University Press, 1999). On race, sexuality, and lynching, see Jacquelyn Dowd Hall, " 'The Mind That Burns in Each Body': Women, Rape, and Racial Violence," in *Powers of Desire: The Politics of Sexuality*, ed. Ann Snitow et al., 328–49 (New York: Monthly Review Press, 1983); *The Crucible of Race: Black/White Relations in the American South since Emancipation* (New York: Oxford University Press, 1984).

3. See Janine Kim, "Are Asians Black?: The Asian-American Civil Rights Agenda and the Contemporary Significance of the Black/White Paradigm," *Yale Law Journal* 108 (1999): 2385–2412.

4. See W. Fitzhugh Brundage, *Lynching in the New South: Georgia and Virginia, 1880–1930* (Urbana: University of Illinois Press, 1993); Michael W. Suleiman, ed., *Arabs in America: Building a New Future* (Philadelphia, PA: Temple University Press, 1999); Tetsuden Kashima, *Judgement without Trial: Japanese American Imprisonment during World War II* (Seattle: University of Washington Press, 2003).

5. Muneer Ahmad, "Homeland Insecurities: Racial Violence the Day after September 11," *Social Text* 20 (2002): 103.

6. See Muneer Ahmad, "A Rage Shared by Law: Post-September 11 Racial Violence as Crimes of Passion," *California Law Review* 92 (2004): 1259–1330.

7. U.S. Civil Rights Act of 1957, section 101–115.

8. The Midwestern advisory committees reviewed in this chapter are as follows: Illinois, Indiana, Michigan, Minnesota, North Dakota, Ohio, and Wisconsin. For some regional perspective, I also looked at hearings held in California and New York, and metropolitan Washington, DC Minutes and other USCCR records were directly obtained from the USCCR via a Freedom of Information Act request.

9. USCCR, "Anniversary Update on Commission Activities Related to September 11," September 2002, 1.

10. Metropolitan Washington Joint Committee to the USCCR, "Civil Rights Concerns in the Metropolitan Washington Area in the Aftermath of 9.11 Tragedies: Muslims, Sikhs, Arab Americans, South Asian Americans, and Muslim Women," April 25, 2002, Annandale, Va., 354.

11. Metropolitan Washington, "Civil Rights," 354.
12. Akram and Johnson, "Race," 2002, 295–355.
13. Metropolitan Washington, "Civil Rights," 374–75.
14. Metropolitan Washington, "Civil Rights," 374.
15. Metropolitan Washington, "Civil Rights," 375.
16. Metropolitan Washington, "Civil Rights," 354–55.
17. Metropolitan Washington, "Civil Rights," 456.
18. Metropolitan Washington, "Civil Rights," 457–58.
19. Michigan Advisory Committee to the USCCR, "Civil Rights Issues Facing Arab Americans in Michigan," 2001, 17; USCCR, "Briefings on Boundaries of Justice: Immigration Policies Post-September 11," October 12, 2001, Washington, DC, 55. In his written statement to the USCCR briefing, James Zogby of the Arab American Institute continued: "The morning after September 11, I received a harrowing death threat at my office. The caller left this message: 'Jim, you towelhead, all Arabs must die. We will slit your throats and kill your children.' My daughter, a college student, received two threatening phone calls. My nephew, also a college student, was affected. My brother, John, received two bomb threats at his office." See "Briefings on Boundaries," 55.
20. Indiana Advisory Committee to the USCCR, "Civil Rights Issues Facing Muslims and Arab Americans in Indiana Post-September 11," May 30, 2002, 10.
21. Wisconsin Advisory Committee to the USCCR, "Briefing on Civil Rights Issues Facing Muslims and Arab Americans in Wisconsin Post-September 11," April 11, 2002, Milwaukee, 2.
22. Wisconsin, "Briefing," 5–6.
23. Ohio Advisory Committee to the USCCR, "Civil Rights Facing Muslims and Arab Americans in Ohio Post-September 11," November 14, 2001, Columbus, 20.
24. New York State Advisory Committee to the USCCR, "Civil Rights Issues and Post 9–11 Law Enforcement/Community Relations in New York Fact-Finding Forum," May 21, 2003, New York, 39, 36. Some federal state bodies, though, performed better than others. For example, the legal advisor to a local chapter of the American Arab Anti-Discrimination Committee in metropolitan Washington lauded the Equal Employment Opportunity Commission. The commission apparently responded—and once again this is a reaction to something—to rights violations as part of the post-9/11 backlash. See Metropolitan Washington, "Civil Rights," 319.
25. New York, "Civil Rights," 21.
26. Wisconsin, "Briefing," 16–17.
27. USCCR, "Briefings on Boundaries," 2001, 25.
28. New York, "Civil Rights," 2001, 70. Those fleeing also acted in anticipation of the "Safe Third Country" agreement signed by the United States and Canada in 2002. The agreement stipulated that immigrants who arrived in the United States and sought to then immigrate to Canada had to go through U.S. immigration processes and background checks before proceeding to Canada. In addition to special registration and Safe Third Country being new governance technologies available to the authorities,

Vive, an organization primarily concerned with the immigration status of Latin American refugees in the United States, feared that these technologies would ironically lead to the trafficking of immigrants from the United States to Canada. And Vive lobbied the USCCR in an attempt to get the commission to temper what Vive understood to be a rights violation not necessarily covered by a civil rights largely bounded by citizenship. See New York, "Civil Rights," 72.

29. Indiana, "Civil Rights," 6.
30. Wisconsin, "Briefing," 8.
31. USCCR, "Briefings on Boundaries," 2001, 27.
32. Indiana, "Civil Rights," 4–5. One Sikh leader in metropolitan Washington said: "In South Asia there is a fear of going to government because there's corruption and so forth. And also, on top of that, there's shame and embarrassment sometimes. The victims almost blame themselves for the attack having occurred, and they'd like to just wish it away." See Metropolitan Washington, "Civil Rights," 352.
33. Wisconsin, "Briefing," 6.
34. Wisconsin, "Briefing," 8.
35. Illinois Advisory Committee to the USCCR, "Arab and Muslim Civil Rights Concerns since September 11, 2001," March 2002, 18.
36. Illinois, "Civil Rights," 18.
37. Michigan, "Civil Rights," 13.
38. Michigan, "Civil Rights," 13.
39. New York, "Civil Rights," 62–63.
40. Indiana, "Civil Rights," 9.
41. Indiana, "Civil Rights," 30.
42. See Michael C. Dawson, *Behind the Mule: Race and Class in African-American Politics* (Princeton, NJ: Princeton University Press, 1994), 76–80, 82–84.
43. Rita Kastoryano, *Negotiating Identities: States and Immigrants in France and Germany* (Princeton, NJ: Princeton University Press, 2002), 210. Kastoryano continued: "One can see this phenomenon among immigrant communities that are now settled in Western Europe, especially among Muslim populations. Muslims settled in different European countries have a distinct basis for transnational organization: being Muslim in Europe, a member of a religious minority who is seeking legitimacy and recognition both within Europe and the individual countries of settlement."
44. Wisconsin, "Briefing," 11.
45. New York, "Civil Rights," 30.
46. California State Advisory Committee to the USCCR, "Meeting of May 15, 2002," May 15, 2002, San Diego, 35.
47. New York, "Civil Rights," 12. One African American Muslim leader in the Washington, DC, area mentioned an African American Muslim who had difficulty obtaining a job in information technology marketing. Success finally came when the African American Muslim changed his name from "Khalid" to "Ted." See Metropolitan Washington, "Civil Rights," 315.
48. Metropolitan Washington, "Civil Rights," 320–21.
49. NCLR, submission, in USCCR, "Briefings on Boundaries," 37–39.

50. NCLR, submission, 39. The Council continued: "This is particularly troubling because racial profiling not only violates civil rights, it also undermines the ability of law enforcement to enforce the law effectively."
51. NCLR, submission, 40.
52. NCLR, submission, 41.
53. NCLR, submission, 45–46.
54. USCCR, "Briefings on Boundaries," 65–66.
55. USCCR, "Briefings on Boundaries," 69.
56. North Dakota Advisory Committee to the USCCR, "Briefing on Civil Rights Issues Facing Muslims and Arab Americans in North Dakota Post-September 11," May 2002.
57. Wisconsin, "Briefing," 16. Another participant present for the Wisconsin proceedings was aware of how tenuous race and privilege are for some people of color in the United States. The participant, a Filipino, commented on how early Filipino immigrants to the United States were educated, middle class, and constructed as white (however on the margins of white) in certain parts of the United States. At a later point, Filipinos became Asian, Asian American, and Asian Pacific, even as they wanted to be white and accrue all of the accompanying privileges of whiteness. See Wisconsin, "Briefing," 11.
58. Metropolitan Washington, "Civil Rights," 351.
59. Indiana, "Civil Rights," 5. One witness speaking to the Michigan advisory committee told of one travel anecdote. The witness, who was a non-black Muslim, usually gets extra scrutiny. The one time there was no scrutiny was when the ticket agent was an African American Muslim. See Michigan, "Civil Rights," 20.
60. Indiana, "Civil Rights," 15.
61. Metropolitan Washington, "Civil Rights," 313–14.
62. Michigan, "Civil Rights," 12.
63. California, "Meeting," 42.
64. California, "Meeting," 27.
65. California, "Meeting," 29.
66. California, "Meeting," 31. Michael Lichter and Roger Waldinger, as well as other contributors to the volume *Color Lines: Affirmative Action, Immigration, and Civil Rights Options for America*, wrote about new hierarchical boundaries. See Lichter and Waldinger, "Producing Conflict: Immigration and the Management of Diversity in the Multiethnic Metropolis," in *Color Lines*, ed. John David Skrentny, 147–67 (Chicago: University of Chicago Press, 2001).

Chapter 5

1. See, e.g., John Dugard, "The Judicial Process, Positivism, and Civil Liberty," *South African Law Journal* 88 (1971): 181–200; Dugard, *Human Rights and the South African Legal Order* (Princeton, NJ: Princeton University Press, 1978); David Dyzenhaus, "Positivism and Validity,"

South African Law Journal 100 (1983): 454–67; Hugh Corder, *Judges at Work: The Role and Attitudes of the South African Appellate Judiciary, 1910–1950* (Cape Town: Juta, 1984); C. Forsyth, *In Danger for Their Talents: A Study of the Appellate Division of the Supreme Court of South Africa from 1950–1980* (Cape Town: Juta, 1985); H. A. Strydom, "The Legal Theory of Lon L. Fuller," in *Essays on Law and Social Practice in South Africa*, ed. Hugh Corder, 123–44 (Cape Town: Juta, 1988); Dyzenhaus, *Hard Cases in Wicked Legal Systems: South African Law in the Perspective of Legal Philosophy* (Oxford: Clarendon Press, 1991); Stephen Ellman, *In a Time of Trouble: Law and Liberty in South Africa's State of Emergency* (Oxford: Clarendon Press, 1991).

2. Dugard, *Human Rights*, 373–74.
3. Strydom, "The Legal Theory," 138–39.
4. Strydom, "The Legal Theory," 126.
5. Ellman, *In a Time of Trouble*, 232.
6. On literalism, for example, Ellman pointed to Antonin Scalia's use of "original intent" in his U.S. Supreme Court writings. Ellman saw Scalia's supposedly apolitical quest for the original intent of American constitutional framers as an interpretative rationale constraining governmental actions, not an interpretative rationale legitimating the judiciary's support of the legislature and executive. See Ellman, *In a Time of Trouble*, 233, 27, 34.
7. Richard Abel, *Politics by Other Means: Law in the Struggle against Apartheid, 1980–1994* (New York: Routledge, 1995), 305.
8. See, e.g., Albie Sachs, *Protecting Human Rights in a New South Africa* (Cape Town: Oxford University Press, 1990); McCaps Malose Motimele, ed., *Constitution for a Democratic South Africa* (Johannesburg: Skotaville, 1993); Bertus de Villiers, *Birth of a Constitution* (Kenwyn: Juta, 1994); Lourens du Plessis and Hugh Corder, eds., *Understanding South Africa's Transitional Bill of Rights* (Kenwyn: Juta, 1994); Erika de Wet, *The Constitutional Enforceability of Economic and Social Rights: The Meaning of the German Constitutional Model for South Africa* (Durban: Butterworths, 1996); Yvonne Burns, *Administrative Law under the 1996 Constitution* (Durban: Butterworths, 1999); Penelope Andrews and Stephen Ellman, eds., *The Post-Apartheid Constitutions: Perspectives on South Africa's Basic Law* (Johannesburg: Witswatersrand University Press, 2001).
9. Jean Comaroff and John Comaroff, "The Colonization of Consciousness in South Africa," *Economy and Society* 18 (1989): 268. "Structure" and "predicament" took hold as "technological innovations and a 'scientific' rationale" seeped into everydayness with the transformation of the [traditional African rainmaking] "ritual" into a resource merely in need of "technical management." Tswanas were not passively constructed by colonizers seeking to displace indigenous racial constructions with European forms and norms; Tswanas resisted. See Comaroff and Comaroff, "The Colonization," 268, 274. But colonial interactions introduced Tswanas to a pervasive European cosmology, ranging from the bureaucratic rationalization of water management to "a modernist discourse of rights," where white rights prevailed over the rights of black communities. Sue John Comaroff, "The Discourse of Rights in Colonial South Africa: Subjectivity, Sovereignty, Modernity," in *Identities,*

Politics, and Rights, ed. Austin Sarat and Thomas Kearns, 193–236 (Ann Arbor: University of Michigan Press, 1996).

10. Ivan Evans, *Bureaucracy and Race: Native Administration in South Africa* (Berkeley: University of California Press, 1997), 8.

11. Evans, *Bureaucracy*, 85–87, 65–67, 86–118.

12. Evans, *Bureaucracy*, 225–34.

13. Gready and Kgalema, "Magistrates," 150, 157–60.

14. Michel Foucault, *Birth of the Clinic: An Archaeology of Medical Perception* (New York: Vintage, 1975); Gayatri C. Spivak, *A Critique of Postcolonial Reason: Toward a History of the Vanishing Present* (Cambridge, MA: Harvard University Press, 1999); Kimberlé Crenshaw, "Mapping the Margins: Intersectionality, Identity Politics, and Violence against Women," *Stanford Law Review* 43 (1991): 1241–99.

15. Chang, *Disoriented*.

16. Judith Butler, "Appearances Aside," *California Law Review* 88 (2000): 62.

17. Equality Act, 2000, preamble.

18. Joint Committee on the Promotion of Equality and Prevention of Unfair Discrimination, press release, October 29, 1999. Note: All minutes and public submissions cited were electronically obtained from the Parliamentary Monitoring Group (PMG), a nongovernmental organization funded by foundations and international organizations. These documents can be obtained by e-mailing the PMG at info@pmg.org.za.

19. Equality Act, preamble.

20. Equality Act, 10(1).

21. Equality Act, 10(1)(a-c), 10(2).

22. Equality Act, 1(1)(xxii)(a-b).

23. Equality Act, 31(1)(a).

24. Equality Act, section 31(1)(a-b).

25. Equality Act, section 31(4)(a).

26. Amendment Act 52, 2002.

27. Joint Committee, minutes, October 29, 1999.

28. Debates of the National Assembly, January 26, 2000, 398.

29. COSATU, submission, undated.

30. Joint Committee, minutes, December 9, 1999.

31. SACOB, submission, undated.

32. Joint Committee, minutes, November 23, 1999.

33. Joint Committee, minutes, December 10, 1999.

34. Joint Committee, minutes, December 10, 1999.

35. Joint Committee, minutes, November 5, 1999.

36. Equality Act, preamble.

37. FXI, submission, undated.

38. Phyllis Pease Chock, "Ambiguity in Policy Discourses: Congressional Talk about Immigration," *Policy Sciences* 28 (1995): 165–84.

39. Debates of the National Assembly, January 26, 2000, 205.

40. David Roediger, *The Wages of Whiteness: Race and the Making of the American Working Class* (New York: Verso, 1999); Richard Delgado and Jean Stefancic, eds., *Critical White Studies* (Philadelphia, PA: Temple University Press, 1997).

41. Kevin Durrheim, submission, undated.

42. CGE, submission, undated, point 54. The CGE actually proposed a defin-
    ition of gender to be included in the definition chapter of the bill. Its
    proposed definition read: "Gender describes socially determined charac-
    teristics and roles that are attributed to men and women. The social
    relations between men and women that derive from these characteristics
    and roles have the effect of creating or sustaining forms of domination
    and disadvantage. Gender is distinguished from sex, which is biologi-
    cally determined" (point 55).

43. Matsuda et al., Words, 111–32.

44. Joint Committee, minutes, November 5, 1999.

45. CGE, submission, undated, point 62.

46. DEAFSA, submission, undated.

47. The Equality Alliance included the following groups: AIDS Law Project,
    Black Sash, University of the Western Cape's Community Law Center,
    Congress of South African Trade Unions, Freedom of Expression
    Institute, Human Rights Committee, Legal Resource Center, National
    Association of Democratic Lawyers (Human Rights and Advocacy
    Project), National Coalition for Gay and Lesbian Equality, South African
    Municipal Workers Union, Women's Legal Center.

48. Equality Alliance, submission, undated.

49. Joint Committee, minutes, November 22, 1999.

50. IDASA, submission, undated.

51. Joint Committee, minutes, November 22, 1999.

52. Jacquelyn Dowd Hall, "'The Mind That Burns in Each Body': Women,
    Rape, and Racial Violence," in Powers of Desire: The Politics of Sexuality,
    ed. Ann Snitow, 328–49 (New York: Monthly Review Press, 1983).

53. Black Sash, submission, undated.

54. Equality Act, 2000, 1(xxii)(a-b).

55. Equality Act, 2000, 8(a-i).

56. Joint Committee, minutes, November 22, 1999.

57. IDASA, submission, undated.

58. Debates of the National Council of Provinces, January 28, 2000, 205.

59. Debates, January 28, 2000, 205.

60. Debates, January 20, 2000, 206.

61. Jacques Derrida, "Justice, Law, and Philosophy—An Interview with
    Jacques Derrida," South African Journal of Philosophy 18 (2000): 279–86.

62. Pierre Bourdieu, Masculine Domination (Stanford, CA: Stanford
    University Press, 2001).

63. Judicial Services Commission and Magistrates Commission (hereafter
    JSCMC), Bench Book for Equality Courts (Pretoria: Judicial Services
    Commission and Magistrates Commission, 2002); JSCMC, Resource Book
    for Equality Courts (Pretoria: Judicial Services Commission and
    Magistrates Commission, 2002).

64. Amendment Act, 2002, 31(4)(a), 31(6)(a).

65. JSCMC, Bench, section 3.1.

66. JSCMC, Bench, section 3.3.

67. JSCMC, Bench, section 3.3.

68. JSCMC, Resource, 2002, section 1.1.

69. JSCMC, Bench, section 3.2.

70. JSCMC, *Bench*, section 3.2.
71. JSCMC, *Bench*, section 3.2.
72. JSCMC, *Bench*, section 3.2.
73. JSCMC, *Bench*, section 3.2.
74. JSCMC, *Resource*, section 1.1.
75. JSCMC, *Resource*, section 2.2.
76. JSCMC, *Resource*, section 3.3.
77. JSCMC, *Resource*, section 2.3.
78. JSCMC, *Resource*, section 2.4.1.
79. JSCMC, *Resource*, section 2.
80. JSCMC, *Bench*, section 9.
81. JSCMC, *Bench*, section 11.1.
82. JSCMC, *Resource*, section 4.2.
83. JSCMC, *Resource*, section 1.2.
84. *National Council for Gay and Lesbian Equality v. Minister of Justice*, quoted in JSCMC, *Bench*, section 4.1.
85. JSCMC, *Resource*, section 1.2.
86. JSCMC, *Resource*, section 1.2.
87. JSCMC, *Resource*, section 3.2.5a.
88. JSCMC, *Resource*, section 3.2.5a.
89. JSCMC, *Resource*, section 1.3.1.
90. JSCMC, *Bench*, section 24.2.
91. JSCMC, *Bench*, section 24.2
92. JSCMC, *Bench*, section 24.2.
93. JSCMC, *Resource*, section 3.2.5a.
94. See Raymond Williams, *Keywords: A Vocabulary of Culture and Society* (Oxford: Oxford University Press, 1976).
95. Evans, *Bureâucracy*, especially 225–34.
96. JSCMC, *Bench*, section 25.3.
97. JSCMC, *Resource*, section 3.2.5.
98. JSCMC, *Bench*, section 24.3.
99. JSCMC, *Bench*, section 24.3.
100. *Brink v. Kushoff*, 6 BCLR 752 (1996).
101. Case cited in JSCMC, *Bench*, section 24.3.
102. Equality Act, section 1(viii)
103. *National Coalition for Gay and Lesbian Equality v. Minister of Home Affairs*, 12 BCLR 1517 (1998).
104. JSCMC, *Bench*, section 23.

Chapter 6

1. Mbongeni Ngema, "AmaNdiya," Universal Music, 2002. On the history of South Asians in South Africa, see S. Bhana and J. B. Brain, *Setting Down Roots: Indian Migrants in South Africa, 1860–1911* (Johannesburg: Witswatersrand University Press, 1990). On the "AmaNdiya" controversy,

also see Gary Baines, "Racist Hate Speech in South Africa's Fragile Democracy: The Case of Ngema's 'AmaNdiya,'" in *Popular Music Censorship in Africa*, ed. Michael Drewett and Martin Cloonan, 53–70 (Aldershot, England: Ashgate, 2006).

2. D. Pillay, "Singling Out Indians Will Achieve Nothing," *Sunday Times*, July 21, 2002.

3. Bronwyn Harris, "New Song, Same Old Tune," 2002, http://www.csrr.org.zq/index.php?option=com_content&task=view&id=119&Itemid=35 (accessed January 4, 2008).

4. Other BCCSA cases before "AmaNdiya" can be used to help put into perspective the regulation of Ngema's "AmaNdiya." Cases that involve hate speech or racial slurs that might border on hate speech are presented as representative cases and categorized on the commission's Web site under "offensive." Of twenty cases labeled "offensive," nine cases, according to the court, did not meet the standards of hate speech or slurs that might be understood to be hateful. The BCCSA authorities found that four out of the eleven remaining cases constituted hate speech, ranging from the Ngema case to haranguing in a derogatory way Mandela, berating breast cancer survivors, making a joke about the rape of young girls, and calling a black woman a *meid* (literally, "maid"), which is considered the feminine version of *kaffir* (roughly equivalent to "nigger"). (The derogatory remarks made about Mandela in a song came on a public affairs program, where public debate was encouraged, thus no penalty to the member broadcaster.) Two cases were deemed to contravene the broadcasting code, but as slurs where the word "chink" was used and a reference to sexually available women. The remaining five cases were deemed neither a slur nor hate speech. These five cases ranged from calling someone gay an "it" to comments directed to the Sri Lankan cricket team.

5. BCCSA Constitution, section 16(1).

6. BCCSA Constitution, section 16(2).

7. IBA Act 1993, summary.

8. ICASA Act 2000, section 3(3).

9. ICASA Act 2000, section 3(4).

10. BCCSA Constitution, section 3. Note BCCSA documents—its governing documents as well as records of its decisions—were directly obtained from the BCCSA.

11. BCCSA Procedure, Mediation and Adjudication of Complaints, section 1.

12. BCCSA code, section 7.1.1.

13. *Islamic Unity Convention v. the Independent Broadcasting Authority and Others*, 4 SA 294 (CC) (2002).

14. *State v. Mamobolo*, 3 SA 409 (CC) (2001).

15. *Islamic Unity Convention*, paragraph 26 (2002).

16. See Publications Act of 1974, section 47(2)(c-3).

17. *Myburgh v. Radio 702*, 2001/04 Radio 702 (2001); *Fouche v. 94.7 Highveld Stereo*, 2000/18 Highveld Stereo (2000).

18. *Islamic Unity Convention*, paragraph 51 (2002).

19. *Clarke and Others v. East Coast Radio*, 2003/06 East Coast Radio (2003).

20. See, e.g., Dugard, *Human Rights*; Dyzenhaus, "Positivism and Validity"; Corder, *Essays*.

21. *Human Rights Commission of South Africa v. SABC*, 2002/31 SABC (2002), paragraphs 34–38 (2002).

22. *Prinsloo and Venter v. Rippel 90.5FM*, 2002/19 Rippel 90.5FM (2002).

23. *Islamic Unity Convention*, paragraph 51 (2002).

24. *Fouche v. 94.7 Highfeld Stereo*, 2000/18 94.7 Highfeld Stereo (2000).

25. *Johnson v. 94.7 Highveld Stereo*, 2002/07 94.7 Highveld Stereo (2002).

26. *Clarke*, paragraph 7 (2003).

27. *Clarke*, paragraph 7.

28. *Human Rights*, paragraph 35 (2002).

29. Steve Biko, *I Write What I Like* (New York: Harper and Row, 1978); Edward Said, *Orientalism* (New York: Pantheon, 1978).

30. *Human Rights*, paragraph 35.

31. *Human Rights*, paragraph 38.

32. *Human Rights*, paragraph 35.

33. *Human Rights*, paragraphs 35–36.

34. *Human Rights*, paragraph 36.

35. *Human Rights*, paragraph 35.

36. *Human Rights*, paragraph 35.

37. *Human Rights*, paragraphs 36–37.

38. *Human Rights*, paragraph 38.

39. *Human Rights*, paragraph 38.

40. See Sarah Nuttall and Carli Coetzee, eds., *Negotiating the Past: The Making of Memory in South Africa* (Cape Town: Oxford University Press, 1998).

41. Theo Coggin, *Censorship: A Study of Censorship in South Africa* (Johannesburg: Institute of Race Relations, 1983); Kenyan Tomaselli, *The Cinema of Apartheid: Race and Class in South African Film* (London: Routledge, 1989); Christopher Merrett, *A Culture of Censorship: Secrecy and Intellectual Repression in South Africa* (Cape Town: David Phillip, 1994); Abel, *Politics by Other Means: Law in the Struggle against Apartheid*; Coetzee, *Giving Offense: Essays on Censorship*; Margreet DeLange, *Muzzled Muse: Literature and Censorship in South Africa* (Philadelphia, PA: John Benjamin Publishing, 1997).

42. Pierre Bourdieu, "The Essence of Neoliberalism," *Le Monde Diplomatique* 8 (December 1998), English edition: 3.

43. A. Steenkamp, "Film Working Document," June 3, 1988, National Archives, Cape Town, IDP volume 2/342, number R88/6/14.

44. M. N. deVliew, "Film Working Document," June 3, 1988, National Archives, Cape Town, IDP volume 2/342, number R88/6/14.

45. Malan, "Film Working Document," June 3, 1988, National Archives, Cape Town, IDP volume 2/342, number R88/6/14. Only the surname is used here, because the first name is illegible.

46. Chair, "Film Working Document," June 22, 1988, National Archives, Cape Town, IDP volume 2/342, number R88/6/14. I only use "chair" to iden-tify this juror, because the name is not legible. The chair's phone number, 48-9593, might be used in order to identify this member of the group with more precision in the records.

47. H. Botha, "Film Working Document," June 22, 1988, National Archives, Cape Town, IDP volume 2/342, number R88/6/14.
48. A. Niekerk, "Film Working Document," June 22, 1988, National Archives, Cape Town, IDP volume 2/342, number R88/6/14.
49. "Application for Approval/Review," June 22, 1988, 4, National Archives, Cape Town, IDP volume 2/342, number R88/6/14.
50. Letter and application, from L. S. Jacobson to Directorate of Publications, July 5, 1988, National Archives, Cape Town, IDP volume 2/349, number R88/8/130.
51. "Certificate of Approval," Form DP 2D, July 21, 1988, National Archives, Cape Town, IDP 2/342, number R88/6/14. Referencing the debate surrounding classification and certification of *Cry Freedom*, the chair of the second committee classifying the video version of *Mapantsula* wrote in summarizing the *Mapantsula* deliberations that *Mapantsula* "has ... no way near the impact of a film like *Cry Freedom*." See "Application for Approval/Review," Form DP2, June 22, 1988, p. 2, National Archives, Cape Town, IDP volume 2/342, number R88/6/14.
52. "Application for Approval/Review," Form DP2, August 15, 1988, p. 1, National Archives, Cape Town, IDP volume 2/349, number R88/8/130.
53. Nelson Mandela, *Long Walk to Freedom: The Autobiography of Nelson Mandela* (Boston, MA: Back Bay Books, 1995), 577–78.
54. Media activists during this period concerned themselves with getting solar-powered radios in the hands of blacks. Many blacks were without televisions, and even fewer had access to a VHS machine. Many blacks with televisions powered their sets with car batteries.
55. W. J. Botha, "Mapantsula (Theatre Version)," August 15, 1988, point 2.2.1, National Archives, Cape Town, IDP volume 2/349, number R88/8/130.
56. Botha, "Mapantsula," point 2.2.4, emphasis in original.
57. Botha, "Mapantsula," point 2.2.3.
58. Botha, "Mapantsula," point, 2.2.2, emphasis in original.
59. Botha, "Mapantsula," point, 2.2.2.
60. Botha, "Mapantsula," point, 2.2.2.
61. Botha, "Mapantsula," point, 2.2.3.
62. Botha, "Mapantsula," point, 2.2.6.
63. Botha, "Mapantsula," point, 2.2.7.
64. Botha, "Mapantsula," point, 2.2.8.
65. Botha, "Mapantsula," point, 2.2.9.
66. "Notice of Appeal," September 16, 1988, point D2, National Archives, Cape Town, IDP, volume 2/349, number R88/8/130. Quote from J. C. W. van Rooyen (Kobus), *Censorship in South Africa: Being a Commentary on the Application of the Publications Act* (Kenwyn: Juta, 1987), 35.
67. Coetzee, *Giving Offense*, 187.
68. Van Rooyen, *Censorship*, 4.
69. Van Rooyen, *Censorship*, 5.
70. Van Rooyen, *Censorship*, 5.
71. Van Rooyen, *Censorship*, 5.
72. Van Rooyen, *Censorship*, 5.

73. J. C. W. van Rooyen (Kobus), *Publikasiebeheer in Suid-Afrika* (Cape Town: Juta, 1978), 39.
74. Van Rooyen, *Censorship*, 38–39.
75. Van Rooyen, *Censorship*, 16.
76. Van Rooyen, *Censorship*, 3.
77. Van Rooyen, *Censorship*, 46.
78. Van Rooyen, *Censorship*, 104.
79. Supposedly constituting a kind of legal science, judgments of the board looked and read like a legal opinion, complete with One Look as plaintiff and the publications committee of the Directorate of Publications as defendant.
80. Papers, *One Look Productions (Pty) Ltd v. Committee of Publications, Mapantsula* (1988) File, p. 6, Film and Publication Board, Cape Town, R91/12/10. Note: This and related documents were directly obtained from the Film and Publication Board when it was headquartered in Cape Town. At some point, the whole file should be transferred to the National Archives, either to Cape Town or Pretoria.
81. Quoted in van Rooyen, *Censorship*, 56.
82. Van Rooyen, *Censorship*, 57.
83. *One Look v. Committee*, 7.
84. *One Look v. Committee*, 7–8.
85. Van Rooyen, *Censorship*, 102.
86. Van Rooyen, *Censorship*, 102
87. *One Look v. Committee*, 7.
88. *One Look v. Committee*, 7.
89. *One Look v. Committee*, 8.
90. *One Look v. Committee*, 8.
91. *One Look v. Committee*, 8.
92. *One Look v. Committee*, 7.
93. *One Look v. Committee*, 8.
94. *One Look v. Committee*, 8.
95. *One Look v. Committee*, 7–8.
96. E. Theron, "Film Working Document," November 26, 1991, *Mapantsula* File, Film and Publication Board, Cape Town, R91/12/10.
97. Theron, "Film Working Document."
98. Letter, Director of Publications to Film and Allied Workers Organization," November 28, 1991, *Mapantsula* File, Film and Publication Board, Cape Town, R91/12/10. Directorate of Publications officials thought about the police scene, "Especially in a time such as the present, this will cloud the relationship between the police and community."
99. Van Rooyen not only chaired the task group but also was a finalist in the search for the first head of the postcensorship regulatory agency directly sanctioned by the state, the Film and Publication Board. He subsequently received an appointment as head of the South African Broadcasting Complaints Commission, an industry body that has public regulatory functions presented in a self-regulation frame.
100. "Report of the Task Group," 1994, 10, Government Publications, University of Cape Town, G68 E: Home 1/94.

101. See Bernard A. O. Williams, Report of the Committee on Obscenity and Film Censorship (London: HMSO, 1979).
102. "Report," 25.
103. "Report," 25.
104. "Report," 26.
105. "Report," 14.
106. See, e.g., James Robertson, *The Hidden Cinema: British Film Censorship in Action, 1913–1972* (New York: Routledge, 1989); John Hill, *British Cinema in the 1980s: Issues and Themes* (Oxford: Clarendon Press, 1999); Anthony Aldgate, "Defining the Parameters of 'Quality' Cinema for the 'Permissive Society': The British Board of Film Censors and *This Sporting Life*," in *Windows on the Sixties: Exploring Key Texts of Media Culture*, ed. Anthony Aldgate, 19–36 (London: I. B. Taurus, 2000); Annette Kuhn, "Children, 'Horrific' Films, and Censorship in 1930s Britain," *Historical Journal of Film, Radio, and Television* 22 (2002): 197–202.
107. C. E. Wakeford, "FPB Recommendation and Classification," August 13, 1999, 3, *Mapantsula* File, Film and Publication Board, Cape Town, R91/12/10.
108. Wakeford, "FPB Recommendation," 3.

Postscript

1. Delgado and Stefancic, *Must We Defend Nazis?*, 11.
2. See Kimberlé Crenshaw, who has taken her scholarship to the Internet, at http://www.law.ucla.edu/faculty/bios/crenshaw/index.html (accessed June 4, 2007); Bonaventura de Sousa Santos, *Toward a New Common Sense: Law, Science, and Politics in Paradigmatic Transition* (New York: Routledge, 1995).
3. Stuart Hall, "The Problem of Ideology: Marxism without Guarantees," in *Marx: A Hundred Years On*, ed. Betty Matthews, 57–85 (London: Lawrence and Wishart, 1983).
4. Stuart Hall, "Gramsci's Relevance for the Study of Race and Ethnicity," *Journal of Communication Inquiry* 10 (1986): 5–27.
5. See, e.g., Narnia Bohler-Muller, "The *Promise* of Equality Courts," *South African Journal on Human Rights* 22 (2006): 380–404.

Bibliography

Articles and Books (published)

Abel, Richard. *Politics by Other Means: Law in the Struggle against Apartheid, 1980–1994.* New York: Routledge, 1995.

Adelman, Lynn, and Pamela Moorshead. "Bad Laws Make Hard Cases: Hate Crime Laws and the Supreme Court's Opinion in *Wisconsin v. Mitchell*." *Gonzaga Law Review* 30 (1995): 1–27.

Agamben, Giogrio. *Homo Sacer: Sovereign Power and Bare Life.* Translated by Daniel Heller-Roazen. Stanford, CA: Stanford University Press, 1998.

———. *State of Exception.* Translated by Kevin Attell. Chicago: University of Chicago Press, 2005.

Ahmad, Muneer. "Homeland Insecurities: Racial Violence the Day after September 11." *Social Text* 20 (2002): 101–16.

———. "A Rage Shared by Law: Post-September 11 Racial Violence as Crimes of Passion." *California Law Review* 92 (2004): 1259–1330.

Akram, Susan M., and Kevin R. Johnson. "Race, Civil Rights, and Immigration Law after September 11, 2001: The Targeting of Arabs and Muslims." *New York University Annual Survey of American Law* 58 (2002): 295–355.

Aldgate, Anthony. "Defining the Parameters of 'Quality' Cinema for the 'Permissive Society': The British Board of Film Censors and *This Sporting Life*." In *Windows on the Sixties: Exploring Key Texts of Media Culture*, edited by Anthony Aldgate, 19–36. London: I. B. Taurus, 2000.

American Law Institute. *Restatement (Second) of Torts.* St. Paul, MN: America Law Institute, 1965.

Ancheta, Angelo. *Race, Rights, and the Asian American Experience.* New Brunswick, NJ: Rutgers University Press, 1998.

Andrews, Penelope, and Stephen Ellman, edited by *The Post-Apartheid Constitutions: Perspectives on South Africa's Basic Law.* Johannesburg: Witswatersrand University Press, 2001.

Ansell, Amy Elizabeth. *New Right, New Racism: Race and Reaction in the United States and Britain.* New York: New York University Press, 1997.

Armour, Jody. *Negrophobia and Reasonable Racism: The Hidden Costs of Being Black in America.* New York: New York University Press, 1997.

———. "Race *Ipsa Loquitir*: Of Reasonable Racists, Intelligent Bayesians, and Involuntary Negrophobes," *Stanford Law Review* 46 (1994): 781–816.

Baines, Gary. "Racist Hate Speech in South Africa's Fragile Democracy: The Case of Ngema's 'AmaNdiya.'" In *Popular Music Censorship in Africa*, edited by Michael Drewett and Martin Cloonan, 53–70. Aldershot, England: Ashgate, 2006.

Barry, A. et al., eds. *Foucault and Political Reason: Liberalism, Neo-liberalism, and Political Reason*. Chicago: University of Chicago Press, 1996.

Battaglia, Jack M. "Regulation of Hate Speech by Educational Institutions: A Proposed Policy." *Santa Clara Law Review* 31 (1991): 345–92.

Bell, Jeannine. *Policing Hatred: Law Enforcement, Civil Rights, and Hate Crime*. New York: New York University Press, 2002.

Bender, Leslie. "Is Tort Law Male?: Foreseeability Analysis and Property Managers' Liability for Third Party Rapes of Residents." *Chicago-Kent Law Review* 69 (1993): 313–43.

Berlet, Chip, ed. *Eyes Right: Challenging the Right Wing Backlash*. Boston, MA: South End Press, 1995.

Bernstein, Richard. "First Amendment Limits on Tort Liability for Words Intended to Inflict Severe Emotional Distress." *Columbia Law Review* 85 (1985): 1749–85.

Bhana, S., and J. B. Brain. *Setting Down Roots: Indian Migrants in South Africa, 1860–1911*. Johannesburg: Witswatersrand University Press, 1990.

Biko, Steve. *I Write What I Like*. New York: Harper & Row, 1978.

Blakey, Michael L. "Scientific Racism and the Biological Concept of Race." *Literature and Psychology* 45 (1999): 29–54.

Bohler-Muller, Narnia. "The *Promise* of Equality Courts." *South African Journal on Human Rights* 22 (2006): 380–404.

Bourdieu, Pierre. "The Essence of Neoliberalism." *Le Monde Diplomatique* 8 (December 1998), English edition: 3.

———. *Masculine Domination*. Stanford, CA: Stanford University Press, 2001.

Braithwaite, John. "The New Regulatory State and the Transformation of Criminology." *British Journal of Criminology* 40 (2000): 222–38.

Bratich, Jack et al., eds. *Foucault, Cultural Studies, and Governmentality*. Albany: State University of New York Press, 2003.

Brown, Michael P., and Paul Boyle. "National Closets: Governmentality, Sexuality, and the Census." In *Closet Space: Geographies of Metaphor from the Body to the Globe*, edited by Michael P. Brown, 88–115. New York: Routledge, 2000.

Brown, T. "AIDS, Risk, and Social Governance." *Social Science & Medicine* 50 (2000): 1273–84.

Brundage, W. Fitzhugh. *Lynching in the New South: Georgia and Virginia, 1880–1930*. Urbana: University of Illinois Press, 1993.

Bullock III, Charles S. and Susan A. MacManus. "Staggererd Terms and Black Representation." *Journal of Politics* 49 (1987): 543–52.

Burchell, Graham et al., eds. *The Foucault Effect: Studies in Governmentality*. Chicago: University of Chicago Press, 1991.

Burns, Yvonne. *Administrative Law under the 1996 Constitution*. Durban: Butterworths, 1999.

Butler, Judith. "Appearances Aside." *California Law Review* 88 (2000): 55–63.

———. *Excitable Speech: A Politics of the Performative*. New York: Routledge, 1997.

———. *Gender Trouble: Feminism and the Subversion of Identity*. New York: Routledge, 1990.

———. *Precarious Life: The Powers of Mourning and Violence*. New York: Verso, 2006, 50–100.

———. *Undoing Gender*. New York: Routledge, 2004.

Carle, Susan D. "Theoretical Agency." *American University Law Review* 55 (2005): 307–93.

Carmody, Moira. "Sexual Ethics and Violence Prevention." *Social & Legal Studies* 12 (2003): 199–216.

Carrier, Paul. "Augusta Tries to Heal Recent Wounds of Racism." *Portland Press Herald* (July 7, 1996), pp. 1A, 12A.

Chamallas, Martha. "The Architecture of Bias: Deep Structures in Tort Law." *University of Pennsylvania Law Review* 146 (1998): 912–40.

———. "Civil Rights in Ordinary Tort Cases: Race, Gender, and the Calculation of Economic Loss." *Loyola of Los Angeles Law Review* 38 (2005): 1435–68.

———. "Questioning the Use of Race-Specific and Gender-Specific Economic Data in Tort Litigation: A Constitutional Argument." *Fordham Law Review* 63 (1994): 73–124.

———. "The September 11th Victim Compensation Fund: Rethinking the Damages Element in Injury Law." *Tennessee Law Review* 71 (2003): 51–79.

Chamallas, Martha, and Linda Kerber. "Women, Mothers, and the Law of Fright: A History." *Michigan Law Review* 88 (1990): 814–63.

Chang, Robert S. *Disoriented: Asian Americans, Law, and the Nation-State*. New York: New York University Press, 1999.

Chappell, Ben. "States of Exception and Threat Governmentality." *Cultural Dynamics* 18 (2006): 313–34.

Chin, Audrey, and Mark Peterson. *Deep Pockets, Empty Pockets: Who Wins in Cook County Jury Trials?* Santa Monica, CA: Rand Corporation, 1985.

Chock, Phyllis Pease. "Ambiguity in Policy Discourses: Congressional Talk about Immigration." *Policy Sciences* 28 (1995): 165–84.

Clark, Kenneth B. *Dark Ghetto: Dilemmas of Social Power*. New York: Harper & Row, 1965.

Coetzee, J. M. *Giving Offense: Essays on Censorship*. Chicago: University of Chicago Press, 1996.

Coggin, Theo. *Censorship: A Study of Censorship in South Africa*. Johannesburg: Institute of Race Relations, 1983.

Coleman, Jules. *Risks and Wrongs*. New York: Cambridge University Press, 1992.

Comaroff, Jean, and John Comaroff. "The Colonization of Consciousness in South Africa." *Economy and Society* 18 (1989): 267–95.

Comaroff, John. "The Discourse of Rights in Colonial South Africa: Subjectivity, Sovereignty, Modernity." In *Identities, Politics, and Rights*, edited by Austin Sarat and Thomas Kearns, 193–236. Ann Arbor: University of Michigan Press, 1996.

Conover, Pamela J. and Stanley Feldman. "Candidate Perception in an Ambiguous World: Campaigns, Cues, and Inference Processes." *American Journal of Political Science* 33 (1989): 912–40.

————. "How People Organize the Political World: A Schematic Model."
American Journal of Political Science 28 (1984): 95–126.

————. "The Role of Inference in the Perception of Political Candidates." In
Political Cognition, edited by Richard Lau et al., 127–58. Hillsdale: Erlbaum,
1986.

Conroy, John. "Police Torture in Chicago." Chicago Reader (weekly), February
4, 2005. http://www.chicagoreader.com/policetorture/050402. Accessed
June 4, 2007.

Corder, Hugh. *Judges at Work: The Role and Attitudes of the South African
Appellate Judiciary, 1910–1950*. Cape Town: Juta, 1984.

Cortese, Anthony. *Opposing Hate Speech*. Westport, CT: Praeger, 2005.

Crain, Marion, and Ken Matheny. "'Labor's Divided Ranks': Privilege and the
United Front Ideology." *Cornell Law Review* 84 (1999): 1542–1625.

Crenshaw, Kimberlé. "Mapping the Margins: Intersectionality, Identity Politics,
and Violence against Women." *Stanford Law Review* 43 (1991): 1241–99.

Dawson, Michael C. *Behind the Mule: Race and Class in African-American Politics*.
Princeton, NJ: Princeton University Press, 1994.

Dean, Mitchell, and Barry Hindess, eds. *Governing Australia: Studies in
Contemporary Rationalities of Government*. Cambridge: Cambridge
University Press, 1998.

De Genova, Nicholas. *Working the Boundaries: Race, Space, and 'Illegality' in
Mexican Chicago*. Durham, NC: Duke University Press, 2005.

De Lange, Margreet. *Muzzled Muse: Literature and Censorship in South Africa*.
Philadelphia, PA: John Benjamin Publishing, 1997.

Delgado, Richard, and David Yun. "The Neo-Conservative Case against Hate
Speech Regulation—Lively, D'Souza, Gates, Carter, and the Toughlove
Crowd." *Vanderbilt Law Review* 47 (1994): 1807–25.

Delgado, Richard, and Jean Stefancic, eds. *Critical White Studies*. Philadelphia,
PA: Temple University Press, 1997.

————. *Must We Defend Nazis?: Hate Speech, Pornography, and the New First
Amendment*. New York: New York University Press, 1997.

Deloria, Vine. *Red Earth, White Lies: Native Americans and the Myth of Scientific
Fact*. New York: Scribners, 1995.

Derrida, Jacques. "Justice, Law, and Philosophy—An Interview with Jacques
Derrida." *South African Journal of Philosophy* 18 (2000): 279–86.

Desimone, Laura. "Racial Discourse in a Community: Language and the Social
Construction of Race." *Journal of Negro Education* 62 (1993): 414–18.

De Sousa Santos, Bonaventura. *Toward a New Common Sense: Law, Science, and
Politics in Paradigmatic Transition*. New York: Routledge, 1995.

De Villiers, Bertus. *Birth of a Constitution*. Kenwyn: Juta, 1994.

De Wet, Erika. *The Constitutional Enforceability of Economic and Social Rights: The
Meaning of the German Constitutional Model for South Africa*. Durban:
Butterworths, 1996.

Dudziak, Mary L., and Leti Volpp. *Legal Borderlands: Law and the Construction of
American Borders*. Baltimore, MD: Johns Hopkins University Press, 2006.

Dugard, John. *Human Rights and the South African Legal Order*. Princeton:
Princeton University Press, 1978.

————. "The Judicial Process, Positivism, and Civil Liberty." *South African Law
Journal* 88 (1971): 181–200.

Du Gay, Paul et al. *Doing Cultural Studies: The Story of the Sony Walkman.* London: Sage Publications, 1997.

Du Plessis, Lourens, and Hugh Corder, eds. *Understanding South Africa's Transitional Bill of Rights.* Kenwyn: Juta, 1994.

Dyzenhaus, David. *Hard Cases in Wicked Legal Systems: South African Law in the Perspective of Legal Philosophy.* Oxford: Clarendon, 1991.

———. "Positivism and Validity." *South African Law Journal* 100 (1983): 454–67.

Eberle, Edward J. "Cross Burning, Hate Speech, and Free Speech in America." *Arizona State Law Journal* 36 (2004): 953–1001.

———. "Hate Speech, Offensive Speech, and Public Discourse in America," *Wake Forest Law Review* 29 (1994): 1135–1213.

Ellman, Stephen. *In a Time of Trouble: Law and Liberty in South Africa's State of Emergency.* Oxford: Clarendon Press, 1991.

Ernst, Walter, and Bernard Harris, eds., *Race, Science, and Medicine, 1700–1960.* New York: Routledge, 1999.

Evans, Ivan. *Bureaucracy and Race: Native Administration in South Africa.* Berkeley: University of California Press, 1997.

Fitzpatrick, Peter. "Racism and the Innocence of Law." In *Critical Legal Studies*, edited by Peter Fitzpatrick and Alan Hunt, p. 119–32. London: Blackwell, 1987.

Flagg, Barbara J. "Fashioning a Title VII Remedy for Transparently White Subjective Decision Making." *Yale Law Journal* 104 (1996): 535–40.

Flores, Juan. " 'Que Assimilated, Brother, Yo Soy Asimilao': The Structuring of Puerto Rican Identity." In *Divided Borders: Essays on Puerto Rican Identity*, edited by Juan Flores, 182–98. Houston, TX: Arte Publico Press, 1993.

Flynt, Rob. "Clinical Governance and Governmentality." *Health, Risk & Society* 4 (2002): 155–73.

Forsyth, C. *In Danger for Their Talents: A Study of the Appellate Division of the Supreme Court of South Africa from 1950–1980.* Cape Town: Juta, 1985.

Foucault, Michel. *Birth of the Clinic: An Archaeology of Medical Perception.* New York: Vintage, 1975.

———. *Discipline and Punish.* New York: Pantheon, 1977.

———. "Governmentality." In *The Foucault Effect: Studies in Governmentality*, edited by Graham Burchell et al., 87–104. Chicago: University of Chicago Press, 1991.

Frankenburg, Ruth. *Displacing Whiteness: Essays in Social and Cultural Criticism.* Durham, NC: Duke University Press, 1997.

———. *White Women, Race Matters: The Social Construction of Whiteness.* Minneapolis: University of Minnesota Press, 1993.

Fredrickson, George M. *Black Liberation: A Comparative History of Black Ideologies in the United States and South Africa.* New York: Oxford University Press, 1995.

———. *The Comparative Imagination: On the History of Racism, Nationalism, and Social Movements.* Berkeley: University of California Press, 1997.

———. *White Supremacy: A Comparative Study in American and South African History.* New York: Oxford University Press, 1981.

Frohmann, Lisa. "Convictability and Discordant Locales: Reproducing Race, Class, and Gender Ideologies in Prosecuting Decision Making." *Law and Society Review* 31 (1997): 531–56.

Gates, Henry Louis. "War of Words: Critical Race Theory and the First Amendment." In *Speaking of Race, Speaking of Sex: Hate Speech, Civil Rights, and Civil Liberties*, edited by Gates et al., 17–58. New York: New York University Press, 1994.

Geschwender, James A. "Ethnicity and the Social Construction of Gender in the Chinese Diaspora." *Gender and Society* 6 (1992): 480–507.

Gey, Steven G. "What if *Wisconsin v. Mitchell* Had Involved Martin Luther King Jr?: The Constitutional Flaws of Hate Crime Enhancement Statutes." *George Washington Law Review* 65 (1997): 1014–70.

Gilens, Martin. *Why Americans Hate Welfare: Race, Media, and the Politics of Anti-Poverty Policy*. Chicago: University of Chicago Press, 2000.

Glen, Russell W. et al. *Training the 21st Century Officer: Redefining Police Professionalism for the Los Angeles Police Department*. Santa Monica, CA: Rand Corporation, 2003.

Goldberg, David Theo. *Anatomy of Racism*. Minneapolis: University of Minnesota Press, 1990.

Goode, Victor M., and Conrad A. Johnson, "Emotional Harm in Housing Discrimination Cases: A New Look at a Lingering Problem," *Fordham Urban Law Journal* 30 (2003): 1143–1214.

Gotanda, Neil. "A Critique of 'Our Constitution Is Color-Blind.'" *Stanford Law Review* 44 (1991): 1–68.

———. "'Other Non-Whites' in American Legal History: A Review of Justice at War," *Columbia Law Review* 85 (1985): 1186–92.

Gould, Jon B. *Speak No Evil: The Triumph of Hate Speech Regulation*. Chicago: University of Chicago Press, 2005.

Grabham, Emily. "Taxonomies of Inequality: Lawyers, Maps, and the Challenge of Hybridity." *Social & Legal Studies* 15 (2006): 5–23.

Gready, Paul, and Lazarus Kgalema. "Magistrates under Apartheid: A Case Study of the Politicization of Justice and Complicty in Human Rights Abuses," *South African Journal on Human Rights* 19 (2003): 141–88.

Gross, Ariela J. "Litigating Whiteness: Trials of Racial Determination in the Nineteenth-Century South." *Yale Law Journal* 108 (1998): 109–85.

Gutierrez, Gabriel. "Affirmative Action of the First Kind: Social and Legal Constructions of Whiteness and White.... Male Privilege in Nineteenth Century California," *Latino Studies Journal* 11 (2000): 14–48.

Gutto, Shadrack B. "The Criminalization of Hate Speech?" In *Between Speech and Silence: Hate Speech, Pornography, and the New South Africa*, edited by Jane Duncan, 103–27. Cape Town: Idasa, 1995.

Habell-Pallan, Michelle. *Loca Motion: The Travels of Chicana and Latina Popular Culture*. New York: New York University Press, 2005.

Hacker, Andrew. *Two Nations: Black and White, Separate, Hostile, Unequal*. New York: Scribner's, 1992.

Hall, Jacquelyn Dowd. "'The Mind That Burns in Each Body': Women, Rape, and Racial Violence." In *Powers of Desire: The Politics of Sexuality*, edited by Ann Snitow et al., 328–49. New York: Monthly Review Press, 1983.

Hall, Stuart. "Gramsci's Relevance for the Study of Race and Ethnicity," *Journal of Communication Inquiry* 10 (1986): 5–27.

———. "The Meaning of New Times." *New Times: The Changing Face of Politics in the 1990s*, edited by Stuart Hall and Martin Jacques, 116–33. London: Lawrence & Wishart, 1989.

———. "The Problem of Ideology: Marxism without Guarantees," in *Marx: A Hundred Years On*, edited by Betty Matthews, 57–85. London: Lawrence & Wishart, 1983.

———. "The Spectacle of the 'Other.'" In *Representation: Cultural Representations and Signifying Practices*, edited by Stuart Hall et al., 225–57. London: Sage Publication, 1997.

———. "The Whites of Their Eyes." In *Silver Linings*, edited by R. Brunt, 89–93. London: Lawrence and Wishart, 1981.

Haney-Lopez, Ian. *Racism on Trial: The Chicano Fight for Justice*. Cambridge, MA: Harvard University Press, 2003.

———. "The Social Construction of Race: Some Observations on Illusion, Fabrication, and Choice," *Harvard Civil Rights-Civil Liberties Law Review* 29 (1994): 1–62.

———. *White by Law: The Legal Construction of Race*. New York: New York University Press, 1996.

Hardt, Michael, and Antonio Negri. *Empire*. Cambridge, MA: Harvard University Press, 2000.

Harris, Anita. "Discourses of Desire as Governmentality: Young Women, Sexuality, and the Significance of Safe Spaces." *Feminism & Psychology* 15 (2005): 39–43.

Harris, Bronwyn. "New Song, Same Old Tune," 2002. http://www.csvr.org.za/index.php?option=com_content&task=view&id=119&Itemid=35. Accessed January 4, 2008.

Hey, Valerie, and Simon Bradford. "The Return of the Repressed?: The Gender Politics of Emergent Forms of Professionalism in Education." *Journal of Education Policy* 19 (2004): 691–713.

Hill, John. *British Cinema in the 1980s: Issues and Themes*. Oxford: Clarendon Press, 1999.

Hooton, Angela. "A Broader Vision of the Reproductive Rights Movement: Fusing Mainstream and Latina Feminism." *American University Journal of Gender, Social Policy, & the Law* 13 (2005): 59–86.

Human Rights Watch. "Chicago Torture." Undated. http://www.hrw.org/reports98/police/uspo53htm. Accessed June 4, 2007.

Huntington, Samuel P. "The Hispanic Challenge." *Foreign Policy* 141 (2004): 30–45.

———. *The Soldier and the State: The Theory and Politics of Civil-Military Relations*. Cambridge, MA: Harvard University Press, 1957.

———. *Who Are We?: The Challenges to America's National Identity*. New York: Simon & Schuster, 2004.

Ignatiev, Noel. *How the Irish Became White*. New York: Routledge, 1996.

Ilcan, Susan et al. "Spaces of Governance: Gender and Public Sector Restructuring in Canada." *Gender, Place & Culture: A Journal of Feminist Geography* 14 (2007): 75–92.

Jacobs, James B., and Kimberly Potter. *Hate Crimes: Criminal Law & Identity Politics*. New York: Oxford University Press, 1998.

Jenness, Valerie, and Ryken Grattet. *Making Hate a Crime: From Social Movement Concept to Law Enforcement Practice*. New York: Russell Sage Foundation, 2001.

Johannessen, Lene. "A Critical View of the Constitutional Hate Speech Provision." *South African Journal on Human Rights* 13 (1997): 135–50.

Johnson, Kevin R. "'Aliens' and the U.S. Immigration Laws: The Social and Legal Construction of Nonpersons." *University of Miami Inter-American Law Review* 28 (1998): 263–92.

Jones, Marvin. "No Time for Trumpets: Title VII, Equality, and the *Fin De Siecle*." *Michigan Law Review* 92 (1994): 2311–69.

Joyce, Paul. "Governmentality and Risk: Setting Priorities in the New NHS." *Sociology of Health and Illness* 23 (2001): 594–615.

Kalpagam, U. "Colonial Governmentality and the 'Economy,'" *Economy & Society* 23 (2000): 418–38.

Kashima, Tetsuden. *Judgement without Trial: Japanese American Imprisonment during World War II*. Seattle: University of Washington Press, 2003.

Kastoryano, Rita. *Negotiating Identities: States and Immigrants in France and Germany*. Princeton, NJ: Princeton University Press, 2002.

Kelly, Robin D. G. *Yo' Mama's Disfunktional: Fighting the Culture Wars in Urban America*. Boston, MA: Beacon Press, 1997.

Kim, Janine. "Are Asians Black?: The Asian-American Civil Rights Agenda and the Contemporary Significance of the Black/White Paradigm." *Yale Law Journal* 108 (1999): 2385–2412.

King, Lisa. "Subjectivity as Identity: Gender through the Lens of Foucault." In *Foucault, Cultural Studies, and Governmentality*, edited by Jack Z. Bratich et al., 337–52. Albany: State University of New York Press, 2003.

King, Samantha J. "Doing Good by Running Well: Breast Cancer, the Race for the Cure, and New Technologies of Ethnical Citizenship." In *Foucault, Cultural Studies, and Governmentality*, edited by Jack Z. Bratich et al., 295–316. Albany: State University of New York Press, 2003.

Kiss & Tell. *Her Tongue on My Theory: Images, Essays, and Fantasies*. Vancouver: Press Gang Publishers, 1994.

Kitschelt, Herbert. "Linkages between Citizens and Politicians in Democratic Polities." *Comparative Political Studies* 33 (2000): 845–79.

Krieger, Linda Hamilton. "The Content of Our Categories: A Cognitive Bias Approach to Discrimination and Equal Opportunity." *Stanford Law Review* 47 (1995): 1161–1248.

Kros, Cynthia. "Secularity in a World 'Torn by Difference': A Consideration of the French Headscarf Affair from South Africa." *Politikon: South African Journal of Political Studies* (2005): 1–16.

Kuhn, Annette. "Children, 'Horrific' Films, and Censorship in 1930s Britain." *Historical Journal of Film, Radio, and Television* 22 (2002): 197–202.

Kuhn, Thomas. *Structure of Scientific Revolutions*. Chicago: University of Chicago Press, 1962.

Laclau, Ernesto, and Chantal Mouffe. *Hegemony and Socialist Strategy: Towards a Radical Politics*. London: Verso, 1985.

Lane, P. "South Africa's Equality Courts: An Early Assessment." 2005. http://www.wits.ac.za/csvr/papers/paprctp5.htm. Accessed June 27, 2007.

Lawrence III, Charles R. "The Id, the Ego, and Equal Protection: Reckoning with Unconscious Racism." *Stanford Law Review* 39 (1987): 317–88.

Levin, Jack, and Jack McDevitt. *Hate Crimes: The Rising Tide of Bigotry and Bloodshed*. Boulder, CO: Westview Press, 2001.

———. *Hate Crimes Revisited: America's War on Those Who are Different*. Boulder, CO: Westview Press, 2002.

Levit, Nancy. "Critical Race Theory: Race, Reason, Merit, and Civility." *Georgetown Law Journal* 87 (1999): 795–822.

Lichter, Michael, and Roger Waldinger. "Producing Conflict: Immigration and the Management of Diversity in the Multiethnic Metropolis." In *Color Lines: Affirmative Action, Immigration, and Civil Rights Options for America*, edited by John David Skrentny, 147–67. Chicago: University of Chicago Press, 2001.

Lijphart, Arend. "The Political Consequences of Electoral Laws, 1945–1985." *American Political Science Review* 84 (1990): 481–96.

Love, Jean C. "Tort Actions for Hate Speech and the First Amendment: Reconceptualizing the Competing Interests." *Law and Sexuality* 2 (1992): 29–35.

Lublin, David. "Racial Redistricting and African-American Representation: A Critique of 'Do Majority-Minority Districts Maximize Substantive Black Representation in Congress?,'" *American Political Science Review* 93 (1999): 183–86.

McBride, Dwight A. *Why I Hate Abercrombie & Fitch: Essays on Race and Sexuality*. New York: New York University Press, 2005.

McClellan, Frank M. "The Dark Side of Tort Reform: Searching for Racial Justice." *Rutgers Law Review* 48 (1996): 761–98.

Mahoney, Martha. "Segregation, Whiteness, and Transformation," *University of Pennsylvania Law Review* 143 (1995): 1659–84.

Mandela, Nelson. *Long Walk to Freedom: The Autobiography of Nelson Mandela*. Boston, MA: Back Bay Books, 1995.

Marable, Manning. *Beyond Black and White: Transforming African-American Politics*. London: Verso, 1995, 117–30.

Marcus, Gilbert. "Incitement to Hatred: A Southern African Perspective." *Media Law and Practice in Southern Africa* (February 1998): 11–19.

———. "Racial Hostility: The South African Experience." In *Striking a Balance: Hate Speech, Freedom of Expression, and Non-Discrimination*, edited by Sandra Coliver, 208–22. London: University of Essex Press, 1992.

Marcuse, Herbert. *One-Dimensional Man: Studies in the Ideology of Advanced Industrial Society*. Boston, MA: Beacon Press, 1964.

Marotta, Sylvia A., and Jorge G. Garcia. "Latinos in the United States in 2000." *Hispanic Journal of Behavioral Sciences* 25 (2003): 13–34.

Marx, Anthony W. *Making Race and Nation: A Comparison of the United States, South Africa, and Brazil*. New York: Cambridge University Press, 1998.

Matsuda, Mari et al. *Words That Wound: Critical Race Theory, Assaultive Speech, and the First Amendment*. Boulder, CO: Westview Press, 1994.

Merrett, Christopher. *A Culture of Censorship: Secrecy and Intellectual Repression in South Africa*. Cape Town: David Phillip, 1994.

Merry, Sally Engle. "Spatial Governmentality and the New Urban Social Order: Controlling Gender Violence through Law." *American Anthropologist* 103 (2001): 16–29.

Mills, Charles W. *The Racial Contract*. Ithaca, NY: Cornell University Press, 1997.

Morrison, Adele M. "Queering Domestic Violence to 'Straighten Out' Criminal Law: What Might Happen When Queer Theory and Practice Meet Criminal Law's Conventional Responses to Domestic Violence." *Southern California Review of Law and Women's Studies* 13 (2003): 81–160.

Motimele, McCaps Malose, ed. *Constitution for a Democratic South Africa*. Johannesburg: Skotaville, 1993.

Nash, Gary B. *History on Trial: Culture Wars and the Teaching of the Past*. New York: Knopf, 1997.

Neale, Andrew N. "Foucault in Guantánamo: Towards an Archaeology of the Exception." *Security Dialogue* 37 (2006): 31–46.

Newitz, Annalee, ed. *White Trash: Race and Class in America*. New York: Routledge, 1997.

Nielsen, Laura Beth. *License to Harass: Law, Hierarchy, and Offensive Public Speech*. Princeton, NJ: Princeton University Press, 2004.

Nuttall, Sarah, and Carli Coetzee, eds. *Negotiating the Past: The Making of Memory in South Africa*. Cape Town: Oxford University Press, 1998.

O'Brien, M. "Governing Risk and Drug Use in Juvenile Justice Settings." *Contemporary Drug Problems* 28 (2001): 625–49.

O'Byrne, Patrick. "The Micro-fascism of Plato's Good Citizens: Producing (Dis)order through the Construction of Risk." *Nursing Philosophy* 8 (2007): 92–101.

Okizaki, Carrie Lynn H. "'What Are You?': Hapa Girl and Multiracial Identity." *University of Colorado Law Review* 71 (2000): 463–94.

O'Malley, Pat. "Indigenous Governance." In *Governing Australia: Studies in Contemporary Rationalities of Government*, edited by M. Dean and Barry Hindess, 156–72. Cambridge: Cambridge University Press, 1998.

Omi, Michael, and Dana Takagi. "Situating Asian Americans in Political Discourse on Affirmative Action." In *Race and Representation*, edited by Robert Post and Michael Rogin, 271–81. Boston, MA: MIT Press, 1998.

Omi, Michael, and Howard Winant. *Racial Formation in the United States: From the 1960s to the 1980s*. New York: Routledge, 1986.

Perea, Juan F. "The Black and White Binary Paradigm of Race: Exploring the 'Normal Science" of American Racial Thought." *California Law Review* 85 (1997): 1213–58.

Pillay, D. "Singling Out Indians Will Achieve Nothing." *Sunday Times* (South Africa), July 21, 2002.

Pratt, Mary Louise. *Imperial Eyes: Travel Writing and Transculturation*. New York: Routledge, 1992.

Prince, Russell et al. "Governmentality, Discourse, and Space in the New Zealand Health Care System, 1991–2003." *Health & Place* 12 (2006): 253–66.

Rankin, Katherine. "Governing Development: Neo-liberalism, Microcredit, and Rational Economic Woman." *Economy & Society* 30 (2001): 18–37.

Read, E. M. "Put to the Proof: Evidentiary Considerations in Wisconsin Hate Crime Prosecutions," *Marquette Law Review* 89 (2005): 453–74.

Riggs, Damien. "Locating Control: Psychology and the Cultural Production of 'Health Subject Positions.'" *Culture, Health & Sexuality* 7 (2005): 87–100.

Robertson, James. *The Hidden Cinema: British Film Censorship in Action, 1913–1972.* New York: Routledge, 1989.

Robins, Steven. "At the Limits of Spatial Governmentality: A Message from the Tip of Africa." *Third World Quarterly* 23 (2002): 665–89.

Rodriguez, Norma. *Changing Race: Latinos, the Census, and the History of Ethnicity in the United States.* New York: New York University Press, 2000.

Roediger, David R. *The Wages of Whiteness: Race and the Making of the American Working Class.* New York: Verso, 1999.

Rosenberg, David. *The Hidden Holmes: His Theory of Torts in History.* Cambridge, MA: Harvard University Press, 1995.

Sachs, Albie. *Protecting Human Rights in a New South Africa.* Cape Town: Oxford University Press, 1990.

Saenz, Rogelio. *Latinos and the Changing Face of America.* New York: Russell Sage Foundation, 2004.

Said, Edward. *Orientalism.* New York: Pantheon, 1978.

Saito, Natsu Taylor. "Model Minority, Yellow Peril: Functions of 'Foreignness' in the Construction of Asian American Legal Identity." *Asian Law Journal* 4 (1997): 71–95.

———. "Symbolism under Siege: Japanese American Redress and the 'Racing' of Arab Americans as 'Terrorists.'" *Asian Law Journal* 8 (2001): 1–29.

Schauer, Frederick. "Uncoupling Free Speech." *Columbia Law Review* 92 (1992): 1321–57.

Schur, Richard. "The Dialogic Criticism of Richard Delgado: Chicano/a Literature, Equality, and the Rhetoric of Form," *Law and Inequality* 19 (2001): 129–58.

Schweber, Howard. "The 'Science' of Legal Science: The Model of Natural Sciences in Nineteenth-Century American Legal Education," *Law and History Review* 17 (1999): 421–66.

Sharma, Sherri. "Beyond 'Driving While Black' and 'Flying While Brown': Using Intersectionality to Uncover the Gendered Aspects of Racial Profiling." *Columbia Journal of Gender and Law* 12 (2003): 275–309.

Smandych, Russell, ed. *Governable Places: Readings on Governmentality and Crime Control.* Aldershot, England: Ashgate, 1999.

Sniderman, Paul et al., "The New Racism." *American Journal of Political Science* 35 (1991): 423–48.

"Special Section." *Social & Legal Studies* 7 (1998): 539–76.

Spielman, Fran. "Council to Hold Hearings on Alleged Police Torture." *Chicago Sun-Times* (daily), March 24, 2007, http://www.suntimes.com/news/politics/398398,23burge.article. Accessed June 4, 2007.

Spivak, Gayatri Chakravorty. *A Critique of Postcolonial Reason: Toward a History of the Vanishing Present.* Cambridge, MA: Harvard University Press, 1999.

———. *The Post-colonial Critic: Interviews, Strategies, Dialogues.* New York: Routledge, 1990.

Stenson, Kevin. "Sovereignty, Biopolitics, and the Local Government of Crime in Britain." *Theoretical Criminology* 9 (2005): 265–87.

Stepan, Nancy. *The Idea of Race.* London: Macmillan, 1982.

Stinson, James. "Opinion and Representation." *American Political Science Review* 89 (1995): 179–83.

Stoler, Ann. *Race and the Education of Desire: Foucault's History of Sexuality and the Colonial Order of Things.* Durham, NC: Duke University Press, 1995.

Stone, Geoffrey. *Constitutional Law.* Boston, MA: Little, Brown, 1991.

Strydom, H. A. "The Legal Theory of Lon L. Fuller." In *Essays on Law and Social Practice in South Africa,* edited by Hugh Corder, 123–44 (Cape Town: Juta, 1988).

Suleiman, Michael W., ed. *Arabs in America: Building a New Future.* Philadelphia, PA: Temple University Press, 1999.

Takaki, Ronald. *From Different Shores: Perspectives on Race and Ethnicity in America.* New York: Oxford University Press, 1994.

Taylor, Paul C. *Race: A Philosophical Introduction.* Cambridge: Polity Press, 2004.

Terry, Jennifer, and Jacqueline Urla. *Deviant Bodies: Critical Perspectives on Difference in Science and Popular Culture.* Bloomington: Indiana University Press, 1995.

Ticktin, Miriam. "Policing and Humanitarianism in France: Immigration and the Turn to Law as State of Exception." *Interactions* 7 (2005): 347–68.

Tomaselli, Kenyan. *The Cinema of Apartheid: Race and Class in South African Film.* London: Routledge, 1989.

Trankell, Ing-Britt, and Jan Ovesen. "French Colonial Medicine in Cambodia: Reflections of Governmentality." *Anthropology & Medicine* 11 (2004): 91–105.

Tsesis, Alexander. *Destructive Messages: How Hate Speech Paves the Way for Harmful Social Movements.* New York: New York University Press, 2002.

Valdes, Francisco. "Beyond Sexual Orientation in Queer Legal Theory: Majoritarianism, Multidimensionality, and Responsibility in Social Justice Scholarship or Legal Scholars as Cultural Warriors." *Denver University Law Review* 75 (1998): 1409–64.

Valdez, Norberto, and Janice Valdez. "The Pot That Called the Kettle White: Changing Racial Identities and U.S. Social Construction of Race." *Identities* 5 (1998): 379–413.

Van Rooyen, J. C. W. (Kobus). *Censorship in South Africa: Being a Commentary on the Application of the Publications Act.* Kenwyn: Juta, 1987.

———. *Publikasiebeheer in Suid-Afrika.* Cape Town: Juta, 1978.

Vetri, Dominick. *Tort Law and Practice.* New York: Matthew Bender & Company, 1998.

Virtanent, Simon V., and Leonie Haddy. "Old-Fashioned Racism and New Forms of Racial Prejudice." *Journal of Politics* 60 (1998): 311–32.

Voyce, Malcolm. "The Privatization of Public Property: The Development of a Shopping Mall in Sydney and Its Implications for Governance through Spacial Practices." *Urban Policy & Research* 21 (2003): 249–62.

Waltraud and Bernard Harris, eds. *Race, Science and Medicine, 1700–1960.* New York: Routledge, 1999.

Weinrib, Ernest. "The Case for a Duty to Rescue." *Yale Law Journal* 90 (1990): 247–93.

Weinstein, James. *Hate Speech, Pornography, and the Racial Attack on Free Speech Doctrine.* Boulder, CO: Westview, 1999.

West, Cornell. *Race Matters.* Boston, MA: Beacon Press, 1993.

White, G. Edward. "The American Law Institute and the Triumph of Modernist Jurisprudence." *Law and History Review* 15 (1997): 1–47.

——. *Tort Law in America: An Intellectual History*. New York: Oxford University Press, 1980.

Williams, Bernard Arthur Owen. *Report of the Committee on Obscenity and Film Censorship*. London: HMSO, 1979.

Williams, James W., and Randy Lippert. "Governing on the Margins: Exploring the Contributions of Governmentality Studies to Critical Criminology of Canada." *Criminology & Criminal Justice* 48 (2006): 703–19.

Williams, Patricia. *The Alchemy of Race and Rights*. Cambridge, MA: Harvard University Press, 1991.

Williams, Raymond. *Keywords: A Vocabulary of Culture and Society*. Oxford: Oxford University Press, 1976.

Williamson, Joel. *The Crucible of Race: Black/White Relations in the American South since Emancipation*. New York: Oxford University Press, 1984.

Wilson, William Julius. *When Work Disappears: The World of the New Urban Poor*. New York: Knopf, 1996.

Winston, Judith. "Mirror, Mirror on the Wall: Title VII, Section 1981, and the Intersection of Race, Sex, Gender, and the Civil Rights Act of 1990." *California Law Review* 179 (1991): 75–82.

Wriggins, Jennifer B. "Torts, Race, and the Value of Injury, 1900–1949." *Howard Law Journal* 49 (2005): 99–138.

——. "Toward a Feminist Revision of Torts." *American University Journal of Gender, Social Policy, & the Law* 13 (2005): 139–59.

Wu, Frank H. *Yellow: Race in America beyond Black and White*. New York: Basic Books, 2001.

Yamamoto, Eric K. "Critical Race Praxis: Race, Theory, and Political Lawyering Practice in Post-Civil Rights America." *Michigan Law Review* 95 (1997): 821–99.

National Constitutions

Constitution of the Republic of South Africa.

Constitution of the United States of America.

United States Public Documents

Nonarchival, Nonpublished

Augusta Police Department. Papers. Silvers-Hallowell Case (Case # 9622395), 1996.

California State Advisory Committee to the USCCR. "Meeting of May 15, 2002," May 15, 2002.

Chicago Police Department. "Amendment Investigations." General Order 88-17, September 8, 1988.

———. "The First Amendment and Police Actions." General Order 02-10, October 11, 2002.

———. "Hate Crimes/Criminal and Noncriminal Incidents Motivated by Hate," General Order 92-1, Addendum 4, July 3, 1992.

———. "Human Rights and Human Resources," General Order 92-1, July 3, 1992.

Illinois Advisory Committee to the USCCR. "Arab and Muslim Civil Rights Concerns since September 11, 2001," March 2002.

Indiana Advisory Committee to the USCCR. "Civil Rights Issues Facing Muslims and Arab Americans in Indiana Post-September 11," May 30, 2002.

Kennebec County Superior Court. Papers. Silvers-Hallowell Case (Case # CV-96-282), 1996.

Metropolitan Washington Joint Committee to the USCCR. "Civil Rights Concerns in the Metropolitan Washington Area in the Aftermath of 9.11 Tragedies: Muslims, Sikhs, Arab Americans, South Asian Americans, and Muslim Women," April 25, 2002.

Michigan Advisory Committee to the USCCR. "Civil Rights Issues Facing Arab Americans in Michigan," 2001.

New York State Advisory Committee to the USCCR. "Civil Rights Issues and Post 9-11 Law Enforcement/Community Relations in New York Fact-Finding Forum," May 21, 2003.

North Dakota Advisory Committee to the USCCR. "Briefing on Civil Rights Issues Facing Muslims and Arab Americans in North Dakota Post-September 11," May 2002.

Ohio Advisory Committee to the USCCR. "Civil Rights Facing Muslims and Arab Americans in Ohio Post-September 11," November 14, 2001.

United States Commission on Civil Rights. "Anniversary Update on Commission Activities Related to September 11," September 2002.

United States Commission on Civil Rights. "Briefings on Boundaries of Justice: Immigration Policies Post-September 11," October 12, 2001.

Wisconsin Advisory Committee to the USCCR. "Briefing on Civil Rights Issues Facing Muslims and Arab Americans in Wisconsin Post-September 11." April 11, 2002.

Published

Chicago Police Department. "CAPS at 5: A Report on the Progress of Community Policing in Chicago, 1993–1998."

———. "Hate Crime," *Training Bulletin* 35 (November 28, 1994): 3.

———. "What is CAPS?"
http://www.egov.cityofchicago.org/city/webportal/portalContentItemAct ion.do?blockName=Police%2fHow+CAPS+Works%2fI+Want+To&deptMai nCategoryOID=-9965&channelId= 536879037&programId=536879161& entityName=Police&topChannelName=Dept&contentOID=10912&Failed_ Reason=Invalid+timestamp,+engine+has+been+restarted&contentTypeNa me=COC_EDITORIAL&com.broadvision.session.new=Yes&Failed_Page= %2fwebportal%2fportalContentItemAction.do&context=dept. Accessed January 4, 2008.

Judicial Services Commission and Magistrates Commission. *Bench Book for Equality Courts*. Pretoria: Judicial Services Commission and Magistrates Commission, 2002.

———. *Resource Book for Equality Courts*. Pretoria: Judicial Services Commission and Magistrates Commission, 2002.

Maine Revised Statutes Annotated 1997. St. Paul, MN: West Publishing, 1997.

New York State Judicial Commission. *Report of the New York State Commission on Minorities*. New York: The Commission, 1991.

Office of Management and Budget. *Race and Ethnic Standards for Federal Statistics and Administrative Reporting*. Washington, DC: Office of Management and Budget, 1977.

———. *Statistics Policy Directive No. 15*. Washington, DC: Office of Management and Budget, 1977.

Oregon Supreme Court Task Force. "Report of the Oregon Supreme Court Task Force on Racial/Ethnic Issues in the Judicial System." *Oregon Law Review* 73 (1994): 823–942.

United States Department of Justice. "Student Manual: National Hate Crimes Training Curricula." Washington, DC: U.S. Department of Justice, 1998.

Wessler, Stephen. *Addressing Hate Crimes: Six Initiatives That Are Enhancing the Efforts of Criminal Justice Practices*. Washington, DC: U.S. Department of Justice, Office of Justice Programs, Bureau of Justice Assistance, 2000.

———. *Promising Practices against Hate Crimes: Five State and Local Demonstration Projects* (Washington, DC: U.S. Department of Justice, Office of Justice Programs, Bureau of Justice Assistance, 2000).

Wessler, Stephen, and Margaret Moss. *Hate Crimes on Campus: The Problem and Efforts to Confront It*. Washington, DC: U.S. Department of Justice, Office of Justice Programs, Bureau of Justice Assistance, 2001.

Laws

U.S. Civil Rights Act of 1957.
U.S. Civil Rights Act of 1964.
U.S. Equal Pay Act of 1994.

Cases

Alliance to End Repression et al. v. City of Chicago et al., 74 C 3268 (1988).
Alliance to End Repression v. City of Chicago, 237 F. 3d 799 (2001).
American Civil Liberties Union et al. v. City of Chicago et al., 75 C 3295 (1988).
Chicago Lawyers' Committee et al. v. City of Chicago et al., 74 C 1982 (1982).
DeGraffenreid v. General Motors, 413 F. Supp. 142 (1976).
Dillon v. Legg, 68 Cal. 2d 728, 441 P. 2d 912, 69 Cal. Rptr. 72 (1968).
Doe v. Linder Construction Company, 845 S. W. 2d 173 (1992).
Equal Employment Opportunity Commission v. Flasher Co., 986 F. 2d 1312 (1992).
Ex parte Shahid, 205 F. 812 (1913).
Gomillion v. Lightfoot, 364 U.S. 339 (1960).

Hernandez v. Texas, 347 U.S. 475 (1954).
In re Ah Yup, 1 F. Cas. 223 (1878).
In re Takuji Yamashita, 30 Wash. 234 (1902).
Irving v. J. C. Marsh, 46 Ill. App. 3d 162, 360 N. E. 2d (1977).
Mathews v. Diaz, 426 U.S. 67 (1976).
Memphis v. Greene, 451 U.S. 100 (1981).
Palmore v. Sidoti, 466 U.S. 429 (1984).
Payton v. Abbot Labs, 437 N. E. 2d 171 (1982).
R.A.V. v. St. Paul, 505 U.S. 377 (1992).
Stanton v. Stanton, 421 U.S. 7, 16 (1975).
Village of Arlington Heights v. Metropolitan Housing Development Corp., 429 U.S. 252 (1977).
Warren v. Halstead Industries, Inc., 802 F. 2d 746, 752–753 (1986).

South African Public Documents

Archival

Mapantsula file, Film and Publication Board, Cape Town. R91/12/10.
Papers on the theatrical release of *Mapantsula*. National Archives. Cape Town. IDP vol. 2/349, no. R88/8/130.
Papers on the video release of *Mapantsula*. National Archives. Cape Town. IDP vol. 2/342, no. R88/6/14.
"Report of the Task Group." Government Publications. University of Cape Town. G68 E: Home 1/94.

Nonarchival, Nonpublished

Joint Committee on the Promotion of Equality and Prevention of Unfair Discrimination (JCPEPUD) file. Parliamentary Monitoring Group. Cape Town.

Published

Debates of the National Assembly. Cape Town: Parliament of the Republic of South Africa, 2000.
Debates on the National Council of Provinces. Cape Town: Parliament of the Republic of South Africa, 2000.

South African Laws

Group Areas Act 41 of 1950.
Independent Broadcasting Act 153 of 1993.

Native Land Act 27 of 1913.

Population Registration Act 30 of 1950.

Independent Communication Authority of South Africa Act 13 of 2000.

Promotion of Equality and Prevention of Unfair Discrimination Act (Equality Act) 4 of 2000.

Promotion of Equality and Prevention of Unfair Discrimination Amendment Act 52 of 2002.

Publications Act of 1974.

Separate Amenities Act 49 of 1953.

Urban Areas Act of 21 of 1923.

Court Cases

Brink v. Kushoff, 6 BCLR 752 (1996).

Islamic Unity Convention v. the Independent Broadcasting Authority and Others, 4 SA 294 (CC) (2002).

National Coalition for Gay and Lesbian Equality v. Minister of Home Affairs, 12 BCLR 1517 (1998).

State v. Mamobolo, 3 SA 409 (CC) (2001).

Broadcasting Complaints Commission of South Africa (BCCSA) Regulations and Cases

BCCSA Code

BCCSA Constitution

BCCSA Procedure

Clarke and Others v. East Coast Radio, 2003/06 East Coast Radio (2003).

Fouche v. 94.7 Highveld Stereo, 2000/18 94.7 Highveld Stereo (2000).

Human Rights Commission of South Africa v. SABC, 2002/31 SABC (2002).

Johnson v. 94.7 Highveld Stereo, 2002/07 94.7 Highveld Stereo (2002).

Myburgh v. Radio 702, 2001/04 Radio 702 (2001).

Prinsloo and Venter v. Rippel 90.5fm, 2002/19 Rippel 90.5fm (2002).

Index